## DATE DUE

| | |
|---|---|
| NOV 18 1996 | |
| | |
| | |
| | |
| | |
| | |
| | |
| | |
| | |
| | |
| | |
| | |
| | |
| | |
| | |
| | |
| | |
| | |

GAYLORD                                    PRINTED IN U.S.A.

# Frontiers of Hispanic Theology
# in the United States

AAW-6816

*Edited and with an Introduction*
*by*
*Allan Figueroa Deck, S.J.*

ORBIS BOOKS

Maryknoll, New York 10545

The Catholic Foreign Mission Society of America (Maryknoll) recruits and trains people for overseas missionary service. Through Orbis Books, Maryknoll aims to foster the international dialogue that is essential to mission. The books published, however, reflect the opinions of their authors and are not meant to represent the official position of the society.

Copyright © 1992 by Allan Figueroa Deck, S.J.
Published by Orbis Books, Maryknoll, N.Y. 10545-0308
All rights reserved
Manufactured in the United States of America

**Library of Congress Cataloging-in-Publication Data**

Frontiers of Hispanic theology in the United States / edited and with
 an introduction by Allan Figueroa Deck.
   p.  cm.
 Includes bibliographical references and index.
 ISBN 0-88344-826-2
 1. Theology, Doctrinal—United States—History—20th century.
 2. Hispanic American Catholics—Religion.   I. Deck, Allan Figueroa,
 1945-   .
 BT30.U6F   1992
 230'.089'68073—dc20                                          92-14036
                                                                 CIP

*To the coadjutor brothers of the Society of Jesus,*
*outstanding "men for others" and unsung heroes*

# Contents

# Acknowledgments

A debt of gratitude is owed my colleagues in the Academy of Catholic Hispanic Theologians of the United States (ACHTUS). This collection modestly reflects their ongoing efforts to accompany God's people with the resources, gifts, and skill of the theologian. Special thanks are also due to those who generously assisted me with the editing and word processing of the manuscript: Fidel Alvarez, Lisa Floch, Sister Joan Fronc, O.P., and María de Pedraza. Finally, the encouragement and vision of Robert Ellsberg, editor-in-chief of Orbis Books, made this work possible.

ALLAN FIGUEROA DECK, S.J.
Loyola Marymount University
Los Angeles, California
February 12, 1992

# Introduction

*ALLAN FIGUEROA DECK, S.J.*

Until now there have been few professional United States Hispanic theological voices.[1] Virgil Elizondo, within the Roman Catholic tradition, and Justo González and Orlando Costas, within the Protestant tradition, are among the few who come to mind. The emergence of a growing number of professional Hispanic theologians is a change that the publication of this book heralds.

This is, moreover, an event of great significance for theology as a vocation and profession in the United States. For much too long the dominant U.S. theological voices, be they liberal-progressive or conservative-integrist, have reflected the realities and interests of a mainstream that is aging and drying up. The biological life of the U.S. Catholic Church is surely passing to "newcomers": Hispanic, Asian-Pacific, and African American peoples.[2] Sooner or later the intellectual life and leadership must also move in that direction. This trend is now becoming obvious in the case of European and North American theologies where one observes the passing of "giants" like Karl Rahner but does not readily identify their successors. Is the torch being passed to a new generation of theologians in Latin America, Asia, Africa, and their descendants in the First World? The theologians whose works appear here are pioneers of a new theological "frontier."

The ideas behind this collection, my vision as editor, were simple: (1) to provide a collection of essays demonstrating the range and seriousness of theological reflection and writing going on today among these new emergent voices; (2) to promote a dialogue with both the Hispanic communities whose interests and perspectives this theology exemplifies and with mainstream colleagues on seminary and university faculties and within our professional organizations; (3) to affirm a clearer identity for U.S. Hispanic theology as a "bridge" theology suitable for a "bridge" people. These Hispanic writers are committed to the service of their communities within the United States. We are not Latin American theologians "passing through." We are North Americans of Hispanic origin. We have one foot, as it were, in the Third World and another in the First. In a unique way, we as U.S. Hispanics, know *both* worlds as perhaps few others do. For we have struggled in our own minds and hearts, in our flesh, with the complexities of both the Hispanic-American and the Anglo-American worlds – so different and often antagonistic socio-economically and culturally speaking. Ours is a truly bilingual and bicultural theology that simply cannot take the perspective of any one group as the final word. Our deepest intuitions about and approaches to the understanding of the faith tend to be permanently dual (not dualistic), at once Hispanic and North American.

Readers can judge whether the dream that inspired the book has been attained. The articles reveal a breadth of interest, some more scholarly, others more pastoral, that fairly characterizes today's U.S. Hispanic theologian. The participation of most of the contributors on theological faculties and professional associations allows them to formulate the concerns of U.S. Hispanics in ways that engage U.S. mainstream, academic communities. U.S. Hispanic theologians thus articulate new ideas about theological education, methodology, and curricula that challenge the prevailing wisdom, norms, and mind-sets – progressive, moderate, or conservative – regarding theology's role in the life of church and society. This point is made by the various contributors in different ways.

One of the more obvious characteristics of this theology and the theologians who do it is its rootedness in the complex reality – social, economic, political, cultural, and pastoral – of the Hispanic communities. Such involvement is one of its notable strengths. But it is also a source of ongoing tension insofar as this theology desires to influence academia, whose professional demands often mean distancing oneself from the field of battle, from practical concerns, in the name of "intellectual rigor, scholarship, or seriousness." The movement back and forth from theory to praxis is not easy. Most of the writers in this collection have become veterans of just such a career. What has sustained them, undoubtedly, is the conviction that theology is an integral dimension of the life of a vibrant community struggling for that abundant life offered by Jesus Christ. This is the point made with passion and precision by María Pilar Aquino in chapter 2 of this book.

The collection before you gives witness to something new and still untested within North American religious and theological contexts. Arturo Bañuelas calls it "emerging U.S. Hispanic voices in the theologies of the Americas." This development, moreover, represents a qualitative change in the theological landscape, a breakthrough faithfully reflecting the dramatic transformation of the U.S. Catholic Church. No longer is it a church of mainstreamed European immigrants. The demographic trends reveal the birth of a new or "second-wave" church, one of Latin American origin. These trends also point to a rediscovery or recuperation of the oldest and deepest current of North American Catholicism – namely, its Hispanic roots. These roots have consistently been obscured by views of U.S. Catholic history which incorrectly place its origins in Maryland, and narrowly conceive of it as a movement westward.[3] The emergence of theologians working out of a sounder vision of U.S. Catholic Church history is an important step in establishing the crucial importance of today's growing Hispanic presence.

The real identity and destiny of the U.S. Catholic Church as a whole is the issue.

The material conditions that give rise to such a development are frequently overlooked. Perhaps this is so because theology historically became a dialogue between disengaged academics/theoreticians on the one hand and the sources of Christian faith on the other. The engagement and rootedness of the theologian in a given socio-economic and cultural context was seldom viewed as relevant. The data upon which theologians reflected were often suspended in the air, in some eternal realm of ideas. Reality, especially in its socio-economic, political, and cultural dimensions, has too often been *terra incognita* for theologians. The Second Vatican Council did much to change the dominant theological methodology by insisting on the church's, and hence theology's, need to be in dialogue with the world, to stop "looking at the clouds," as it were, and fix its vision on temporal affairs. In a Christian dispensation the worldly cannot be dichotomized from the eternal. Yet theological production and curricula, with some notable exceptions even twenty-five years after the Second Vatican Council, are limited to a dialogue with the Anglo-European world, its philosophical categories and burning issues, not necessarily with the concerns of the vast majority of human beings, the Third and Fourth Worlds. These worlds are in important ways more representative of the human, of the "real," world, than is the First World itself. U.S. Hispanic theology as modestly reflected in the articles in this collection now brings these viewpoints into the heart of modern or postmodern North American culture.

There is something qualitatively different, then, about U.S. Hispanic theology. It is a theology which certainly contrasts with mainstream U.S. theology, but also with the theology of liberation. That difference emerges from a simple glance at the origins and trajectory of this theology. The articles in this collection will clarify even more the character and basic profile of this emergent new "family on the theological block."

The very fact that now it is possible to broach the subject of U.S. Hispanic theology is itself the sign of something new and perhaps unforeseen on the theological horizon. For up to now the sea change constituted by the Hispanic presence has been visible almost exclusively at the grass-roots level, within the context of parish and pastoral care. Fully one-third of today's U.S. Roman Catholics are Hispanic and, if trends persist (and they give every indication of doing so), Hispanics will constitute the majority of Roman Catholics sometime in the first decade of the next millennium.[4]

The assumption, however, has been that the Hispanic presence is fundamentally a practical matter. It is not something that portends anything particularly profound at the level of self-understanding or theory. While the U.S. bishops have shown considerable insight into the consequences of the Hispanic presence in their pastoral letter of 1983, *The Hispanic Presence: Challenge and Commitment*, and more recently in the National Pastoral Plan for Hispanic Ministry (1987), the middle level of church leadership at the pastoral, educational, and intellectual levels has tended to read the situation as an epiphenomenon, a passing (and, for some, unpleasant) phase.[5] This is so at least in part due to the unanalyzed acceptance and dominance of the immigrant analogy/paradigm, that is, the conviction that "those people" will eventually become just "like us" as the forces of assimilation inexorably transform newcomers just as they transformed "our" grandparents. A clear sign of this tendency, perhaps one of its greatest verifications, has been the dearth of intellectual production—books, articles, courses, lectures, and research—on the Hispanic presence as source of significant theological reflection.

As I have noted elsewhere, that presence has in no way been reflected in the world of ideas, in the intellectual life of the U.S. Catholic Church.[6] In theologates and Catholic universities, in the curricula, on the faculties, and in the administrations one is hard pressed to find significant Hispanic elements. But something is happening. One indication of this is the successful course taught by Arturo Bañuelas in the spring of 1991 at the Jesuit School of Theology at Berkeley. This was one of the first courses ever offered specifically on U.S. Hispanic theology. The course generated a fifteen-page bibliography of U.S. Hispanic theological literature. This book is, of course, another indicator of this development.

At the risk of being excessively schematic or anecdotal, I will proceed to profile the background that elucidates the context of the essays before you.

## THE RISE OF U.S. HISPANIC THEOLOGY:
## THE LEGACY OF VIRGIL ELIZONDO

The history of contemporary U.S. Hispanic theology must begin with the work of Virgil Elizondo.[7] A priest of the archdiocese of San Antonio, Elizondo has provided a paradigm for theological scholarship rooted in a love of the Hispanic communities. He began in the 1960s, spurred on by the vision of the late Archbishop Robert Lucey.[8] From the beginning Elizondo demonstrated a keen interest in pastoral and catechetical concerns. His was a reflection grounded in practical realities but fascinated with the sources of Christian faith—scripture and tradition. His writing reflects a remarkable ability to apply those sources in new, imaginative, and pastorally energizing ways. His finest work to date is *The Galilean Journey*, in which he develops the concept of *mestizaje* or miscegenation as a theologically rich approach for understanding the importance of the historical experience of U.S. Hispanics. A synthesis of Elizondo's concept of *mestizaje*, so fertile and influential among U.S. Hispanic writers, is provided in chapter 6 of this volume.

Elizondo's bibliography includes more than seventy items. He is the only U.S. Hispanic theologian with wide recognition in the U.S., Europe, and the Third World as well. While producing a regular stream of books and articles, Elizondo has always been more than a scholar. He is an extraordinary activist. He founded the Mexican-American Cultural Center in San Antonio, participated in numerous national and international conferences, became a famous lecturer, and served on the board of several national and international theological associations such as *Concilium*, EATWOT (the Ecumenical Association of Third World Theologians), and ACHTUS (the Academy of Catholic Hispanic Theologians of the U.S.). For several years he has been rector of the cathedral in San Antonio where he has inaugurated many new outreach programs for the local community. Of special note are the meticulously planned Holy Week ceremonies. At the cathedral he has produced a weekly Sunday liturgy that is broadcast throughout the country on Spanish-language television.

For approximately twenty years Elizondo was the sole, highly visible U.S. Hispanic theologian. That is one of the reasons why in 1989 the Academy of Catholic Hispanic Theologians of the U.S. (ACHTUS) decided to give its first annual award for outstanding contributions to a theology of and for U.S. Hispanics to Elizondo, and to name it the Virgil Elizondo Award.

It would be difficult to exaggerate the importance of Elizondo's contribution to U.S. Hispanic theology. In addition to the work on *mestizaje*, Elizondo was one of the first theologians to view popular religiosity as a *locus theologicus*. In this he pioneered an implicit theological method that takes the anthropological concept of culture quite seriously. Undoubtedly this interest was the fruit of Elizondo's reading of *Gaudium et Spes*, especially paragraphs 56 and the following. In several articles and in a small, highly readable book entitled *La Morenita*, Elizondo reinterpreted the story of Our Lady of Guadalupe as a myth in the deepest anthropological sense of the word, a myth which allows us to get at the heart of the Mexican and the Mexican-American culture and identity. In this Elizondo actually anticipated the criticism that was going to be made of liberation theologians for their disregard for the anthropological core of popular culture. A theology which purports to be "of the people" cannot take seriously only or mainly the socio-economic and political factors; it must attend to the people's religion, to their devotions, rituals, and customs. Among the Latin American peoples that means paying attention to their profound interest in the Virgin Mary. The contribution that Elizondo has made to the understanding of the Guadalupe event as it is celebrated and lived by Hispanics of Mexican origin shows that he possessed the insight long before many of his contemporaries.

Like Latin American liberation theologians, however, Elizondo has attempted to view popular religiosity, especially its strong Marian character, as a fundamental feature of any truly liberative approach to the issues of society and political economy. Elizondo is a theologian squarely committed to action on behalf of justice, to a faith doing justice. His concerns, then, go beyond what may at times appear to be a romantic interest in quaint, sometimes alienating, and often dying popular religious customs. It is fair to say, however, that his writings have tended to reflect more interest in pastoral, catechetical, and anthropological issues than in socio-economic and political issues. Personally and in terms of his considerable commitments, Elizondo sees his work as that of an organic intellectual rooted in the horizon of the Hispanic poor for whom *mestizaje* and popular religiosity are key root experiences.

This schematic overview of Elizondo's work shows that his approach has been highly influential. Two interwoven features of the "new generation" of U.S. Hispanic writers, the ones writing in this volume and others as well, are the interest in popular religiosity and the commitment to the social struggles of the people. This means that the starting point for most contemporary U.S. Hispanic theologians is the socio-economic, political, or cultural realities grasped with the aid of the corresponding social sciences. Theirs is a theology explicit about its commitments and social location, much like Third World and women's theologies. In this regard, the emerging U.S. Hispanic theology like liberation, women's, and black theologies, has been called an "advocacy theology." This often pejorative epithet still has currency among some "mainstream" theologians who naively persist in holding, implicitly or explicitly, that there is some serious, intellectually rigorous, neutral, objective, serenely uncommitted theology "out there," and that theirs is most likely it. The persistence of this attitude contributes to the enduring marginalization of Hispanics and their theologians, which shows itself, at best, in patronizing and, at worst, in disdainful ways.

## The Legacy of Latin American Theology

At the same time that Elizondo was beginning his career as writer, lecturer, and teacher, currents of Latin American theology began to influence U.S. Catholic thinkers. Elizondo was the first U.S. Hispanic to personally know Latin American theologians such as Gustavo Gutiérrez, Juan Luis Segundo, Enrique Dussel, Leonardo Boff, Jon Sobrino, and Ricardo Antoncich. His friendship with Gustavo Gutiérrez was especially important and is reflected in the numerous lectures and teaching engagements Gutiérrez has accepted over the years at the Mexican-American Cultural Center in San Antonio. Over time Elizondo had the opportunity to meet and deepen friendships with many of these Latin American theologians. Certainly one of those occasions was at the annual meetings of *Concilium* in Belgium, as well as at numerous theological gatherings in Latin America, Asia, and Africa. While Elizondo was communicating to his U.S. audience some of the concerns and approaches of these Latin American theologians and recasting them from the unique perspective of U.S. Latinos, a younger generation was listening.

Liberation theology then, especially its praxis-oriented methodology, was embraced by a new generation of U.S. Hispanic thinkers with enthusiasm and hope. The many common points between the Latin American situation and the U.S. Hispanic one—marginality, powerlessness, discrimination, and outright oppression—suggested to thoughtful U.S. Hispanics that in the brilliant writings of Latin American sisters and brothers there was something of special relevance. We admired what they were accomplishing and desired to emulate them.

Corresponding to this fascination with Latin American theology was a similar attraction to the "new" church, the "people's church," being heralded by the bishops' conferences of Medellín (1968) and Puebla (1979). The Latin American theologians were producing an articulate, theologically grounded vision of church and society. The institutional church, through the often episcopally sanctioned basic ecclesial communities, was facilitating the creation of institutional bases that incarnated that vision of God's reign.

U.S. Hispanic theologians have thus deepened their respect for the accomplishments of Latin American and other third-world theologies. They have acknowledged an important debt. Yet there has been a gradual recognition of the need to do something different: to affirm the originality of theology grounded on the unique experiences of Hispanics specifically in the U.S. Gustavo Gutiérrez reminded us over and over again of the need to do this. He suggested that it was not a question of replicating the work of Latin Americans in the considerably different North American context, but of truly taking their *method* seriously—that is, doing theology out of *this* particular U.S. Hispanic reality. The resulting theology would surely be something fresh and original.

Virgil Elizondo has already taken the lead in this search for the specificity of U.S. Hispanic theology with his discussion of the role of *el rechazo* or "rejection" in the experience of Hispanics of Mexican origin in the borderlands. This is an element in his more elaborate concept of *mestizaje*.

In recent years U.S. Hispanic theologians have begun to pursue the implications of their people's being "a bridge" within North American culture. Here one sees a clear element of contrast with Latin American theology. It is the bridge or dialogical nature of U.S. Hispanic theology that seems to set it apart from mainstream U.S. theology, from mainstream feminist theology, and perhaps even from black theology. There are three areas where in my view the bridge character is revealed. The first area has to do with the context of modernity, where U.S. Hispanic theologians function. The second refers to the distinctive situation of U.S. Latinas and their prototypal participation in the elaboration of U.S. Hispanic theology. The third area revolves around the issue of the relative importance of different analytical tools of the social sciences and differing social science methodologies in the analysis of reality, the first moment in liberation methodology.

## U.S. HISPANICS CONFRONT THE CULTURE OF MODERNITY

Let us consider the first issue: the import of the culture of modernity as contextualizing the U.S. Hispanic reality. The key point here is that U.S.

Hispanics encounter the culture of modernity *at the source* and not in some derivative or "watered down" fashion as is the case in the Third World. What that means in terms of theological reflection and intellectual life is one of the central concerns of Roberto Goizueta (chapter 1). His theological writings focus on issues of method and hermeneutics. He deals with the epistemological suppositions of the dominant North American theological milieu, Roman Catholic and Protestant, and the interface of that epistemology with that of U.S. Hispanic theologians. Goizueta pursues the issues of ontological individualism and pluralism as they are understood and sometimes reflected by mainstream theologians. He critiques these conceptions and values from the vantage point of a committed U.S. Hispanic.

Goizueta's background in fundamental theology allows him to dialogue with mainstream colleagues. In the process he proposes some interesting, new directions for U.S. Hispanic theology in dialogue with mainstream U.S. theology. U.S. Hispanic theologians are not outsiders but distinctive voices within the North American context. Goizueta's thought challenges mainstream U.S. theology, whether liberal, progressive, or conservative, Catholic or Protestant, in the sense that paradigms rooted in the experience of the Third World make claims that possibly go to the heart of Anglo-American and European theologies. As long as Latin American theology was precisely that—Latin American—it remained somewhat foreign, perhaps exotic, even intriguing. But its claims on the dominant theologies and the way of life those theologies ground and enhance remain minimal. Goizueta issues a challenge to mainstream theologians on their own ground, on their own turf. This is perhaps what is most interesting, problematic, and to some thinkers even disconcerting about his approach.

Goizueta's critique of the prevailing understanding of pluralism among North American intellectuals is telling. His contribution to this book is a fine example of how this young, promising theologian approaches underlying philosophical and methodological issues from the unique standpoint of a committed, organic U.S. Hispanic intellectual. His work represents a distinctive, new moment for U.S. Hispanic theology, a moment that reflects the peculiar position of U.S. Hispanics somewhere between the First World ("in" modernity but somehow still not "of" it) and the Third World ("of" it but not "in" it). His thought runs the risk of being rejected by both those worlds insofar as its social class and cultural location reflect a *tertium quid*. It therefore seems foreign and peculiarly threatening to the status quo, the hegemonic intellectual and ideological forces (of whatever stripe) of either Latin America or the U.S..

In chapter 2 María Pilar Aquino cautions us against the unanalyzed acceptance of or complicity with the culture of modernity. She claims that U.S. Hispanic theologians may inadvertently succumb to this modernity's enchantments and thus lose their critical edge.[9] She is challenging U.S.

Hispanic theologians to go back to their roots, their people, their identity. This means taking a stand, and in that sense not being a "bridge."

## Hispanic Women's Voices at the Ground Floor

The second bridge character of U.S. Hispanic theology is manifested in the unusually prominent role that women have had in this emergent theology. One of Bañuelas's students, Eduardo Fernández, documented the fact that approximately 25 percent of the current generation of U.S. Hispanic theological writers are women. It is doubtful that even today such a significant percentage of women theological writers could be found in the Latin American context.

The number of Latina women doing theology is gradually rising. Theologians like Gloria Loya, Rosa María Icaza, and María Pilar Aquino who have contributed to this volume exemplify this. But there are others as well, as the select bibliography found at the end of this book demonstrates. Especially notable among these are María de la Cruz Aymes, Marina Herrera, and Ada María Isasi-Díaz. Aymes's work has been limited to catechetics and pastoral issues, and goes back to the 1960s. For many years she conceived of herself as a "mainstream" writer-educator. In 1990 she was awarded the Virgilio Elizondo Award of the Academy of Catholic Hispanic Theologians of the U.S. In her acceptance speech the Mexican-born woman religious shared the story of her "conversion" to the U.S. Hispanic reality. For most of her career as a leading, internationally known catechist she had prescinded from issues of Hispanic identity in the United States—that is, from her people's social and cultural questions. Her exposure to the thought of Virgil Elizondo and the work of the Mexican-American Cultural Center was decisive in her *conscientización* or conversion to a new view of her people and of herself as teacher and writer. This is reflected in her literary production of the 1980s to the present.

Marina Herrera was the first U.S. Hispanic (born in Santo Domingo) woman to earn the doctorate in theology. Her numerous writings go back to the mid 1970s. She deserves recognition, therefore, as one of the first U.S. Hispanic theological writers along with Elizondo himself. Herrera, like Aymes, is an accomplished religious educator. She identified with cultural and women's issues from the beginning of her career. This is reflected in her bibliography, which includes articles on catechesis, multicultural ministry, and the Hispanic woman.

Ada María Isasi-Díaz is a Cuban American who began writing in earnest in the late 1970s. She has an excellent theological background, having earned the doctorate in social ethics at Union Theological Seminary. Isasi-Díaz has specialized in a U.S. Hispanic women's theology and published along with Yolanda Tarango the only booklength monograph to date in this crucial area. Currently on the faculty of Drew University, she has been active in the women's ordination movement. Perhaps more than any other

U.S. Latina, Isasi-Díaz has moved in ecumenical circles and thus is an invaluable resource in the almost nonexistent area of ecumenism among Roman Catholic and Protestant Hispanics.

In the area of U.S. Hispanic liturgy, prayer, and spirituality, Rosa María Icaza (chapter 8) is certainly a leader. She has served for many years on the faculty of the Mexican-American Cultural Center and is at this writing president of the Instituto de Liturgia Hispana. In addition to teaching and writing, Icaza has been a leader in promoting the inculturation of liturgy within Hispanic contexts in countless parishes and dioceses.

There are other Latinas who have begun to teach and write. Jeanette Rodríguez-Holguín was born in Ecuador and raised in New York. She earned the doctorate at the Graduate Theological Union and is currently teaching at Seattle University, where she is also director of a graduate program. She is specializing in Hispanic women's issues. Her thesis was on Guadalupe as a potentially liberative symbol for Hispanic women.

Ana María Pineda, born in El Salvador and raised in San Francisco, is completing the doctorate at the Universidad de Salamanca while teaching and directing the Hispanic ministry program at the Catholic Theological Union in Chicago. Pineda has contributed articles to *New Theology Review*. Her doctoral dissertation focuses on the permanent diaconate among U.S. Hispanics and promises to be one of the few substantive pastoral/theological reflections on a subject that has not received the attention it deserves.

Gloria Inés Loya (chapter 7) is currently teaching Hispanic studies and supervising field ministry at the Jesuit School of Theology at Berkeley. She can be included among the women who are beginning to write during and after the arduous process of acquiring the doctorate. Loya's article on a U.S. Hispanic women's liberation theology is included in this collection and synthesizes a section of her doctoral dissertation at the Universidad de Salamanca.

The presence of a significant number of women in the gestation of this new U.S. Hispanic theology is unthinkable outside the context of the United States. It is here that women – "mainstream," white women – have achieved more recognition in the field of theology than anywhere else in the world. That recognition is the fruit of a considerable theological production that is respected for its high quality. Undoubtedly the issues and concerns developed by U.S. women have in various ways encouraged Latinas to pursue the theological vocation within their own distinctive cultural and social settings. They have done this without losing sight of the growing theological production of Latin American women such as Elsa Tamez, María Clara Bingemer, and many others. This dual indebtedness – to U.S. mainstream feminism on the one hand and to a Latin American counterpart on the other – suggests and evokes once again the bridge character of U.S. Hispanic theology.

### U.S. Hispanic Culture and Socio-Political Liberation

A third way in which U.S. Hispanic theology manifests its bridge character and originality is more implicit than explicit. It has to do with (1) the importance given to certain elements of Marxist analysis and (2) the explicit call for radical change that at times was quite influential in Latin American theology. While seldom if ever critiquing the emphasis on economic, structural, and social class analyses of their Latin American counterparts and their passionate calls for socio-economic and political transformation, U.S. Hispanic theologians have gravitated toward *cultural* analysis, especially to popular culture as epitomized by popular religiosity. Such a tendency has a muting effect, at least in the short term, on the urgent calls for radical change. María Pilar Aquino in her article in this collection critiques this approach and warns us about its pitfalls and inadequacies.

The thought of Elizondo certainly moves with the cultural, anthropological reality more than with any other, and therefore may be viewed as somewhat more "culturalist" than "liberationist." Orlando Espín, as cogently demonstrated in chapter 4 in this book and in much of his other writings, has insisted, however, on the value of popular religiosity as the least invaded or colonized source for the doing of a U.S. Hispanic theology. In his view it can and must be linked to the liberation struggle. For popular religiosity is a special instance of a first moment, a response, precisely to the initial oppression of indigenous and African cultures in the Americas.

A review of the literature reveals that the single most recurrent topic in U.S. Hispanic theology is the practical, pastoral reality and issues of evangelization, ministry, and catechesis. The second most popular topic is women's issues, and the third is popular religiosity and spirituality. Interestingly enough, to this writer's knowledge no one has investigated the lack of a more rigorous socio-economic and political analysis of the U.S. Hispanic realities as a starting point for theological reflection. Aquino does provide us with some suggestive leads. In any event, this lack is notable and a contrasting feature with much Latin American theology. This lack may be a source of a valid critique of U.S. Hispanic theology. That theology has perhaps unintentionally fallen into the trap of viewing reality in the pragmatic and functionalist fashion severely criticized by Gregory Baum. At a plenary session of the Catholic Theological Society of America he expressed this concern in these words:

> The question raised is whether post-conciliar American theology has surrendered to liberal values and the liberal political philosophy associated with the American dream? . . . Has a certain sense of discontinuity made post-conciliar theologians forget the cautions against liberalism contained in pre-conciliar theology? . . . Is American theology generated out of an identification with the middle class? . . . The question must, therefore, be asked whether and to what extent American Catholic theology has become part of the liberal ideology that legitimizes American society . . . as a model for the rest of the world.[10]

Roberto Goizueta has pointed to the pervasive tendency among mainstream Euro-North American thinkers to romanticize and hence dismiss the realities of the poor and powerless, among them U.S. Hispanics.[11] One example of this is the stereotyping of Hispanics as carefree and fiesta-oriented, as a kind of "ornamental" people. They are nice to have around. Their food is tasty enough and their music often exhilarating. But do they have anything to say? Anything substantive or intellectually, socially, politically, or economically challenging or profound to offer? Goizueta was speaking of the dilemma of the U.S. Hispanic intellectual who is a kind of nonentity, a contradiction in terms, because of the stereotypical, folkloric view in which Hispanics are held by the dominant society and into which they sometimes willingly allow themselves to be ensnared. Women have helped us understand a comparable mechanism at work in patriarchal society with its implicit axiom about women being "seen but not heard." Certainly the African-American theologians as well as women could speak volumes about this romanticizing phenomenon.

One may ask why U.S. Hispanic theologians have not read the abundant historical and social science literature of Chicano nationalism of the 1970s in a more frontal fashion. This literature was a counterpart of the social class and economic analyses coming out of Latin America. It was often inspired by the theory of dependency, a form of Marxist analysis influential in Latin America a decade or more ago. Chicano nationalism inspired an entire generation of U.S. Hispanic intellectuals in the social sciences. Many of them are today professors at leading secular universities. U.S. Hispanic theologians, in contrast, tended to reflect a pastoral, church-oriented, and perhaps even a clerical vision of themselves. They may appear to an outside viewer to function more as companions of people within church than as companions of people within society. Hence the neglect of the social class, political, and economic coordinates.

Yet this lack of a more constant and coherent socio-economic and political interest in U.S. Hispanic theology is more implicit than explicit. It is seemingly unintentional. This deficiency may be addressed in future U.S. Hispanic theology. The possibility is suggested by changes in the use of social analysis among Latin American theologians in the wake of *perestroika*, *glasnost*, and the worldwide collapse of socialism. Gustavo Gutiérrez and Jon Sobrino, for example, have turned more and more to issues of spirituality, to cultural and anthropological concerns, without necessarily abandoning their epistemological option for the poor.

U.S. Hispanic theology, since it has focused on pastoral and religious issues more than on any others, is relatively unencumbered by the heavy ideological concerns of Latin American theology. It has done so in a practical, nontheory-laden way. Consequently, it may have something to offer Latin American theology—for instance, a more practical understanding of how basic ecclesial communities constitute a new way of being church in the highly mobile, urban, and modernized context of U.S. Hispanics. This is a context that becomes less and less foreign to Latin Americans even if they never leave their nation of birth, given the dramatic urbanization underway throughout that continent. On the other hand the critique of U.S. Hispanic theology on the grounds that it fails to take a more clearly liberationist perspective and remains more in the "culturalist" camp may find a resolution as Latin American theology struggles with a new, more mature synthesis of how to use practical tools for analyzing reality in all its diversity and depth—socially, politically, economically, and of course culturally. The excesses of the past have been acknowledged as Latin American theologians strive to move beyond the accomplishments of the past twenty-five years, while owning up to the sometimes strident and inflexible ideology of a vaguely socialist flavor that lost contact with the reality it was claiming to elucidate.

To acknowledge such excesses does not at all imply the canonization of free market, neocapitalist ideologies and practices. Pope John Paul II's encyclical *Centesimus Annus*, for example, vigorously criticizes capitalism and insists on the need to modify it.[12] Hispanics may contribute to this new maturity and search for viable socio-economic and political alternatives while gaining insights from their Latin American colleagues. All of this, once again, brings home the bridge or dialogical nature of the relationship of U.S. Hispanic theologians with their Euro–North American colleagues on the one side and their Latin American colleagues on the other.

## ACHTUS: Midwife of U.S. Hispanic Theology

The historical evolution of theological reflection from the unique perspectives of Hispanics in the United States owes much to the Academy of Catholic Hispanic Theologians of the United States (ACHTUS). Its origins and trajectory read like a Who's Who of that theology and help clarify the problems and possibilities for the doing of such a theology.

It is hard to say who originally had the idea of founding an association of U.S. Hispanic Catholic theologians. Certainly the idea had been vaguely discussed in the 1970s, perhaps in the context of the *encuentros* sponsored by the Secretariat for Hispanic Affairs of the United States Catholic Conference or at other important moments in the Hispanic ministry movement of the 1970s and 80s. Nothing happened, however, until 1985 when this writer renewed his friendship with Arturo Bañuelas. I had met Arturo twelve years before, at a meeting of Hispanic seminarians at Immaculate Conception Seminary in Santa Fe, New Mexico. We saw or conversed with each other only a few times in the intervening years. We both followed each other's work in Hispanic ministry. Arturo had found some of my articles on the rights of undocumented immigrants useful in his ministry. I had heard of Arturo's leadership in his diocese and work on the board of the Mexican-American Cultural Center.

Our meeting in Rome in the fall of 1985 was the result of circumstance. Arturo was completing the doctorate in fundamental theology at the Gregorian University and I was beginning the doctoral program in missiology.

On our first meeting in so many years one of us broached the subject of the need for an association of U.S. Hispanic theologians. We spoke passionately about the need but also understood some of the obstacles.

It seemed to us that the lack of articulate Hispanic theological voices was a basic and alarming symptom of the marginality that characterized the Hispanic presence in the U.S. Catholic Church. While the Hispanic communities' lack of "hands on" pastoral care and outreach was of deep concern to us, the failure to raise up a more critical and theologically grounded voice seemed to us to be especially serious in the North American Catholic Church context. The fuller participation of Hispanics in the church especially at the levels of policy and planning, a fairer distribution of the church's resources, and a more valid vision of the U.S. church's identity and destiny would never come about without the contribution of thinkers and theologians. But not just *any* thinkers and theologians. We were concerned about professionals interested in and capable of doing what Clodovis Boff calls "feet-on-the-ground" theology.

We knew there were many pitfalls. One of them was a kind of anti-intellectualism we had noted among some of our Hispanic colleagues. One of the words used to describe this anti-intellectualism is *basismo*—that is, the idea that only the poor themselves, the grass-roots people of the "base," are qualified to do this theology. All other efforts, especially those that reek of academe, are suspect. This *basismo* could also be compounded with a suspicion of elitism. Here we have two priests (in Rome of all places!) plotting to initiate yet another theological men's club. This view struck us as understandable given the reality of ivory-tower theology, of elitism, clericalism, and sexism in church and society. However, we also saw ourselves as being qualified, as having some credibility, to begin such an effort. We both were committed and had a record of social justice activism and serious involvement in grass-roots ministries. It also seemed to us that one of the best ways to acknowledge our debt as theologians to persons like Gustavo Gutiérrez and a host of other Latin American theologians was by doing in our context what they had done in theirs. Few, if any, were accusing them of being elitist, ivory-tower intellectuals.

Another factor that entered into our conversation was the relationship of theologians, specifically Hispanic theologians, not this time to the base or grass-roots communities, but rather to the bishops, especially the U.S. Hispanic bishops and other key leaders. Both Bañuelas and I felt that there was something lacking in the reflection that Hispanic leaders—lay, clerical, or episcopal—had thus far been able to produce. This concern was brought home by a simple comparison between the elaborate, sophisticated processes and resources brought to bear on the U.S. bishops vis-à-vis their famous pastoral letters on war and peace and on the U.S. economy on the one hand, and the relatively simple, unsophisticated tone of their pastoral letter on the Hispanic presence on the other. We were not belittling the significance of the pastoral letter on Hispanics, but pointing to something that is rather evident: the dearth of theological and other reflective, intellectual expertise among the U.S. Hispanic leadership. That is what our ACHTUS project wanted to do something about.

One of the final considerations that influenced our "dream" was a factual matter. *Are* there any U.S. Hispanic theologians? We knew of just a handful and realized that the "dream" might not get off the ground unless we did more research. That would have to await our return to the United States.

On returning to the United States in 1987 the project was taken up in earnest. By that time we had identified others who also shared this vision and helped make it a reality: María Pilar Aquino, Roger Luna, Roberto Goizueta, C. Gilbert Romero, Virgil Elizondo, and Orlando Espín. These, plus Arturo Bañuelas and I, met in January 1988 at the Jesuit School of Theology at Berkeley. It was there that the decision was made to move ahead with bylaws and statutes for the new academy and to initiate a membership campaign. The first meeting of the board of directors took place in Ruidoso, New Mexico, in November 1988. The first officers were elected and the first annual meeting of the academy planned for June 1989. The decision was made to inaugurate the Virgilio Elizondo Award and confer the first award on Elizondo himself. This was done at the June 1989 meeting at the Graduate Theological Union in Berkeley, California.

An issue that concerned ACHTUS from the very beginning was how to be sensitive toward and inclusive of women. We were pleased that the academy had at least one foundress: María Pilar Aquino. But soon other women theologians joined as regular or associate members: Marina Herrera, Jeanentte Rodríguez-Holguín, Ada Isasi-Díaz, Zoila Díaz, Gloria Inés Loya, Ana María Pineda, and Carmen Cervantes. The Second Annual Virgilio Elizondo Award, as mentioned above was given to María de la Cruz Aymes.

A second concern of ACHTUS was how to be inclusive of the diverse Hispanic national groups. We recruited members from every major Hispanic community in the country. As a result the forty-four regular and associate members of ACHTUS in 1991 reflect rather faithfully the distribution of U.S. Hispanics according to national origin (Mexican, Cuban, Puerto Rican, Dominican, Central American, and South American). The recruitment effort was quite successful in that it brought almost two-thirds of all U.S. Hispanic Catholics with or completing doctorates in some theological discipline into the academy.[13]

A third issue of some concern to ACHTUS members was the need to assert the difference between Latin American theology and U.S. Hispanic theology. Several members have had the experience of being recognized as followers of some liberation theologian or an exponent of liberation theology in the United States. We wanted to move beyond that stereotype to create something rooted in the historical praxis of U.S. Hispanics who certainly have much in common with their Latin American progenitors but who need theology appropriate to their distinct circumstances. ACHTUS members such as Arturo Bañuelas reminded us of the original Hispanic roots of U.S. Catholicism. He expressed a special interest in defining and developing what he calls a "borderlands" theology that originated in the first evangelization of the Southwest four hundred years ago.

A final major concern of ACHTUS was ecumenism. It seemed that an academy purporting to be Roman Catholic must take seriously the Second Vatican Council and its challenge of promoting Christian unity. Yet the group was sensitive to the negative experience that U.S. Hispanic Catholics have had of an aggressive and disrespectful proselytism on the part of some Protestant sects. For the time being it was decided that the academy would stress its Roman Catholic character in pursuit of a firmer and clearer identity. From the beginning, however, the academy had excellent relations with Hispanic Protestant colleagues, most of them from the historical, mainline churches. Some ACHTUS members are actively involved in *La Comunidad*, an ecumenical association of Hispanic scholars of religion, organized at the American Academy of Religion (AAR) and promoted by the Fund for Theological Education. ACHTUS and Protestant Hispanic theologians have had occasion to dialogue and even collaborate on projects at meetings of ACHTUS, of *La Comunidad*, and at the annual Hispanic summer program sponsored by the Fund for Theological Education. ACHTUS members have regularly written in *Apuntes*, the only journal of U.S. Hispanic theology in the country. It is edited by Justo González and published at Perkins School of Theology at Southern Methodist University. In light of the academy's interest in Christian unity, the board of directors conferred the 1991 Virgilio Elizondo Award on Justo L. González, a Methodist, who is, without a doubt, one of the most prolific and accomplished U.S. Hispanic theologians—Roman Catholic or Protestant. Finally, ACHTUS decided to cosponsor an ecumenical conference on Hispanic theology called "Faith Doing Justice," which took place at Union Theological Seminary in New York City in October 1991. This was one of the first major ecumenical U.S. Hispanic theological conferences ever held.

Having completed this cursory review of the origins of U.S. Hispanic theology, now it is time to turn to the theologians themselves as reflected in the nine chapters of this collection. They offer a glimpse of how the Christian faith is again understood and actualized in the complex and pluralistic North American setting. Their reflections are nurtured by the profound faith of the Hispanic communities. For the first time these communities are acquiring, through these and many other writers, a theological voice. That voice promises to shed new, unexpected light on what Christian discipleship means in the changing circumstances of ecclesial life in contemporary North America. Theirs is certainly not a definitive voice or the last word. This is, after all, just a beginning for what promises to be a crucial, revitalizing dialogue engaging the attention of intelligent U.S. Christians for many years to come.

NOTES

1. There is no consensus among persons of Latin American origin in the United States regarding the most appropiate umbrella term. Church and government agencies have tended to use "Hispanic." In the western United States university, professional, and political leaders have preferred the term "Latino." The simple truth is that no single term is adequate. This editor therefore uses Hispanic and Latino interchangeably. Each contributor has made his or her own option in this regard.

2. The use of the word "newcomer" with reference to Hispanics is really quite inappropriate. The Hispanics were the first Europeans to settle in several parts of what is now the United States.

3. One of the few studies of the Hispanic Catholic in what is now the United States is the collection of essays edited by Moisés Sandoval, *Fronteras*, San Antonio: Mexican-American Cultural Center, 1983. The Cushwa Center at the University of Notre Dame has undertaken an ambitious project to advance the historical knowledge about Hispanics in the U.S. Catholic Church. Three volumes are being planned with publication beginning in 1992. Jay Dolan is the chief editor of this series.

4. See Allan Figueroa Deck, *The Second Wave*, Mahwah, N.J.: Paulist Press, pp. 9–10.

5. See *The Hispanic Presence: Challenge and Commitment*, Washington, D.C.: USCC, 1984, and *The National Pastoral Plan for Hispanic Ministry*, Washington, D.C.: USCC, 1987.

6. See Deck, *Second Wave*, Foreword, pp. xi–xvi; and "Opening the Door to Life in the Church," a collection of reflections on the challenge of the Hispanic presence, in *Origins*, vol. 19, no. 12, August 17, 1989.

7. It should be noted that the very first U.S. Hispanic theologian was really the nineteenth-century Cuban-American priest of the archdiocese of New York, Felix Varela. His was a brilliant but isolated example of theological reflection on the part of a U.S. Hispanic. See Felipe J. Estévez, *El perfil pastoral de Felix Varela*, Miami: Editorial Universal, 1989, and by the same author, *Felix Varela, Letters to Elpidio: A Critical Translation*, Mahwah, N.J.: Paulist Press, 1989.

8. For the life of Archbishop Lucey and its relevance to the growth of Hispanic ministry, see Stephen A. Privett, S.J., *The U.S. Catholic Church and Its Hispanic Members: The Pastoral Vision of Archbishop Robert E. Lucey*, San Antonio: Trinity University Press, 1988.

9. The issue of modern culture's influence on the evangelization of Latin America is being discussed more and more under the heading of the "new evangelization." The fifth centenary of Columbus's arrival in the New World has inaugurated a debate about modernity and evangelization. See, for instance, Leonardo Boff, *New Evangelization*, Maryknoll: Orbis Books, 1991. U.S. Hispanic thinkers in the very center of modern culture—that is, in the United States—have much to contribute.

10. Gregory Baum, "The Social Context of American Catholic Theology," in *Proceedings of the Forty-First Annual Convention*, Catholic Theological Society of America, p. 94.

11. See Roberto Goizueta's presentation in the section entitled "New Vitality: Theology and the Challenge of Black, Hispanic, and Feminist Theologies in North America," at the third plenary session of the forty-sixth annual convention of the Catholic Theological Society of America (1991) to be published in the *Proceedings*.

12. Pope John Paul II, *Centesimus Annus*, Washington, D.C.: USCC, 1991, nos. 33 and 42.

13. For further information on the members of ACHTUS, see *The Directory of the Academy of Catholic Hispanic Theologians of the United States* for 1991, available from the ACHTUS National Office, 1050 N. Clark St., El Paso, Texas 79905.

# Chapter One

# United States Hispanic Theology and the Challenge of Pluralism

## ROBERTO S. GOIZUETA

As we approach the twenty-first century, the so-called Christian world stands at an axial point in its history. Johann Baptist Metz speaks of three epochs in the history of the church and theology: "the epoch of Jewish Christianity, the epoch of Hellenism and European culture and civilization," and finally "the epoch of a culturally polycentric genuinely universal church."[1] We are presently witnessing the transition from the second to this third epoch, the shift from a Eurocentric to a polycentric Christianity. Today any analysis of the church and of theology must, in Metz's words,

> start from the fact that the church no longer simply "has" a third world church outside Europe but that it "is" a third world church with its origins and its history in the West and Europe. . . . And this is of great importance not just for the life of the church but for the fate of theology, since the church's social history affects the intellectual history of theology.[2]

Metz's penetrating observations raise a number of questions for third-world Christian theology in general and U.S. Hispanic theology in particular. The first set of questions, concerning ecclesiology, is born out of the relationship between the "origins and history" of the church on the one hand and its present reality on the other. A second set of questions, concerning theological method, is born out of the relationship between "the church's social history" on the one hand, and "the intellectual history of theology" on the other. Finally, a third set of questions, concerning the socio-cultural *ground* of both ecclesiology and theological method, is born out of the relationship between first-world societies and third-world societies. In other words, the church does not *have* a social history, rather social

1

history "has" the church, which in turn "has" theology.

I will examine these questions in order to then adumbrate the conditions of the possibility of what Metz calls a "culturally polycentric, genuinely universal church." In so doing, I will be speaking as a U.S. Hispanic and a Roman Catholic. My reflection is rooted either directly or indirectly in that experience and, from that perspective, bears on ecclesiological debates taking place within global Catholicism. As the socio-cultural questions ground the ecclesiological and methodological, they will not be addressed independently of these but will, in an integral fashion, inform my reflections on ecclesiology and methodology. Moreover, the ecclesiological and methodological questions that emerge within the socio-cultural matrix of U.S. Hispanic theology will be interpreted as presenting important challenges not only to the dominant society, churches, and theologies, but also to U.S. Hispanic theology itself.

## ECCLESIOLOGICAL QUESTIONS

What does it mean to say that the contemporary church is a third-world church with origins and history in the West and Europe? At the outset, we must begin by asserting the importance of the conjunctive preposition, for the contemporary, third-world church is not parallel to or absolutely different from the church of West European history and origins. That is, the polycentric church of today does indeed have a history, and that history remains ambiguous. Thus, institutionally and historically, these are the same church.

Yet the conjunctive preposition "with" in Metz's statement also implies *dis*junction. There is indeed something distinct about the contemporary church. What is distinct, however, is not so much its institutional structure (at least in the Roman Catholic Church) as its praxis—that is, its way of being church. This is particularly true of large sectors of the church. This practical transformation has yielded new ecclesiologies which, in turn, are now creating pressures for institutional change. The transformative praxis representative of the third-world church is, thus, essentially and intrinsically communal or social, for it represents a new way of being *ekklesia*.[3] This social praxis incorporates both an institutional dimension ("with its origins and its history in the West and Europe") and a grass-roots, communitarian dimension (e.g., base ecclesial communities). These are not opposed to each other but are, rather, dialectically related.

From within his own Brazilian context, Leonardo Boff explains the relationship between these two dimensions of the church:

> We should not view the grassroots church as a church running parallel to that of the larger institution. ... The antagonism does not lie between institution and community. It lies between a Christendom system (a church tied to the classes exercising hegemony in civil soci-

ety) and a people's church. In Brazil, and in Latin America in general, one can see a noticeable convergence between the larger church, structured as a network of institutional services, and the church as a network of grassroots communities. From the larger church the latter gets the symbolic capital of the faith, its links with apostolic tradition, and the dimension of universality. The larger church, in turn, benefits from the grassroots church. From the latter it gets concrete embodiment on the local and personal level, insertion among the common people, and links with the most urgent human causes revolving around justice, dignity, and participation. The two are geared toward each other, in mutual consideration and acceptance. They are not two churches. They are one and the same Church ... made concrete at different levels of society and confronting specific problems. The grassroots level is not at all allergic to the presence of priests and bishops in its midst; indeed, it cries out for them. But it demands of them a new style in exercising their ministry of union and communion. It is to be simpler, more evangelical, more functional, and linked with the people's cause.[4]

Boff thus warns against any attempt to understand Latin American popular Catholicism, with its emphasis on grass-roots communities, as an alternative to the institutional church, with "its origins and its history in the West and Europe." The *fundamental* difference between the traditional, European church and the emergent third-world church is not one of structure but of social praxis. In fact, as Boff points out, the structural differences are complementary. In other words, what is fundamentally "new" about the emergent third-world church is the social praxis (i.e., the way of *being* church in the world) that grounds, informs, and hence only indirectly reforms the institutional structure. Jon Sobrino likewise insists that "the line along which today's church is divided or united is not that of authority and obedience but that of the understanding and practice of the faith."[5] "The understanding and practice of the faith" yields new ecclesiologies which, in turn and only indirectly, create pressures for institutional change. Ecclesiological conflicts cannot be addressed directly, but only in their articulation with the social praxis of Christians. Sobrino contends:

The problem of unity and division is seen not as an intraecclesial problematic but as the reality of the Third World. It is seen as a reality outside the church, but one that is the source of the currents uniting and therefore also dividing Christians.[6]

The historical movement from social praxis, through ecclesiology (models of the church), to institutional renewal has a number of ramifications and precludes certain understandings of polycentric, third-world Christianity, some of which understandings have unfortunately gained currency in

European and North American circles. These *mis*understandings mask an underlying cultural imperialism that distorts the European and North American reception of third-world ecclesiologies.

Before directly addressing these misunderstandings, it will be necessary to digress in order to outline, in at least a cursory fashion, the socio-cultural presuppositions that inform many dominant ecclesiologies. Failure to advert to these cultural matrices has been the source of serious distortions of contemporary third-world ecclesiologies, which distortions, whether wittingly or unwittingly, have often served to legitimate the suppression of grass-roots ecclesial movements throughout the Third World. These cultural, and therefore epistemological, presuppositions, most pervasive and powerful in North America though also evident in some European circles, are the historical concomitants of the liberal, individualist, Enlightenment tradition in Western thought.[7]

The close historical connection between the emergence of capitalism, with its liberal individualist worldview, and the historical development of Protestantism has, of course, been hypothesized and argued by Max Weber and others.[8] The religious emphasis on the individual, implicit in what Paul Tillich has called the "Protestant principle," has sometimes formed an alliance with individualist economic ideologies.[9] Although, as Tillich is quick to point out, Protestantism has itself often lost sight of the Protestant principle, he nevertheless demonstrates how it has informed the historical development of Protestantism. As numerous scholars have observed, Protestantism has in turn been very closely identified with Northern European cultures and, especially, Euro-American culture.[10] In his provocative analysis of the social impact of Western individualism, Paul Wachtel observes:

> Over the past few hundred years, for a number of reasons, the sense of rootedness and belonging has been declining. In its place has appeared a more highly differentiated sense of individuality, implying both greater opportunity and greater separateness. In Protestant countries, this development was symbolized by the view that man faces God ... not through the mediation of (and hence as part of) the mother church, but as a separate and isolated individual.[11]

Referring to the United States, John Wilson speaks of Protestantism as our "common religion."[12] "Evidence that Protestant Christianity became the functional common religion of the society," he suggests, "would overwhelm us if we sought it out."[13] The Protestant principle, therefore, is not coextensive with or limited to Protestantism, but is also very much alive within, for instance, Anglo-American Catholicism—witness the Vatican's ongoing disputes with the United States hierarchy and persistent suspicions of "Americanism." Conversely, writes the Protestant Hispanic-American theologian Justo González, "all Hispanic-Americans have a Roman Catholic background."[14] The result is that, as Glen Caudill Dealy observes, Latin

American Protestants "often appear to think and act like Catholics" when seen through the lenses of Euro-American Protestantism.[15]

In the United States, the Protestant emphasis on the individual believer and the individualism of the prevailing economic ideology are both, in turn, buttressed by the individualism of the liberal, Enlightenment political tradition. The historical relationship between the economic ideology, the liberal political philosophy, and the Protestant principle is the bedrock upon which the Western cult of the individual has been constructed. The religious emphasis on the individual as the fundamental *locus theologicus* reinforces post-Enlightenment, political individualism, which in turn reinforces liberal capitalist, economic individualism. (This is not to suggest that these traditions presuppose anthropologies that are identical in every way, but simply that their emphasis on the individual, whether he or she be conceived as a believer, an entrepreneur, or a voting citizen, as foundational has led them, whether wittingly or unwittingly, into historical alliance.)[16] In the process all three traditions, in themselves important safeguards of individual freedom, have been distorted and their very real benefits muted. A distorted religious individualism legitimates bourgeois, privatized religion.[17] A distorted political individualism legitimates moral relativism. A distorted economic individualism legitimates a war of all against all. And all three, in their interrelationship, legitimate a social order that undermines the very values which these traditions themselves uphold—namely, the priority of the individual vis-à-vis religious, political, and economic systems.[18]

Individuals come to understand themselves as "separated and isolated" not only vis-à-vis the present, with respect to their contemporaries (communities and institutions), but also vis-à-vis the past, with respect to their ancestors (tradition).[19] As Paul Wachtel observes:

> The individual is portrayed as *influenced* by the society in which he lives, but he is not really perceived as an organic part of it. . . . The "community" . . . is a temporary and voluntary association of separate individuals.[20]

Relationships, whether to other individuals or to institutions, are chosen rather than assumed. And those that are assumed must themselves be freely chosen before they can exert any claim upon the individual (witness the ongoing argument over infant baptism vs. adult baptism). It follows, then, that all relationships are at all times renegotiable.

The true dichotomy here is not between individualism and collectivism, but between an anthropology that perceives the individual as prior and only extrinsically related to the social—whether the family, the community, or the institution—and an anthropology that perceives the individual as intrinsically social by nature and definition.[21] (I will later argue that this distinction is at the heart of Anglo-American distortions of theologies emerging in Latin American and U.S. Hispanic contexts.) Alasdair MacIntyre contends:

> The essence of individualism is not so much to emphasize the individual rather than the collective ... as to frame all questions according to an ostensible antithesis between the individual and the collective.[22]

In the United States, this antithesis has functioned to legitimate the "consumer society." The individual, whose freedom liberalism, capitalism, and the Protestant principle have rightly sought to safeguard, now becomes a pawn of the socio-cultural and economic systems in which he or she participates. What had been an end is now but a means, and vice versa.[23] In the name of individual freedom, the individual has been loosed from preexistent ties to community and tradition, has become increasingly mobile both physically and psychologically, has been afforded the "freedom to choose," has, in the process, surrendered the very communal and traditional bonds (at least as a priori, constitutive dimensions) that have heretofore provided the necessary ground and frame of reference *from which* to choose, and has, therefore, been set psychologically adrift, a manipulable pawn in the hands of the dominant ideology and its purveyors. Despite the necessity of maintaining the vitality of the Protestant principle in the face of bureaucratic and self-perpetuating ecclesiastical structures, the historical articulation of this principle within the socio-cultural matrix of our consumer society has therefore had some unfortunate, if unintended, consequences. In itself a crucial dimension of Christian faith and tradition, the Protestant principle is distorted by the ambient social ideologies and in turn lends them credence. In the process, individual believers come to see themselves as consumers of religion, shopping for the right church just as they shop for the right toothpaste, clothes, car, or spouse. If one's faith community is not something that defines who one is, much as one's family does, but is rather something that one "joins," then one is always free to leave when one's needs are no longer being met. What is at stake is not one's very identity, given at least in part by the community, but merely one's ability to opt for a community in which one's presumably autodetermined identity can be actualized.[24] One joins a church much as one would join a garden club, a political party, or the Rotary. And in the process individuality gives way to social conformity.

In their book *Habits of the Heart*, Robert Bellah and associates note the paradoxical connection between this unchecked individualism (or, in the authors' words, the "socially unsituated self") and social conformity:

> As Tocqueville observed, when one can no longer rely on tradition or authority, one inevitably looks to others for confirmation of one's judgments. Refusal to accept established opinion and anxious con-

formity to the opinions of one's peers turn out to be two sides of the same coin.[25]

Furthermore, when the socially unsituated self, with its supposedly unique and irrefutable desires, instincts, and feelings ("I'm OK; you're OK"), is the ultimate ground of decision-making, whether as to career, spouse, or religious affiliation, questions of value can no longer be decided by appeal to either rational argument or tradition. The criterion for deciding competitive value claims becomes, not the inherent worth of the claims themselves, since there is no mutually accepted reference point from which to judge these, but rather one's ability to realize one's value claims:

> In the absence of any objectifiable criteria of right and wrong, good or evil, the self and its feelings become our only moral guide. . . . But while everyone may be entitled to his or her own private space, only those who have enough money can, in fact, afford to purchase the private property required to do their own thing.[26]

Hence, the ideology of economic individualism[27] readily becomes the arbiter of political and religious individualism, or the hermeneutical cipher through which these latter are interpreted in our culture.

There is little doubt that, prescinding from a discussion of social costs, our traditions of individualism have been instrumental in preserving important rights and freedoms. More problematic, however, has been their often symbiotic historical interrelationship. While, for instance, our liberal political tradition takes for granted the need to preserve checks and balances within political institutions, this same need is not as strongly perceived in the *relationship* between the political sphere and other spheres of modern life. Indeed, the political, economic, religious, and cultural are deemed to be separate and independent (e.g., the separation of church and state). Our blindness to their concrete, historical interrelationship prevents us from perceiving how these, instead of checking and balancing each other, reinforce each other in such a way that the virtues of individualism are often obscured under the personal and social disintegration so often wrought by an unchecked individualism.[28]

As indicated above, this individualism inevitably affects the Christian's self-understanding and his or her understanding of the church. It therefore comes as no surprise that ecclesiologies emerging in third-world cultures would have a difficult time gaining acceptance among Anglo-Christians in North America. The difficulties are manifested not only in the outright rejection of these ecclesiologies, but, perhaps more importantly, in the misrepresentations and distortions that characterize their reception within the dominant society, often even when that reception is ostensibly sympathetic. Whether we reject third-world theologies and ecclesiologies or support them, our perception of them will inevitably be colored by the individualism of our culture, an individualism alien to the third-world cultures in which they were born. If we are not methodologically attentive to this epistemological bias, we are bound to impose our own preconceptions, questions, and problems on these theologies and ecclesiologies, thereby distorting them.

Tracing its roots to pre-Reformation Iberian, Native American, and African traditions, the mestizo worldview of Latin American cultures in general and U.S. Hispanic cultures in particular is less individualistic than organic in character.[29] Although an individual is always free to leave behind his or her familial, geographical, and religious roots, such a rejection is made much more difficult by the individual's own self-understanding as one who is formed and, indeed, defined by these very roots. To deny one's family, one's community, or one's faith would be, in a very real way, to deny one's self—this in contradistinction to the belief, more typical of the dominant culture in the United States, that one *must* distance oneself from one's family, community, or faith precisely in order to *assert*, or more precisely to *forge* one's self, one's *own* identity. This latter axiom is reflected, for instance, in the common belief that, in order to be a "healthy" individual, one must at one time or another undergo an "identity crisis" or, in analogous religious language, a "crisis of faith." In Latino cultures, the fundamental social entity is not the individual, but the family or group. In general, a Latino or Latina will not hesitate to criticize his or her formative group, but the criticism will not be perceived in most cases as a sign of rejection, rather as an implicit affirmation of his or her commitment and ties to the group. These commitments and ties are appreciated as the very conditions of the possibility of criticism and conflict.[30]

In sum, the ecclesiologies originating in Latino cultures presuppose an organic worldview, just as Anglo-American ecclesiologies presuppose a fundamentally individualistic anthropology. In a genuinely multicultural, polycentric church, an awareness of these epistemological differences can be a source of insight and conversion, if we become conscious of them and attentive to the manifold ways in which these different cultural and ideological perspectives color our perception of ecclesial movements in the Third World. If not, these epistemological differences will continue to be sources of misunderstanding, thereby preventing genuine dialogue. Furthermore, such a distorted perception will generate caricatures of these movements, which caricatures will all too easily become fodder for the opponents of popular ecclesial movements.[31]

One important example of the way such distortion works can be found in the Base Ecclesial Communities of Latin America and the misperception North Americans often have of the ecclesiology underlying that movement. Leonardo Boff's description of the relationship between the Base Ecclesial Communities (CEBs) and the institutional church, quoted above, reflects precisely the kind of organic worldview I have described as common to Latin American and U.S. Hispanic cultures. While these *dimensions* of the universal church embody different ecclesiological models, they do not represent two churches, one communitarian and the other institutional, one respectful of the individual and the other hopelessly bureaucratic and autocratic. On the contrary, argues Boff, "the two are geared toward each other."[32] He goes on to say that "the grassroots level is not at all allergic to the presence of priests and bishops in its midst; indeed, it cries out for them."[33] In a similar vein, Sobrino insists that "the church of the poor does not disdain the typical ecclesial means of achieving internal unity; on the contrary, it makes them possible."[34] He goes on to assert:

> If the church lacked the institutional dimension . . . it would rob the church of the positive contribution of so many human beings who may have nothing to offer but their suffering, their ignorance, their wretched poverty. . . . It is certain that without the institutional element the church could not exist at all, especially not as a church of the people, a church of the poor.[35]

The notion of "base" is not *fundamentally* an ecclesiological category, but a social, cultural, political, and economic category. Otherwise one would be hard pressed to explain the participation of so many bishops and priests in the CEBs.

Within the context of an individualistic anthropology there can be a tendency to understand the so-called popular church as comprised of voluntary associations of likeminded individuals who have set themselves in opposition to the institutional church, rather than, as is in fact the case, in opposition to oppressive social forces—and only indirectly in opposition to the church, insofar as it is allied with these forces. Such a misinterpretation is already reflected at an etymological level, when, for instance, the term "comunidades eclesiales de base" is translated as "Basic Christian Communities," the most common English translation of the term. By translating the word *eclesial* as "Christian" we obscure the institutional dimension of Base Ecclesial Communities.

In his book *Church: Charism and Power*, Boff explains why the institutional church is necessary. He uses the terms "charism" and "power" in a way analogous to Tillich's use of the terms "Protestant principle" and "Catholic substance," as well as other scholars' use of the terms "prophetic" and "priestly"—namely, as dialectically related dimensions of the one church.[36] "Power (i.e., the ordering principle in the church)," he suggests, "can be a charism, as long as it serves everyone and is an instrument for building justice in the community."[37] The appended caveat reveals the source of Boff's uneasiness with the institutional church. He is critical, not of the institutional church per se, but of the politically oppressive manner in which the church has often functioned historically. Correctly used, the power of the institutional church is necessary precisely so that the church can carry out its liberative and salvific role in society. This is the message that the very presence of the CEBs in its midst continues to convey to the institutional church. "Because of the grassroots communities," asserts the Brazilian theologian, "the whole church has presently adopted a firm option favoring the liberation of the oppressed, the defense of human rights (of the poor in particular), and the overall transformation of society into more socialized forms."[38]

That this option has not been consistently firm and unambiguous does not mean that it is without significance, particularly in the context of many Latin American societies. Lacking a tradition of the separation of church and state, the church here has traditionally played an important public role. The post-Medellín church is often the only public institution capable of effectively confronting military, political, and economic elites. Whatever its many flaws—and some have had truly horrific consequences—the institution, though at times in collusion with the enemies of freedom, is also in many cases the champion of individual rights and the defender of the poor.[39]

Likewise, the *locus theologicus* of U.S. Hispanic theology is not the base community, or popular religiosity, *as opposed to* the institutional church, but the U.S. Hispanic community's popular religiosity *in dialectical relation to* the institutional church; popular religiosity is at the same time an expression of the "official" tradition and a critique of that tradition.[40] To interpret popular religiosity and base communities as if these were fundamentally anti-institutional phenomena would be to impose on them an Enlightenment interpretation which could only perpetuate the suffering undergone by Latino cultures in the face of modern, "enlightened" societies.

For this reason, it can be not only epistemologically dangerous but indeed politically dangerous to read present tensions between the institutional church and U.S. Hispanics through the lenses of an individualistic worldview and anthropology. In a society such as ours, with its relative if not exclusive emphasis on the individual conscience as the ultimate authority, these tensions tend to be interpreted as tensions between competing magisteria, rather than as tensions between competing *models* of authority. In the first instance, the very authority, indeed the existence of the institutional hierarchy would be challenged—in accord with the anti-institutional suspicions of post-Enlightenment, liberal individualism. In the second instance, however, what is challenged is not corporate authority qua authority but that authority's self-understanding, its structural role, and its historical exercise of power in alliance with the dominant societies, classes, and cultures.[41]

Thus, the doctrinal conservatism of U.S. Hispanic and Latin American theologies, sometimes criticized by progressive North American theologians,[42] is a result not only of the fundamentally practical orientation of their theological method but also of their fundamentally organic worldview and ecclesiology. It is that worldview and ecclesiology that underlie, for instance, Clodovis Boff's assertion that the magisterium is "the legitimate tribunal in the discernment of the faith," and his insistence that the relationship between the institutional church, the believer, and the professional theologian is "organic, not independent, much less contradictory."[43] In a statement guaranteed to raise eyebrows among even his most ardent supporters in the United States, Clodovis suggests that "the real fathers and mothers of the theology of liberation are the hierarchical church, in the context of an oppressed, Christian, Latin American people."[44] Note that implicit in this latter statement is the notion that "the context of an oppressed, Christian, Latin American people" is not per se antithetical to the hierarchical church. Whether or not such a fidelity to the hierarchy is either valid or warranted, we must respect it and be aware of the cultural and ideological presuppositions — again, whatever their intrinsic validity — that are the source of our uneasiness with such statements of fidelity. One can and must question both the validity of such an ecclesiology and its ability to promote justice. However, to proffer such a critique and to do so honestly one must first understand the underlying cultural and ideological presuppositions and, in order to do that, one must first understand one's own presuppositions.

Moreover, to read third-world ecclesiologies through the lenses of liberal individualism would be not only to misread them but also to miss the true radicality of their critique: to be marginalized is to live on the edge — of society and its institutions, including the church. A grass-roots ecclesial movement that does not take seriously the decidedly unromantic need for structure and institution, key dimensions of what Leonardo Boff means by "power," will inevitably go the way of the hippies and yippies of the 1960s, and will have as much lasting impact on the lives of the poor. Genuine concern for the individual precludes either a simple identification or a simple opposition between the individual and the collective, both of which alternatives reinforce the power of the collective over the individual. As Alasdair MacIntyre suggests:

> Those who continue to base their thinking on this false antithesis even if . . . they champion the claims of the collective against the individual, remain within the basic categories of individualist thought and practice.[45]

It is in this light that Anglo-Americans who sympathize with popular ecclesial movements and affirm the value of popular religion can all too easily become unwitting accomplices to the authoritarian, bureaucratic forces that are suspicious of popular religious movements. Both the sympathizers and the opponents often share the presupposition that there is an inherent dichotomy between individuals and grass-roots communities ("we") on the one hand and the institution ("it") on the other. What then divides these two camps is that, whereas the liberal sympathizers cast their lot with "the people," the autocrats cast their lot with the bureaucratic institution. And each side reinforces the stereotypes of the other. In a 1988

*New York Times* interview, Gustavo Gutiérrez expressed dismay at the "car-icatures" of liberation theology that are often put forth in the name of liberation theology.[46] These caricatures can be blind to the *dialectical* rela-tionship that exists between popular religion and institutional church. In the context of U.S. Hispanic ecclesiology, Orlando Espín and Sixto García point to the dialectical relationship between the "official" tradition of the church and the tradition embodied in popular Catholicism:

> When careful examination is made of the "official" and "popular" versions of Tradition, the two will be found to be *essentially* the same, though culturally and symbolically expressed in different manners.[47]

A genuinely polycentric Christianity must incorporate such a dialectic for two reasons. (1) In order to avoid the pitfalls of either a naive anti-institutionalism, which would condemn grass-roots ecclesial movements to the ash heap of so many utopian historical projects, or a naive institution-alism, which would undermine the self-identity of these movements and the particularity of their ecclesiologies. (2) In order to avoid the pitfalls of either a co-optation of third-world ecclesial movements by first-world churches, without the necessary analysis of the ways in which different socio-cultural presuppositions influence our ecclesiologies, or a coercive repression based on those very differences.

## THEOLOGICAL QUESTIONS

### *Theological Pluralism and Liberal Individualism*

The emergence of liberation theology as a movement genetically linked to the Base Ecclesial Community movement in Latin America found fertile ideological ground in the organic worldview indigenous to the mestizo cul-tures of that continent. It is no coincidence that even the most influential *opponents* of liberation theology in Latin America—for example, Alfonso López Trujillo—are often themselves perceived as radicals by U.S. stan-dards, for these critics share the liberation theologians' own rejection of ideological individualism. Their opposition to liberation theology is rooted less in a defense of the individual than in a defense of the "common good." It comes as no surprise, then, that North American neoconservatives, like Michael Novak, extend their criticism of Latin American liberation theology to include the Latin American *critics* of liberation theology, for these are also deemed dangerous to "the American way of life."[48] In this sense, Novak has been much more perceptive than other North American critics. In fact, when reading his works one has the impression that Novak's opposition to Latin American liberation theology is based less in his fear of that theol-ogy's putative identification with Marxist ideology than in his fear of its thoroughly Catholic worldview, which, as he correctly observes, has traditionally been at odds with liberal individualism.[49] He quotes, for instance, Pope Paul VI, who, in *Octogesima Adveniens*, taught that "at the very root of philosophical liberalism is an erroneous affirmation of the autonomy of the individual in his activity, his motivation and the exercise of his liberty."[50] Underlying Catholic social teaching is a personalistic anthropology that understands the "person" (not the "individual") as intrinsically social.

Theologies (whether Catholic or Protestant) developed in the predominantly Protestant, Anglo-American context are likely to reflect different presuppositions, which are themselves quite valuable to a polycentric theological perspective. The problem is not so much with the presuppositions themselves—though, as discussed above, these must be questioned rather than merely assumed—as with the failure to appreciate their methodological import, and the concomitant, often inadvertent depreciation of third-world cultures resulting from such a failure, as when Anglo-American theologians, with the best intentions, "adapt" liberation theology to the North American context without giving due attention to the fact that the very notion and process of "adaptation" is itself culturally conditioned. Concepts such as "adaptation," "sensitivity," and "openness" are themselves culturally defined and interpreted from culturally defined anthropologies.

Here I would again point to the danger of understanding the individual as only extrinsically related to social groups, from among which he or she is "free to choose." This, it seems to me, is an almost inevitable corollary of any anthropology that, whatever its name, tends to "frame all questions according to an ostensible antithesis between the individual and the collective."[51] Again, both the liberal individualist and the statist or collectivist options agree on this point. However, while the former promotes the "freedom to choose," the latter suppresses it. The very strength of the liberal individualists' "marketplace of ideas" as an ideological tradition in our country has in some circles provoked a backlash. As in the case of many fundamentalist Christian groups, it itself presupposes an individualist anthropology, though of a different order and with a different intent.[52]

When an "openness" to other theologies is not grounded in a methodological attentiveness to the many ways in which that openness is conditioned by our own social, cultural, political, and economic context—that is, the many ways in which, because of our very humanity and historicity, we are necessarily *closed*—the resulting pluralism will be neither genuinely open nor genuinely pluralistic. That is, the other theological perspectives will be admitted into the theological arena only as *already* interpreted within the implicit, dominant perspective and only as "one perspective" that, precisely qua "perspective," can make no claims on the dominant theology. The marginalized theology is thus admitted into the theological debate, but only as a *marginalized* theology, or, in common parlance, only as a token. Consequently, the rules presupposed and enforced in such a dialogue are none other than those of the dominant worldview, which will admit third-world theologies into the dialogue but only insofar as these are already implicitly interpreted according to the prevailing individualistic ideologies. U.S. Hispanic theology, for instance, will be studied, but only as *"U.S. Hispanic* theology"—that is, only as *one* theology peripheral to the study and articulation of Theology, with a capital "T." Such a pluralism insists on the historicity of third-world theologies, but is curiously ignorant of its own historicity. It yields a relativism that insists on the partial and perspectival nature of all truth claims except those of post-Enlightenment, liberal, individualist "pluralism" itself—as defined, of course, by the theological establishment—which is the one absolute a priori.

One North American theologian who has warned against this danger is David Tracy, who articulates the epistemological implications for theology of Metz's observation that the church no longer "has" a third-world church, but, indeed, "is" a third-world church. Even the *post*modern thinkers concern for "otherness," suggests Tracy, can mask an underlying imperialism:

> But even this turn to the other and the different by the modern West is too often made with the secret wish that we are still the centre and can name those others. The others remain at the margins. Marginal from where? From the centre which no longer holds. . . . The other envisaged from the self-named centre is too often a projected other: one projected either by the new fears of the loss of privilege and power of the modern bourgeois subject, or the hopes for another chance of the neo-conservative, or the desires for escape from modernity of the post-modern non-self. A fact seldom admitted by the moderns, the anti-moderns, and the post-moderns alike—even with all the talk of otherness and difference—is that there is no longer a centre with margins. There are many centres. Pluralism is an honourable but sometimes a too easy way of admitting this fact. Too many forms of modern Western theological pluralism are historicist, but too a-historical as well as curiously a-theological in their visions to allow for the unsettling reality of our polycentric present. There is a price to be paid for any genuine pluralism—that price many pluralists seem finally either unwilling to pay or unable to see. . . . The others are not marginal to our centres but centres of their own.[53]

By definition, a genuine polycentrism rejects the existence of *a* center, the very center presupposed by the notion of *margin*alization.

In some ways, liberal pluralism, which presupposes the individual's unfettered "freedom to choose," is a greater danger to a genuinely polycentric Christianity than either fundamentalist or institutional authoritarianism. There is nothing more seductive than good intentions and a good heart. For generations, the United States has been trying to force democracy and pluralism, or rather its brand thereof, down the throats of Latin Americans. There is nothing more pernicious than absolutism in defense of pluralism, for the inherent contradiction undermines the credibility of pluralism, thereby preventing the emergence of authentic pluralism. Where absolutism is itself an ideology, it can be combatted; where it is a way of life masked by a "pluralistic" ideology, it is virtually unassailable.

## Toward an "Analogical Catholicity of Theology"

What kind of theology, then, is appropriate to a polycentric church? In addressing this question, I refer to Enrique Dussel's attempt to articulate the conditions of the possibility of an "analogical catholicity (*mundialidad*) of theology."[54] "European theology," he argues, "is not universally valid in its univocal or dominating sense; but neither are theologies equivocal, or valid for their own region alone."[55] A univocal theology admits differences, but these are perceived as mere "specifications or individuations" of "some *univocal* Christian experience or theology, which in fact arose in a given culture and is lived in a certain geopolitical region."[56] Such differences are seen as accidental and extrinsic to Christian experience per se.[57] Equivocal theologies, on the other hand, "would have nothing in common. In that case the 'pluralism' would be without any unity."[58] Analogous theologies are rooted in a common faith and tradition but, because faith and tradition have no existence apart from their historical incarnation in a particular time and place, these theologies "also have a distinct (not just different) moment where they are diverse."[59] These distinctions, suggests Dussel, are ontological, for they are grounded in the analogy of being.[60]

Given the Latin American church's historical relationship to the European church, Dussel reserves his greatest criticism for univocal theology, which is "imperialist, war-bent, and child-killing."[61] "Nothing," he writes, "endangers the unity of the church more than neurotic, univocal uniqueness."[62] I would extend Dussel's critique to include an equally strong warning against a pluralism of equivocal theologies, which, when it degenerates into mere relativism, is dangerous not only to the unity of the church but also to the self-identity of the very theologies which such a pluralism would like to respect. Too often, at least in the context of North American society, those who promote theological pluralism are blind to the ways in which an ideology of pluralism can mask and legitimate the control that the dominant theology continues to exert over theological discourse.

Ironically, a pluralism of equivocal theologies, none of which is perceived as having any claims on any other, can (1) forestall dialogue among the theologies and (2) camouflage the effective control still being exercised by the dominant theology. (Perceived equivocity can hide an underlying univocity, thereby contributing to the historical efficacy of the latter.) Dialogue is preempted when equivocal theologies, each perceived as valid within — and only within — its own historical *locus theologicus*, are precluded from entering into mutually critical dialogue. When each theology is its own standard of truth, there is no possibility of mutual critique. This occurs, for instance, when the validity of U.S. Hispanic theology is accepted, but only for U.S. Hispanics. In a way, such an argument is more disarming than an explicit, open rejection of U.S. Hispanic theology. If the truth spoken by U.S. Hispanic theology can make no claim on non-Hispanics, then why should the latter bother engaging in dialogue? Any dialogue predicated on this kind of pluralism would be little more than mutual backslapping.[63]

Pluralism can also become an instrument for exercising greater control over the parameters of theological discourse, while at the same time creating the appearance of genuine dialogue. As indicated above, other theological voices are admitted into the dialogue, but only as marginalized voices.[64] A specific way in which this form of exclusion is institutionalized in our theological and divinity schools is, ironically, by adding courses in areas such as "liberation theology," "U.S. Hispanic theology," "black theology," and "feminist theology," but preventing the issues raised in those courses from becoming integrated into the courses of the required, core curriculum. Theological schools point with pride to their catalogues, which are sometimes filled with such courses. Yet these courses, almost always electives, are at an inherent disadvantage in attracting the vast majority of students, who are already overwhelmed with their required courses in Tillich, Barth, Niebuhr, Rahner, and others. The result is that what appears to be theological pluralism is in fact the same required, basic, or core theological curriculum, promoting the same European theologies, but to which are now added a certain number of optional, marginalized courses, taught by marginalized faculty, and usually attended by marginalized students.

The theological academy cannot begin to talk about genuine theological pluralism until third-world theologies are addressed and studied, not merely as third-world theologies, but as fundamental theology, as systematic theology, as scriptural theology. In other words, the possibility of moving toward an analogical catholicity of theology, or a genuine theological pluralism, will not depend solely on our willingness to allow other voices into the theological discussion. That is not enough. The academic establishment must also be willing to divest itself of the power to set the parameters and define the rules of the discussion. In short, it must relinquish the power to define the nature of pluralism.[65]

## Theory and Praxis

At the same time, third-world theologians must themselves be willing and able to engage that very establishment if they are to articulate an effective critique of the dominant theologies' hegemony. If heretofore marginalized theological voices are to be included as equal partners in theological dialogue, those voices must be attentive to the demands not only of their *locus theologicus* in oppressed communities but also to the conditions of the possibility of actually *being heard* in such a dialogue. This fact presents a number of methodological problems for third-world theologies, generally, and for U.S. Hispanic theology specifically.

U.S. Hispanic theology, on the one hand, is born out of the praxis of Latino communities and, as such, attempts to be a *teología de conjunto*; the theological subject is not the *ego* but the *communio*. This is not to suggest that the professional theological task can be undertaken by the community, but that that task is organically related to the community, taking the community as its starting point; though as "individual," the theologian does not undertake his or her task qua individual, but qua member of the community. His or her authenticity is either affirmed or denied by that community.

On the other hand, U.S. Hispanic theology is also necessarily characterized by a certain *non*identity with the praxis of the community. By virtue of his or her education and training, the theologian necessarily functions at an epistemological distance from the constituent community. That distance is methodologically ambiguous in that it represents both an accession to the dominant social system and the condition of the possibility of a critique of that system. In order to challenge the dominant society and its structures, the U.S. Hispanic theologian must be heard within that society. To be heard, one must first be credible. Yet, to be credible, the Latino or Latina must submit to criteria of credibility which may be quite alien to the historical experience of their constituent communities. In short, for U.S. Hispanic theologians to challenge effectively the dominant society's criteria of truth and rationality, those same theologians must first prove their own credibility by meeting those very criteria (e.g., the theologian must attend a "prestigious" graduate school, earn a doctorate, publish "serious" books and articles in "reputable" journals).

Caught on the horns of this dilemma, some Latino theologians, along with other third-world theologians, are tempted to reject the claims of theory in favor of the claims of praxis, thereby seeking to erase that epistemological distance which they perceive as an obstacle to their identification, or solidarity, with their communities. Implicit in this dichotomous rendering of the theory-praxis relationship is, again, the dominant, post-Enlightenment, Western worldview, reflected, in this case, in the anthropological and epistemological dualism which is presupposed as methodologically axiomatic. The rejection of theory in favor of praxis will often translate into a rejection of the theological academy, or the professional theological enterprise, in favor of social activism; the intellectual enterprise is identified with "theory" and social activism is identified with "praxis." Fearful of co-optation, the theologian rejects the professional theological enterprise altogether, opting for a life of "praxis." Though putatively more in touch with "the people," this theological methodology—a temptation for all praxis-based theologies—reflects the Cartesian mind-body, theory-praxis dichotomy. It is fundamentally at odds with U.S. Hispanic experience and has, in fact, served as an ideological instrument of that community's oppression. By rejecting reason, or intellect, as inherently oppressive, the unreflective activist, or *basista*, unwittingly promulgates the stereotype of the Latino as only a body (laborer), or a heart (emotional, lover of fiestas), with no mind or capacity for rational thinking.

U.S. Hispanic theology, grounded in the organic worldview of Latino culture, must reject such a dichotomy, insisting on a holistic anthropology that distinguishes but does not separate theory and praxis, mind and body. There is no pure praxis any more than there is pure theory. U.S. Hispanic theology does not reject reason, rather it rejects the dominant culture's conceptualist and instrumentalist *models* of reason and criteria of reasonableness. U.S. Hispanic theology seeks to uncover the irrationality of what the dominant society calls reason. And, again, this will not occur until U.S. Hispanic theologians are able not only to join in the theological enterprise (as already defined by the theological establishment), but, indeed, to name and define the very nature of that enterprise.

There can be no more *practical* task than this, for Western reason has, for centuries, functioned as a socio-historical, ideological instrument of oppression, turning whole peoples into instruments in the service of its designs, and turning persons into mere objects to be manipulated in the service of some "greater" end. The liberation of reason is an important dimension of the socio-historical process of liberation. Any rejection of reason per se presupposes, and hence promotes, the very dichotomous anthropology that has been a source of so much suffering for U.S. Hispanics.

U.S. Hispanic theology finds its roots in the praxis of U.S. Hispanic communities. That praxis reflects an instinctive and implicit repudiation of the conceptualist dichotomies underlying modern, Western anthropologies and epistemologies, whether dichotomies of mind-body, intellect-affect, or individual identity-communal identity. As the praxis of whole human persons, hearts and minds, spirits and bodies, it has a reflective moment. The task of U.S. Hispanic theology is to bear witness to the significance of that moment *within* the socio-historical struggles of U.S. Hispanic communities.

More than ever, the poor need the very best theological scholarship. Only if we Latino theologians can use our education and skills to combat the forms of (ir)rationality that govern the institutions that oppress "the people" will those people forgive us for having distanced ourselves from them in the pursuit of our professional education and training. That distance will then be revealed in all its ambiguity, as *both* a temptation to co-optation *and* the condition of the possibility of an effective challenge to the conceptualist and instrumentalist models of rationality that legitimate the oppression of our people.

In their attempt to engage the dominant society and culture in a critical manner, thereby hoping to make possible the emergence of an authentic pluralism, U.S. Hispanic theologians thus confront the tension inherent in their identity: the tension between being a U.S. Hispanic and a U.S. theologian. To seek a premature resolution of that tension is to reject our historical task, our particular, concrete way of being in solidarity with our people; it is to reject our particular contribution to the emergence of a "culturally polycentric genuinely universal church."[66]

A polycentric church demands a new theological subject, or, more properly, new theological subjects. The liberal, modern, Western ego—no matter how "pluralistic" or "open"—can no longer function presumptively as the epistemological center.[67] This is the challenge of U.S. Hispanic theology. At the same time, U.S. Hispanic theology is itself challenged to embrace the responsibility of bringing the historical praxis of U.S. Hispanic communities into critical relationship with the dominant culture and its institutions, thereby helping to forge a truly liberative pluralism.

## NOTES

1. Johann Baptist Metz, "Theology in the Modern Age, and before Its End," in *Different Theologies, Common Responsibility*, Claude Geffré et al., eds. (Edinburgh: Clark, 1984), p. 16.

2. Ibid.

3. This is a crucial point, for, as I will discuss below, it will become one of the methodological presuppositions which, though central to third-world theologies of liberation, will be overlooked by many first-world interpreters, especially sympathetic interpreters, of these theologies.

4. Leonardo Boff, "Theological Characteristics of a Grassroots Church," in *The Challenge of Basic Christian Communities*, Sergio Torres and John Eagleson, eds. (Maryknoll, N.Y.: Orbis, 1981), p. 139.

5. Jon Sobrino, *The True Church and the Poor* (Maryknoll, N.Y.: Orbis, 1984), p. 197.

6. Ibid.

7. The term "liberal" is used here to denote an individualistic political philosophy and a contractual social theory which trace their roots to John Locke, Adam Smith, John Stuart Mill, the Enlightenment, the French Revolution, and the American Revolution. Both "conservatives" and "liberals" in the United States are heirs to this liberal tradition. For an insightful—and arguably classic—interpretation of this tradition in its historical context, see Sheldon S. Wolin, *Politics and Vision* (Boston: Little, Brown and Co., 1960).

8. See Max Weber, *The Protestant Ethic and the Spirit of Capitalism* (New York: Scribner's, 1956). For more recent analyses of the historical connection between liberal individualism and Protestantism, though from different cultural and philosophical perspectives, see Otto Maduro, *Religion and Social Conflicts* (Maryknoll, N.Y.: Orbis, 1982) and Robert Bellah et al., *Habits of the Heart* (New York: Harper and Row, 1985).

9. Paul Tillich, *Systematic Theology* (Chicago: University of Chicago, 1951–63), esp. part V, sec. II; John Dillenberger and Claude Welch, *Protestant Christianity* (New York: Scribner's, 1954), pp. 313–14. It is important to note that Tillich argues for the necessity of both the Protestant principle and the "Catholic substance." Furthermore, it would be an error to assume that the individualism underlying the Protestant principle is identical to that underlying liberal capitalism. While an in-depth comparison of these is beyond the scope of this chapter, such a comparison

is articulated and developed in Bellah et al., *Habits,* pp. 142-63.

10. Ibid. See also Weber, *The Protestant Ethic and the Spirit of Capitalism,* esp. pp. 95-183. For convincing analyses of the fundamental role played by Protestantism in American culture, see, for instance, Martin Marty, *Righteous Empire* (New York: Dial Press, 1970) and Robert Handy, *A Christian America* (New York: Oxford University Press, 1971).

11. Ibid., p. 61. Wachtel adds a caveat: "This does not mean, of course, that *some* sense of community, and *some* secure ties to others do not remain. We could not survive without such ties" (p. 61).

12. John F. Wilson, "Common Religion in American Society," in *Civil Religion and Political Theology,* Leroy S. Rouner, ed. (Notre Dame: University of Notre Dame Press, 1986), pp. 111–24.

13. Ibid., p. 113.

14. Justo González, *Mañana: Christian Theology from a Hispanic Perspective* (Nashville: Abingdon, 1990), p. 66.

15. Glen Caudill Dealy, *The Public Man: An Interpretation of Latin American and Other Catholic Countries* (Amherst: University of Massachusetts Press, 1977), p. 87.

16. For an analysis of the distinction between religious individualism, or what Bellah et al. call "biblical individualism," and other individualistic ideologies, see Bellah et al., *Habits,* pp. 142–63.

17. See Johann Baptist Metz, *Faith in History and Society* (New York: Seabury, 1980), pp. 32–47. Metz warns against projecting onto the Reformation our own individualistic, privatized religious ideology, arguing that the "middle-class, privatistic subjectivity" which has so influenced Western religion was not itself a product of the Reformation (p. 36).

18. For insightful, though differing, analyses of the complex historical and sociopsychological interrelationships among the various aspects of American individualism, see Paul L. Wachtel, *The Poverty of Affluence* (New York: Free Press, 1983) and Bellah et al., *Habits.*

19. Ibid., p. 61.

20. Ibid., p. 118. Wachtel's criticism here is directed more specifically at the writings of Charles Reich, which, according to Wachtel, reflect the exaggerated individualism of modern American society.

21. Or, in the words of Bellah et al., "the improvisational self (i.e., atomic individual) chooses values to express itself; but it is not constituted by them as from a pre-existing source" (p. 80).

22. Alasdair MacIntyre, "Durkheim's Call to Order," *New York Review of Books,* March 7, 1974, p. 26.

23. Ibid., pp. 60–62.

24. See Virgilio Elizondo, Foreword, in Justo González, *Mañana,* pp. 14–15.

25. Bellah et al., *Habits,* p. 148.

26. Ibid., p. 76.

27. I use this term as a way of specifying, within the economic context, what Bellah et al., mean by "utilitarian individualism" (*Habits,* pp. 55–84).

28. Japan is an example of a society where the influences of capitalist individualism are, in Wachtel's words, "kept somewhat in check by a unique and longstanding cultural tradition of strong ties of mutual obligations and expectations. . . . In the United States the anticommunal forces of the competitive market place are reinforced, rather than checked, by prevalent cultural values" (ibid., p. 168).

29. Virgilio Elizondo, Foreword, in Justo González, *Mañana*, p. 13.

30. One of the most intriguing aspects of Anglo-American religion to Latinos is the ease and regularity with which Anglo-Americans switch from one religion to another, or from one denomination to another (see Elizondo, Foreword, in Justo González, *Mañana*, pp. 14–15). Likewise, Latinos are often astounded to hear that what they perceive as mere argumentation and, hence, a way of "making connections" in a relationship, is perceived by non-Latinos as an emotionalism and conflict that threatens relationship. The expression of anger, which for Latinos is often one way of reinforcing relational ties, is perceived as hatred by those accustomed to identifying relationship with nonconflict; conflict is here assumed to signal the breakdown of the relationship and is thus often seen as a just reason for opting out of the relationship.

31. Ibid. See also Roberto S. Goizueta, "Liberation Theology: Retrospect and Prospect," *Philosophy and Theology* 3 (Fall 1988), pp. 25–43.

32. Boff, "Theological Characteristics," p. 139.

33. Ibid.

34. Sobrino, *True Church*, p. 104.

35. Ibid., p. 217.

36. Leonardo Boff, *Church: Charism and Power* (New York: Crossroad, 1986), pp. 159–61.

37. Ibid., p. 161.

38. Boff, "Theological Characteristics," pp. 139–40.

39. The same could be said of traditionally Catholic countries within the communist bloc.

40. Orlando Espín and Sixto García, " 'Lilies of the Field': A Hispanic Theology of Providence and Human Responsibility," *Proceedings of the Forty-Fourth Annual Convention*, Catholic Theological Society of America, 1989, pp. 70–90.

41. Goizueta, "Liberation Theology," p. 38.

42. E.g., David Tracy, *Blessed Rage for Order* (New York: Crossroad, 1975), pp. 242ff. and Schubert Ogden, *Faith and Freedom* (Nashville: Abingdon, 1979).

43. Clodovis Boff, *Theology and Praxis* (Maryknoll, N.Y.: Orbis, 1987), p. 201.

44. Leonardo Boff and Clodovis Boff, *Liberation Theology: From Confrontation to Dialogue* (San Francisco: Harper and Row, 1986), p. 20.

45. MacIntyre, "Call to Order," p. 26.

46. Gutiérrez interviewed in Peter Steinfels, "New Liberation Faith: Social Conflict is Muted," *New York Times*, July 27, 1988.

47. Orlando Espín and Sixto García, p. 75.

48. Michael Novak, *Will It Liberate? Questions About Liberation Theology* (New York: Paulist, 1986), pp. 23, 137.

49. Michael Novak, *The Spirit of Democratic Capitalism* (New York: Simon and Schuster, 1982), pp. 239–50; Goizueta, "Liberation Theology," p. 39. By "Catholic" I mean the worldview or ethos described above, which permeates the culture and which, therefore, informs not only Roman Catholic, but also, to some extent, Protestant theology in Latin America, in the same way as the values imbedded in the predominantly Protestant culture of the U.S.A. inevitably affect Roman Catholic theology done in the U.S.A. In fact, one might even argue that Latin American Catholics have more in common with Latin American Protestants than they do with Anglo-American Catholics. (See notes 14 and 15 above.)

50. Quoted in Novak, *The Spirit of Democratic Capitalism*, p. 246.

51. See note 19.

52. See note 13.

53. David Tracy, "On Naming the Present," in *On the Threshold of the Third Millennium*, The Foundation, ed. (London: SCM, 1990), p. 67.

54. Enrique Dussel, "Historical and Philosophical Presuppositions for Latin American Theology," in *Frontiers of Theology in Latin America*, Rosino Gibellini, ed. (Maryknoll, N.Y.: Orbis, 1979), pp. 184–212.

55. Ibid., p. 185.

56. Ibid., p. 190.

57. Ibid.

58. Ibid.

59. Ibid., p. 191.

60. Ibid., pp. 195–96.

61. Ibid., p. 196.

62. Ibid.

63. See Goizueta, pp. 39–40.

64. See Tracy, "On Naming the Present," p. 66.

65. Ibid.

66. See note 1.

67. Tracy, "On Naming the Present," pp. 66–85

*Chapter Two*

# Perspectives on a Latina's Feminist Liberation Theology

## *MARÍA PILAR AQUINO*

The purpose of this article is to present certain elements that may contribute to the dialogue and development of a theological perspective that accompanies and sheds light on both the experience of faith and the emancipatory praxis of Latina women in North America.[1] The reflections I offer here stem from a fact that only recently has caught the attention of theologians: the growing involvement of women in the various areas that constitute the ecclesial and social life of their Latino communities. These women are gradually becoming conscious of the responsibility they have in view of their present situation of oppression and are taking steps to give direction and guidance to their own destiny. This fact underscores the need to create a theological perspective capable of accompanying the experience of Christian Latina women congruent with both a liberating Christian vision and the characteristics of their own reality.

In this chapter I want to emphasize some of the methodological aspects of such a perspective. To do so, I will point out various fundamental elements inherent to the theological task from the perspective of women. First among these elements is the aim of this task and its immediate references to other ways of doing theological reflection. I am interested here in giving priority to the break evident in the theologizing of women with respect to the liberal-progressive theologies[2] that are currently produced within the North American context. As will be indicated later, I enter into a debate with these theologies because of their visible influence on the orientation of recent Hispanic theology. Next, I focus on five central aspects of the theological task.

### A LATINA'S FEMINIST LIBERATION THEOLOGY

Every theological task is in itself a response to the questions that the Christian community asks about its faith and its historical and eschatological journey stemming from its own historical circumstances. As logos, the human word about God, theology is developed from a specific hermeneutical horizon derived from the socio-cultural context out of which it arises, from the theological tradition in which it is inscribed, from the basic preoccupations that accompany it, and from the challenges to which it wants to respond. Accordingly, I want to say, provisionally, that theology from the perspective of Latina women in North America must be developed with the aim of responding, from the horizon of Christian faith, to the fundamental questions that arise from the historical experience and spiritual legacy of women in their present reality. From the beginning, it is necessary to state that although a greater dialogue is urgent and necessary about its presuppositions, objectives, method, and content, this theology must formally incorporate into its construction the vision and aim of God's liberating purpose for creation, history, the world, and humanity.

In other words, the aim of theology from the point of view of women must share the aim of God's re-creative activity in history and must be inspired by it. Moreover, it must illuminate and activate the response of faith by the one who embraces it. In accordance with the core of the liberating biblical vision, this aim is on the path toward the attainment of the fullness of life, human integrity, shared solidarity, complete liberation, and common enjoyment of the goods of the earth. The biblical formulation of this aim is found succinctly in John 10:10: "I have come that they may have life, and that they may have it abundantly."

This observation constitutes a methodological determination that lends a distinctive character to the theological task of women. While traditional theological reflection evolved into an exercise that "regulates the faith" of the church according to a patriarchal, hierarchical, and exclusivist model,[3] women propose to exercise the intelligence of the faith as a collective endeavor that realizes and anticipates *life*. The allegory of the shepherd and the sheep in John 10:1–21 presents the polemic between the religious leaders, "guardians of the faith," and the vision that the Johannine community has with respect to the correct way of "being with" and assisting the community of believers. This vision is derived by the Johannine Community from Jesus Christ himself. What is more important, the text presents the ultimate objective of "pastorship": while the guardians of faith lead to perdition and death, the model of the shepherd leads to *life*.

In terms of doing theology, Latina women in the United States have proposed to give historical form to their ancestral clamor for life. They no longer wish to follow the foreign voices that rarely have succeeded in alleviating their suffering and, what is worse, have ignored both their spiritual powers and their historical strength. The exclusion of women by those who have done theology until very recently—men, whites, clerics, celibates, intellectuals, from the middle and upper classes—has created a discourse that instead of attracting women is losing them. In regard to the ignoring of the real existence of women and the silencing of their voices by the religious leadership, it may be said that "the thief comes only to steal, slaughter, and destroy" (John 10:10). If Christian reflection takes seriously the liberating gospel vision, all theological endeavor must incorporate as its own the imperative of the attainment of *life* and the complete restitution of women as subjects with full rights within the church and society.

Although I have not yet explained what might be the "content" of God's re-creative activity according to the experience and viewpoint of women, it at least helps to clarify that not just any theology, any way of understanding revelation, any way of understanding God, or any way of explaining the situation of women, is congruent with the interests, the expectations, the questions, and the hopes of Latina women, oppressed *as women, as poor, and as a subordinate race*. It helps also to emphasize that the theological task from the perspective of Latina women in North America must serve not just any group of women, but *these women in particular*. They want to embrace and make known their own situation, from their own condition and consciousness as women; they want to participate actively in the construction of a new order, and they want to "own" their obligations vis-à-vis the structural misery that afflicts them. Therefore, such a theological task must take on the liberating longings of these women and must activate their emancipatory praxis in accordance with the liberating aims of the Christian faith.

Theology from the perspective of Latina women recognizes itself as *liberation theology* and understands itself within the arena of common inspiration of both *feminist liberation theology* and *Latin American liberation theology*.[4] Furthermore, the theological viewpoint of Latina women grants central importance to the cultural aspects that interact with the identity of a people—the Hispanic people of Latino communities—their own identity, their experiences of faith, and their struggles for survival.[5] In reality, these liberation theologies—feminist and Latin American—involve a particular focus with respect to the relationships between faith and culture in that they constitute the proper framework for critically discerning the cultural challenges that Latina women face. Both not only offer a theoretical framework from which the expectations of oppressed women are understood, but they are also what best makes possible the historical, cultural, and spiritual strength of these women. That is why they are the immediate reference of this *new axis* of liberation theologies, created out of the political, cultural, and spiritual reality of Latina women.

Consequently, like all *liberation theology*, the theological task that Latina women develop cannot be understood apart from its own historical circumstances, nor can it avoid dialogue with contemporary theological movements. However, as with liberation theologies, this task consciously and critically distances itself from the postulates and aims of the current *liberal progressive* theological movement of the developed Western world.[6] This movement blatantly demonstrates its disinterest in the world of the poor and oppressed. Without minimizing the multiplicity of present-day theologies, the various axes of this theological movement are derived from what is generically called modern theology.[7] The theological viewpoint that stems from the very situation and consciousness of women, although it recognizes its methodological accomplishments and its conceptual richness, tries to overcome the limited scope of this theology because of its contextualization in the First World. It is important to emphasize this point because I believe that among some Hispanic male theologians there is a preoccupation with clarifying the relationship between *modern* theology and the growing *Hispanic* theology. From their point of view, the questions to which modern theology aims to respond are the questions that concern the Latino communities; as such, this would be its primary partner in dialogue. As a Latina woman, I do not believe this is the case. Basically, the position that grants priority to *modern theology*—in its liberal strands—leads to disinterest in and postponement of the questions to which the liberation theologies want to respond.[8] Thus, the *distancing/break* present in the women's theological perspective can be indicated in various areas; here I allude to only a few of them.

## The Social and Hermeneutical Locus for Reflection

Liberal-progressive theology is born in the geopolitical arena of the developed capitalist countries, but it does not question the presuppositions of this order nor the supposed supremacy of the racial and sexual paradigms of the Western world. In fact, such development and supremacy have only been possible at the cost of the underdevelopment of other peoples, as well as the subordination of women and of the indigenous, black, and mestizo races.

The theology that Latina women are developing also arises from the arena of the First World, but it is being elaborated from the opposite side of triumphal modernism with its sophisticated technology, its "logo-logical" rationalism, its secularist tendencies, its assumption of being "the" road to humanization, and its sexist parameters. The current of thought I am developing here stems from a commitment to transform the misery produced by "modernism" in patriarchal and imperialistic capitalism, examples of which are the following: the asymmetrical distribution of labor on the basis of sex; unbalanced access to social goods, such as health, education, housing, and entertainment; the growing impoverishment of the majority as opposed to the scandalous wealth of the upper classes; systematic racial and sexual segregation; the exclusion of minorities from power and decision-making positions; the deep anguish due to militarism and the threat of nuclear war; the frustration and disappearance of the paradigms of progress whose visible results are victimization, inhumanity, and injustice in the name of this same progress; growing ecological destruction, religious manipulation, and destructive individualism; physical alienation and spiritual deprivation prompted by chemical and religious dependencies; the primacy of the strong and violent; the promotion of a life-style clothed in fear and interior emptiness; in summary, inhumanity and oppression. These affect women in particular, and their effects are most visible in the situation of women of the Third World.

The theological viewpoint of Latina women seeks to respond to the real needs of those who suffer the consequences of this "world order." As such, it overcomes the conciliatory and abstract character of liberal-progressive theology to embrace *oppressed women* — as women, as poor, and as a subordinate race — as the locus from which to shape its reflection. Moreover, this theology affirms that the option for these women is strictly linked to revealed mystery and belongs to the fundamental core of Christian revelation.[9] Therefore, this option, which is more than merely ethical, is the *epistemological and hermeneutical locus of faith and of theology.*[10] Furthermore, this position in favor of oppressed women allows liberation theology to widen its call. That is to say, from this locus it calls nonpoor Latina women who suffer some form of oppression (cultural or sexual) to join the majority and thus share in the gospel promises.

The desire to articulate faith from this position does not in any way mean the negation of the intrinsic solidarity that must exist among all women of the earth. It is true that we are all joined by an infinite hope and by an immemorial suffering, but it is also true that the needs of educated, racially privileged, or middle- and upper-class women cannot compare with the suffering, needs, and hopes of the vast majority of poor and oppressed women. The option for these women is not defined negatively but positively. What is meant here is that *from these women*, the poor, the real meaning of liberation, of faith, and of hope is best understood. These women best clarify what life is all about and how, from them, we can all free ourselves from that which generates death and diminishes life.

## The Challenges Faced by a Latina's Feminist Liberation Theology

At the center of this theological perspective is the concern for eliminating the oppression of women — that is, the radical transformation of the causes of their suffering.[11] Therefore, the central challenge has to do especially with the discernment of paths toward the *liberation* of the impoverished majority and toward the complete emancipation of oppressed women. The axis that directs this task is based on the fundamental principle of *life*. It is from this basic challenge that other challenges are derived, which demand greater dialogue and precision with the aim of directing our energies toward the strengthening of common ends on social as well as ecclesial levels.

In this sense, women have proposed to take responsibility for the historical and spiritual journey of their people as well as their own. To do so requires the development of a common task in view of the social, spiritual, ethical, pastoral, and theological challenges that stem from our own reality.

Within Latino communities, it is common to find those whose regionalism based on national origin, instead of strengthening the potential of these communities—with their diversity, richness, and uniqueness—weakens, breaks up, and isolates them. These positions are most often found in the debate surrounding the "identity" of these communities. In fact, there are those who, instead of promoting the bonds of solidarity, the capacity for struggle and resistance, ancestral wisdom, and the profound humanism of our peoples, busy themselves with dividing Latino communities because of their "differences." For these individuals, diversity is "a problem," a source of polarization that prevents coming together in the common struggle for survival. These positions are influenced by the patriarchal Western culture that prefers schism to a complexity that enriches. I believe that these positions are distractions or deviations and must be fought. If we Latina women agree on *what we want, where we are going, and with whom we want to share our journey*, without a doubt, we will be on that path that leads to realizing our own identity. This means that the challenge posed by the question of *who we are*, as women, will be faced not on the theoretical field of thought but from liberating praxis.

The primary goal of the theology that is developed by Latina women in North America is not the attainment of greater positions of power within the established order, or greater access to economic opportunities, or achieving the learned ideal of "liberty or freedom." This, in the liberal thinking of patriarchal North American capitalism, means the "liberalization" of capital as the driving force of history; "freedom" to accumulate and to become rich at the expense of the needs and hunger of the majority of humanity; "freedom" to impose oneself militarily and culturally on other disadvantaged countries in the name of its own concept of democracy, which in reality deprives women and the poor of decision-making about their own destiny; "freedom" to obtain high levels of well-being at the expense of the multiple labor and suffering of women; "freedom" to use and grant social and ecclesiastical power, condemning women to a subordinate place in public and in private; "freedom" to create labels for men and for women, alienating the latter even from their own bodies. Consequently, the primary challenge stems from the longing for liberation, not from the desire for abstract ideals. The theology that women are developing believes that "freedom" is possible only through a process of *liberation* that affirms them as subjects in their own right. The emphasis here falls on liberation because that is what can guarantee the attainment of *true life* for them, for the earth, and for those who depend on them. Hence, a thorough process of global transformation toward this liberation is necessary.

### Theology in Dialogue: Interlocutors

Liberal-progressive theology dialogues with the individual, the "learned man" who has lost the meaning of God. This current of thought, if it critiques a "God-less secularism," admits secularization as desired by God and seeks a language, secularized as well, to proclaim God in this world fed by information, technology, and the means of social communication. It emphasizes the emancipation of mundane realities from the world of the sacred. It is directed toward those who are concerned about making compatible the living of faith with responsible maturity, centered around the autonomy of human thought and action. As such, this theology dialogues with the individual whose faith is threatened by the highly secularized social surroundings and leads to the loss of the meaning of life.

This is certainly not the situation of oppressed Latina women. Without ignoring the very real advance of the phenomenon of secularization, which must be addressed by theological reflection, and without underestimating the sometimes alienating character of popular religiosity, it may well be said that religious views and the experience of faith have played a primary role in the lives of these women. In their faith they have found the source with which to recognize their own values, to raise their self-esteem, and to resist the aggressive process of religious, spiritual, and cultural colonization.

The subject who stands before modern liberal theology is modern humankind drowning in pessimism, to whom theology wants to prove the credibility of the gospel as the source of salvation. The subjects who dialogue with the theology developed by Latina women on the other hand are oppressed women steeped in hope, who in their emancipatory praxis demonstrate the liberating strength of the Gospel. A given fact in North American ecclesial experience is the spiritual and cultural richness of these women.[12] Therefore, what this theology reclaims is the liberation from all oppression that affects women as poor women of a subordinate race. It dialogues with these women for whom physical and spiritual death comes before their time.

Moreover, there are other subjects who stand before theology as developed by these women: *their polemical interlocutors* — that is to say, those social, theological, and ecclesiastical sectors that not only oppose them but prevent the emergence of women and their participation in the areas of social, political, and ecclesial decision-making. This theology must show that the grace of God and the strength of the Spirit are causing the transformational practices of these women. They are not drowning in pessimism, but as Julia Esquivel has said, they are inundated by resurrection.[13] Liberal-progressive theology polemicizes against the mythic mentality; the liberation theology of Latina women in North America polemicizes against the oppressive rationalism of the androcentric-patriarchal systems that today are combined with imperialist capitalism. On the other hand, it is true that the religious practices and the moral conscience of women have been used by ecclesiastical and political authorities to encourage the submission of women, but it is no less true that today these women have begun to reject this sexist view of the Christian faith. With this approach, women are rescuing the very core of the liberating gospel faith in the heart of a world that has hidden the true face of God.

## The Finality of Theological Knowledge

The purpose here is to explore methodologically the way to exercise theological knowledge in view of reality and the goal of this task. Returning to the text of John 10, it seems clear that the "guardians of faith" are producing discourses foreign to the life of the flock; their voice does not speak to the expectations of the sheep (verse 5). Although the guardians know that the wolf exists, they set aside the danger and the threat that the wolf represents for the life of the sheep; that is, they do not recognize the wolf's mortal character, because the life of the flock is not important to them. Their discourses hide the conflict present in real life, and in this way they become like the wolf: robbers and thieves. With the *hiding of what is real*, they leave the flock at the mercy of the wolf, who catches and scatters the sheep (verses 12–13). They are leaders whose knowledge leads to perdition. Within the perspective of the Johannine community, the same thing does not happen with Jesus, model of the shepherd, nor with the sheep. In this case, the model of the shepherd not only knows of the existence of the wolf and robbers, but is also aware of the death and misery that they produce in real life; the true shepherd knows how to "enter through the gate" and, together with the sheep, seek practical alternatives that lead to the life and well-being of the flock (verses 2–3, 9). The text does not say that, once outside, the sheep return to the same fold, but rather they leave their present situation to go where there are fresh pastures, where they are safe, and where they can come and go as they please (verse 9). "I know mine and mine know me" (verse 14). Between both parties there is established a process of mutual knowledge whose function is to open up concrete paths toward the fullness of life (verses 14–15, 10–11). Knowledge, in this case of the sheep and the model of the shepherd, acquires a practical liberating function.

As in all human endeavors, knowledge can oppress or liberate. Therefore, the theology developed from the perspective of Latina women emphasizes the need to make explicit the liberating dimension of theological knowledge. The reason for this emphasis is that this theology *assumes the suspicion* that present-day theological reflection—traditional as well as liberal-progressive or neoliberal theologies, and even in many cases Latin American liberation theology—makes abstract, subsumes, and holds back the vision, interests, and knowledge of women. This suspicion extends to all areas of Christian tradition, exegetical investigation, the traditional sources of faith, and even traditions within the sacred scriptures themselves, inasmuch as they extend and justify the vision of the androcentric-patriarchal order.

The ways of developing theological knowledge have tended, on the one hand, to ignore real historical oppression, hiding the words of women. On the other hand, they have justified and perpetuated oppressive socio-cultural paradigms. As long as the strands of present-day modern theologies continue to understand themselves from the paradigms of the superiority of the Western androcentric culture and from the geopolitical center of the world in imperialist capitalism, they will be ever more incapable of perceiving the impoverishment and inhumanity to which poor women of a subordinate race are subjected. In the very exercise of theological knowledge, their ignorance of *true reality* is evident. By not letting themselves be affected by reality, they produce abstract and unreal discourses, of absolutely no efficacy for historical transformation. Their task, in effect, plays a political role of supporting patriarchal imperialistic capitalism and its religious connections. Women's theologizing must be critical and self-conscious of its aim, presuppositions, and objectives because it, too, is exposed to this danger.

If the intelligence of faith is a knowledge that wants to be *Christian*, it must be liberating. That is, theological knowledge itself must have the self-understanding that it is a theoretical-practical path leading toward human fullness and integrity of each and every person (man and woman) and people (collectivity). It must illuminate and make possible the struggles that seek to eliminate the "wolves" and the "robbers" of history, even those that exist within ourselves. The function of the theological task must be liberating. The question of the specific "hows" for the development of a feminist liberation theology from the perspective of Latina women is what must be explored.[14] In what follows I want to underscore some specific aspects that indicate the *distance/break*[15] between the theological perspective of Latina women and current liberal-progressive theology.

First: *reason alone vis-à-vis sentient intelligence.*[16] A first aspect of the break that women's theologizing makes with respect to other theological tasks refers to the way of articulating the process of knowledge. The concept "sentient intelligence" refers to the fact that human apprehension of reality is not dualistic, as was believed by the Greeks and subsequent Western thinkers. They always contrasted intelligence (*nous*) and sense (*aisthesis*), but in fact both constitute two moments of one act in the human apprehension of reality.[17] Knowledge, therefore, is not limited to the exercise of pure reason nor does thought acquire self-consistency. On the contrary, women emphasize the structural unity between knowing and sensing in the same act of theologizing. Reflection is not separated from lived experience, and so, for women, theology does not consist of the speculative exercise of the *logos* on the *logos*. The theology that women develop has to do with the *real world*, with vital physical and spiritual needs, with integrity of the body and expansion of the spirit, within the limits and possibilities of daily life. It takes on the multiple dimensions of human existence.

Second: *the logic of androcentric thought vis-à-vis theological realism.* The theological perspective of women incorporates *what is real* about human and social reality in its construction. It believes that reality is necessary for the development of its theological content. Therefore, although it gives preferential treatment to questions that stem from oppressed women, it does not disregard the reality of its members, or the earth and humanity as a whole. While androcentric thought hides the vision and experience of women, the theology that women develop incorporates human and social reality as it presents itself in its unity and diversity. This aspect signals the rupture that is established with traditional modes of knowing, inasmuch as they prevent recognition of the situation of women, due to their exclusive logic. Even liberation theology in general, when it ignores women, is abstracted from reality itself and is incapable of speaking of reality "as it is."

Third: *continuity with the established order vis-à-vis its transformation.* From the point of view of women, the function of theology today is not only to explain and interpret the meaning of faith, but to assist in the transformation of reality itself. In general, it can be said that the perspective of some Hispanic ecclesial sectors influenced by current liberal-progressive theologies has flowed into two movements. On the one hand, it has been believed that the fundamental problem of Latino communities in North America primarily has to do with culture. As such, it depends on systems of thought to find solutions—that is, the area of values, of religious meanings, of conceptual development. Their solutions, therefore, remain on the level of thought. On the other hand, although their theology attempts to change the mythical aspects of Hispanic religiosity, in reality they propose to maintain and preserve the androcentric values and traditional religious meanings in such a way that they may survive in this secularist society. Their theological vision seeks to reconcile the experience of faith with the current unbalanced order.

Even in the area of language, there are those who seem to push the idea that Latino communities should speak English only. For them, English is the language of power, the language of money, which everyone understands. This position deprives the people of the advantage of being bilingual, and more deeply deprives them of a vital means for their own cultural identity. The theological viewpoint of women, on the contrary, in tune with the currents of thought that subscribe to *critical-practical reason*, emphasizes the transforming finality of theology. According to their view, theological knowledge is not conceived as a task at the service of the gradual fulfillment of the present, in continuity with it. It deals with *transforming reality* from a specific experience of faith with which the true meaning of faith is recovered and the liberating aspects of Latino cultures are also recovered.

Fourth: *the logic of Narcissus vis-à-vis the global connection of social status.* The theological perspective of women emphasizes the conflictual nature of present-day patriarchal capitalism. For these women patriarchal neocolonialist capitalism is neither a panacea nor the realization of the promised land. Therefore, they do not contemplate its beauties, as Narcissus contemplated his own. The present order does not project, not even tangentially, an orientation toward greater justice, greater solidarity, or greater sharing of the goods of the earth. This would mean its destruction. In reality, as Julio Lois indicates, to claim to be innocent in view of the great problems of injustice and oppression that shadow a large part of humanity—particularly oppressed women—can be done only out of cynicism, bad faith, or ignorance.[18] The theological discourse of women must reclaim the life and liberation of their sisters whatever their specific place either right here or beyond the Rio Grande. To ignore the global articulation of social status within the very exercise of theological reflection, as liberal-progressive theologians do, discredits it as a theology in any way respectful of the gospel's liberative dimensions.

Fifth: *the fear of naming the demons vis-à-vis the commitment to exorcise them.* One of the major characteristics of modern liberal theology, which the vision of some Hispanic sectors echoes, is the fear of naming directly the mechanisms of domination. This theology is highly sensitive to the East-West contradiction, but yet it hides the central contradiction of North-South. Even within these contradictions, it does not perceive those that destroy women or other oppressed peoples and races.

Women are interested in exorcising the "demons" and in eliminating the evils that follow in their wake. They understand that the exercise of thinking about faith from their own consciousness and from their own situation interpreted analytically assumes the naming of the mechanisms of domination, confronting them and transforming them. Their theological task promotes the emancipatory praxis of women, and therefore clarifies the causes that prevent it. Within the theological vision of women, one cannot avoid the convergence and mutual reinforcement of three combined systems: patriarchalism present in society, the church, and theology; present-day imperialistic capitalism; and the neocolonialism of white Western culture.

Sixth: *the abstraction of the global vis-à-vis the globalization of daily life.* Contemporary theologies, which are elaborated mostly by men, are characterized by abstraction from daily life. Some, focusing their interest in the public sphere, pass over oppressive relationships in the private sector and hide the *micro-physical relationships* of power exercised in the domestic sphere, where women usually have the worst role. Daily life for these theologians does not have epistemological value, does not form part of their comprehension of "reality," and therefore does not affect their theological endeavor. What happens here, in effect, is that they grant to daily life a *natural* character and assume as "natural" the sexist division of labor, the separation of the public and private spheres, and male superiority. Women do not believe this is the case.

The theological perspective of Latina women understands that it is in daily life that the true life of individuals unfolds and that *this* is where global transformations take shape. Daily life has to do with the totality of existence; the totality of social relationships is reproduced and multiplied therein. Daily life, moreover, is where the actual exercise of male power is best discovered. Asymmetrical relationships within the private and domestic sphere are repetitive, continuous, and systematic; that is why they take on a "daily" character. In this sense, daily life plays an ineluctable political role in the theological task of women. If theological reflection proposes the creation of new models of social relationship, if it wants to design models of human relationships in solidarity, then it must help break the inertia of daily life. The processes of liberation within society cannot be isolated from the processes of liberation within the private sector.

For Latina women, the importance of daily life is even greater given that, because of their own inherited patriarchal culture, women contribute enormously to the perpetuation of male superiority. Socialization within today's nuclear family underscores the preferential treatment toward males to the detriment of women. Consequently, daily life is relevant, because it is the arena where the processes of oppression-liberation are experienced. Here, as well, is where transformations reflected and echoed in the social sphere are verified. For women, on the other hand, the struggles to transform daily life imply the widening of their own self-concept. Among other things, it means raising self-esteem, recovering the sense of their own bodies, experiencing sexuality as a liberating and integral dimension of self, valuing creativity itself, and making decisions for themselves. With the ruptures and sufferings that this process implies, daily life is the area for articulating one's inner life and commitments in the public sphere.

### Some Methodological Characteristics

It is not unfamiliar to anyone in the field that traditional theology has tended to be skeptical about the historical processes and political dimension of the Christian faith. But this has been only an illusion. Theology itself has not been able to save itself from historical events. In the name of its supposed "purity," it has granted legitimacy to asymmetrical societies and turned a deaf ear to the prophetic movements that opposed it. For their part, liberal-progressive and neoliberal theologies have also made theirs the historical mediations of faith, but this time to demonstrate the compatibility of the Christian faith with the present established order. Both these positions ignore the hermeneutical structure of all knowing, which is neither neutral nor unbiased.

The theology developed by Latina women in North America is characterized by the centrality of *the liberating praxis of women* and understands itself in reference to this praxis. This theology starts from the commitment of Christian women on the path toward the transformation of oppression, pain, and inhumanity into liberation, true happiness, and human integrity for them and for those who depend on them. With this praxis these women are promoting the universal attainment of basic physical and spiritual needs for all creation, because today's reality structurally gives rise to the daily weakening of women, promotes the pursuit of life by taking the life of others, and leads to the lack of concern regarding the loss of life experienced by women and the poor.

This has to do, then, with a critical reflection on the liberating praxis of Christian women, where women discover the presence of divine revelation. It is in this liberating praxis that women *seek, recognize, and name* God's manifestation. This is the distinctive note that makes the reflection of women *theological.* There may be other forms of reflecting critically about the emancipatory praxis of women, but what Latina women emphasize is that this praxis is motivated by and makes formal reference to the Christian faith. In this sense, for the theological perspective of women, praxis is the place of verifying faith. Historical praxis has its own rules — independent of its reference to faith — and theology has its own grammar and its own autonomy. As such, it may give rise to false teachings in its search for the truth of faith if it ignores the ethical and praxical dimension of theological intelligence. Both, nevertheless, are articulated dialectically, and mutually enrich and correct each other. Therefore, it would not be methodologically correct to set up an automatic equation between theology and praxis.[19]

The theology that Latina women are developing claims for itself the role of critic. This has to do with a critical reflection in four areas: first, with respect to the traditional sources of revelation, because they have obscured the historical and spiritual itinerary of women; second, with respect to historical reality, because it does not "speak for itself" but requires the analytical sciences to uncover the oppressive mechanisms that directly affect women's experience; third, with respect to the Western cultural paradigms that legitimize the superiority of colonizers, because they have sought the obliteration of the ancestral wisdom of our indigenous people, including the authority of women; and finally, with respect to the very presuppositions of theology, which may also be subject to criteria and systems prejudicial toward women.

As the critical reflection on the liberating praxis of women, the use of a dialectical and feminist analytical instrument is indispensable for this theology. The dialectical tool helps it clarify the mechanisms of oppression inherent in capitalist society; the feminist one allows it to recognize, analytically, the oppressive structural mechanisms derived from the patriarchal system and from the androcentric vision within society, the church, and theology. Both focuses are necessary to identify the causes of the multiple oppression that women suffer, and to find, in the proper light, the ways of eradicating them. In addition, the analytical instrument allows this theology to overcome the empirical view of reality, or the naive approach to it. Moreover, it helps it to perceive more clearly the questions that social reality poses for faith and for theology. The dialectical feminist instrument, in short, allows for the coherent analysis and explanation of the alternatives that women face, congruent with the liberating gospel vision and their own interests in liberation. Even more so, this analytical focus finds greater convergence with the global view of the Christian faith and its ethical demands.[20]

In this sense, everything that has to do with the life of women, their struggles and hopes—not only those practices directly related to the religious realm—becomes the privileged area for the reflection of women. This means that theology must take into account all the aspects that comprise the life of women, in which religious expressions occupy a primary place but must be contextualized in a wider scope. It is important to underscore this aspect, because, in my opinion, within the Hispanic theological-pastoral movement it is thought that the existence of Latina women is defined almost exclusively in terms of the symbols of traditional popular religiosity. This position causes the displacement of problems; solutions to the multiple oppression of women are sought that are exclusively cultural. I believe that this supposition is reductionist and dangerous, because it limits the praxis of women to religious pragmatism. Popular religiosity is, without a doubt, a challenge that this theology must face, but it must not ignore other areas of oppression/liberation in the life of women.

For Latina women, Christian faith is not a fragmentary aspect of their life or of their own cultural identity. The struggle of these women for a new earth and for new ways of being and living in the church, where they can participate as members in their own right, is inspired by their convictions of faith, and affects their whole life. To state just a few of their activities, many Latina women are committed to human rights groups, to the defense of the undocumented, to solidarity movements, to peace, to ecological, artistic, and cultural movements, to liberating evangelization groups, to the affirmation of indigenous communities, to the defense of civil rights, to the affirmation of women, young people, children, and the aged, and so on. Consequently, theological reflection must take into account their multiple interests as believers, as poor, and as women, together with their religious and cultural values.

Liberation theology from the perspective of Latina women emphasizes the liberating historical praxis of women because it understands that this is a necessary dimension for the shaping of its theological content. This has to do, properly speaking, with the "internal regulation" that grants theological pertinence to the discourse of women. This assertion underscores three fundamental aspects. First, the liberating praxis of women becomes the *hermeneutical perspective* for reading and interpreting God's liberating activity in the life of women within their present reality. Second, this praxis is the hermeneutical criterion for rediscovering and reconstructing the historical journey and spiritual legacy of the women who have preceded us. This praxis can be placed within biblical history as well as outside it. Third, theology takes its theological themes from this praxis so that all subjects of systematic reflection are viewed from this vantage point. Therefore, the liberating praxis of oppressed women, besides its ethical character, forms part of theological knowledge and so acquires epistemological value.

In this way, the theological focus of women recognizes the fact that God's liberating activity is present in the life of women. Such a revelation takes place in their emancipatory praxis and in their struggles for survival, even when it is not yet verbalized coherently. This means that *women's praxis itself produces a kind of theological essence*, creates space for the formulation of new content, and helps to overcome the exclusivist nature of the content that already exists. In this sense, the theological task from the perspective of Latina women is in opposition to those who believe that the "theological word" is not yet found in the life of women. It discards the view that theology is "something that comes from outside" to provide "knowledge" to the ignorant and illiterate mind of women. On the contrary, we are speaking of a solidarity that shares in the achievements, failures, and hopes of oppressed women. This theology wants to be at the service of their struggles, helping so that the "theological word" already present, yet often incipient and unarticulated, may grow, mature, and bear fruit itself. This means, in effect, embracing the liberating praxis of women as the *formal locus* to shape this theology.

## CONCLUSION

The theological task from the perspective of Latina women, in short, takes on the fundamental human and Christian criterion of all theology that claims to be Christian: *life*. This fundamental principle stems from the core liberating gospel vision and from historical prophetism. It is demanded by the present situation of oppressed women. This criterion is not to be confused with a patriarchal stereotype about women according to which they, because of their biological condition, should dedicate themselves solely to procreation or biological life. The gospel understanding of life assumes the recovery as well as the restoration of all the spiritual, physical, and social energies found in women's condition. It means, in effect, a universal principle that must give power to human life, without which not even biological functions can survive.

To understand the need for the affirmation of life amid so much death every day, and to convert it into a constitutive principle of the theological task, implies a prior position on the part of the theologian. This position combines two corollary attitudes: on the one hand, basic honesty about reality; on the other hand, the fundamental openness to the real manifestation of God in the lives of the poor and oppressed. Real life, material and spiritual, is certainly a divine gift, but it does not eliminate the responsibility of struggling to attain it fully for all creation.

The feminist liberation theology that Latina women are developing claims for itself the recovery of the age-old complicity that exists between women, the earth, and life. Because life is a divine gift, the theological task that takes on the struggle for life understands itself, in the same way, as a gift of the Spirit placed at the service of the liberating path of women toward their complete corporal, psychological, historical, and spiritual fulfillment. With this struggle, women are saying that whoever has crucified them, whoever has taken the life of the poor and oppressed, and whoever rules the destinies of the world, does not have the last word. Their faith tells them that justice will prevail.

*Translated from the Spanish by John W. Diercksmeier*

## NOTES

1. I am aware of the debate surrounding the term used to name ourselves as part of a social entity. Lara Millán presents the advantages and disadvantages of the terms that make reference to the Hispanic/Latino/Chicano community. See "Chicano, Latino or Hispanic?" *Proclama* 1 (May 1990), pp. 6–8. This contribution is necessarily conditioned by my own origins, by the social vision to which I subscribe, and by the theological tradition with which I identify myself. In dealing with my own faith experience, my hope, and all that makes up my identity, the *official view* of the political and religious leaders who have opted for the term Hispanic certainly does not express my reality. Latina, besides referring to the vast majority of mestiza women, allows for extending the arms of solidarity to the south, beyond any border.

2. I understand "liberal-progressive theologies" to be a widespread theological movement that synthesizes both *modern reason* as well as *liberal philosophy* in the articulation of theology. Although it has surpassed traditional theology, it is primarily centered in the creation of a discourse that justifies the convergence of the established social order with Christian faith. I use the term "liberal" as a technical term in reference to the ideology supportive of the capitalist economic system. "Liberal-progressive theologies," in my understanding, are opposed to liberation theologies. They do not seek to transform reality but to develop it "progressively" within the present structural order. The most complete expression of this current of thought is represented by P. Berger and Michael Novak.

3. "The regulation of faith requires ideally a participation of the entire community in the always imperfect, provisional, and partial definition of what is believed. Twenty centuries of church history prove that no ecclesiological model has been able to assure this participation. What is referred to as the episcopal and clerical structure of the Church that was imposed in the early centuries has not favored this communitary regulation, because it has conferred on the bishops and clergy a power and a science that discourages any active and creative participation by the communities. ... It has also contributed to falsifying the rules for the regulation of faith within the very Church itself" (Evangelista Vilanova, *Historia de la Teología Cristiana*, vol. 1 [Barcelona: Herder, 1987], pp. 128–29). See the excellent introduction to the doctrine of the *sensus fidelium* by Orlando Espín in this collection.

4. See the contribution of Ada Isasi-Díaz and Yolanda Tarango, *Hispanic Women: Prophetic Voice in the Church* (San Francisco: Harper & Row, 1988).

5. If the *intelligence of faith* maintains dialectical relationships with the cultural world in which it is born and develops, it keeps however its own internal rules, its

own pertinence. In this sense, theology is not an a priori product of culture. Thus, the dialectical relationships that faith and culture maintain must be further explored.

6. With this statement I am not saying that in the so-called First World there are no liberation theologies, because in fact there are. I am referring here to the theologies that consciously or unconsciously exclude the vision, aims, challenges and methodology of all liberation theologies. Centered in itself this theological movement manifests a lack of sensibility toward the present asymmetries: North/South, classism, racism, sexism, and neocolonialism.

7. In Latin American liberation theology it is now common to use the title *modern theology* to refer to the theologies that "spring from the drying up of the fundamental question of classical theology and from the appearance of the new questions of modernity" (João Batista Libanio, *Teología de la Liberación: Guía didáctica para su estudio* [Santander: Sal Terrae, 1987], p. 88). *Modern theology* has been developed historically in view of the challenges of the first and second Enlightenment. While it is true that this theology has been developed primarily in Europe, its influence on North American theology is considerable. Here I am using the same meaning given this terminology in Latin American theology. See Jon Sobrino, "Teología de la Liberación y Teología Europea Progresista," *Misión Abierta* 4 (Madrid: Loguez, 1984), pp. 11–26; idem, "El Conocimiento teológico en la Teología Europea y Latinoamericana," in *Resurrección de la verdadera Iglesia* (Santander: Sal Terrae, 1981), pp. 21–53; Juan José Tamayo-Acosta, *La Teología de la Liberación* (Madrid: Ediciones de Cultura Hispánica, 1990); idem, "La teología progresista europea ante la Teología de la Liberación," in *Implicaciones sociales y políticas de la Teología de la Liberación* (Madrid: Escuela de Estudios Hispanoamericanos e Instituto de Filosofía, 1989), pp. 111–31.

8. This observation is particularly true in the case of feminist, Latin American, and black liberation theologies. The issue was raised at the June 20–24, 1990, conference called *¡Somos un Pueblo!* sponsored by Aquinas Center of Theology at Emory University. The organizer of this conference, Dr. Roberto Goizueta, has edited a collection of the presentations to be called by the same name and published by Fortress Press in 1992.

9. For further reading on the indissoluble relationship between God and the poor and Jesus Christ and oppressed women, see Elizabeth Schüssler Fiorenza, *In Memory of Her: A Feminist Theological Reconstruction of Christian Origins* (New York: Crossroad, 1985); also Jorge Pixley and Clodovis Boff, *Opción por los Pobres* (Madrid: Paulinas, 1987).

10. Roberto Goizueta also discusses this in his contribution to this collection (chap. 1).

11. See Ada Isasi-Díaz and Yolanda Tarango, *Hispanic Women*, p. 3.

12. Although it has not been sufficiently recognized, it is true that the national process of the Encuentros Hispanos (I, II, and III), pastoral ministry, religious education, and diocesan programs directed at the Hispanic community have come about and take place due to the effort and the work of women. In many cases, they are the ones who have promoted and led these processes in spite of the fact that they have also been excluded from the decision-making.

13. See Julia Esquivel, *El Padre Nuestro desde Guatemala y otros poemas* (San José, Costa Rica: DEI, 1981), pp. 37–40.

14. This is what A. Isasi-Díaz and Yolanda Tarango attempt to do in their study, *Hispanic Women*.

15. J.J. Tamayo-Acosta has discussed the contrast between liberation theologies and European progressive theologies. His study is appropriate for our own reality given that the theologies developed in Europe and the United States share the geopolitical position of countries of the center as well as sharing the progressive-liberal position. I am interested in how the feminist liberation theology contrasts with progressive-liberal theologies. See Juan José Tamayo-Acosta, "Recepción en Europa de la Teología de la Liberación" in Ignacio Ellacuría and Jon Sobrino, eds., *Mysterium Liberationis: Conceptos fundamentales de la Teología de la Liberación*, vol. 1, (Madrid: Trotta, 1990), pp. 51–77.

16. For me, the philosophical contribution of X. Zubiri has been foundational with respect to the diverse modes of understanding. See Xavier Zubiri, *Inteligencia Sentiente* (Madrid: Alianza Editorial, 1980); idem, *Inteligencia y Logos* (Madrid: Alianza Editorial, 1982).

17. Idem, *Inteligencia y Logos*, pp. 50–51.

18. See Julio Lois, *Jesucristo Liberador* (Salamanca: Universidad Pontificia, 1988), p. 39.

19. This is what I perceive in the work of Ada Isasi-Díaz and Yolanda Tarango, *Hispanic Women*, pp. 2–3.

20. Liberal-progressive theology, on the contrary, privileges the functionalist analysis of society. Consequently, this theology tends toward the harmonization and integration of faith within today's structures. At most, it proposes some corrections or certain improvements so that this system may function better. The pastoral consequences of this are obvious: the attempts to correct "dysfunctional" religious practices so that they fit into the present order and thus can be maintained as an organic and balanced whole.

# Chapter Three

# Tradition and Symbol as Biblical Keys for a United States Hispanic Theology

## C. GILBERT ROMERO

It is premature to begin speaking of a U.S. Hispanic theology in the sense of formulated propositions supported by a fully developed methodology. Unlike the blacks and feminists of the 1960s and 1970s, for whom overt and covert oppression were catalytic experiences, U.S. Hispanics of the 1980s were unable to move beyond the reactionary stage of protest, and picket in the face of oppression in order to respond in a theologically cohesive way. Perhaps now U.S. Hispanics are beginning that process of articulation.

Why the need for a theological articulation? Theology as religious language gives voice to the mute witness of oppression, and validates that experience with a response in the world of values where dignity is paramount. Blacks and feminists having developed their theologies have since become forces to be reckoned with vis-à-vis the wider society in light of those theologies. I hope that the 1990s will be such a time for U.S. Hispanics to validate their experiences and culture, and develop a theology (theologies?) which will enable them to be a force confronting oppression in the wider society. This essay offers a contribution in that direction.

My hypothesis is that tradition and symbol as constitutive elements of *religiosidad popular* can serve as biblical keys for establishing a U.S. Hispanic theology. First, a clarification of terms. Hispanics in the U.S.A. are a varied lot — geographically, ethnically, culturally, and ideologically. In this essay the umbrella term "Hispanics" refers principally to Mexican-Americans in the Southwest. What is said of them may be modified and appropriated by other groups. *Religiosidad popular* is the pious exercise of common devotional practices which are culturally rooted in Hispanic Catholicism, and are often at variance with official Catholic liturgy. Tradition and symbol are those elements of a culture that best define and express the identity of a people.

## SCRIPTURE AND THE CONTEMPORARY CATHOLIC

For the believing Catholic the Bible plays a crucial role. Not only are the sacred scriptures the principal font for worship and devotion, but they serve as the primary source for belief as well. Catholic theology is rooted in scripture.

One of the major difficulties over the years has been and continues to be a lack of familiarity with the scriptures on the part of the common people. This patent unfamiliarity has had unfortunate consequences, not the least of which has been the inability to withstand the onslaught of fundamentalist pelting with isolated biblical quotes. In order to cope with the resultant weakening of faith, the Catholic Church responded in varying ways. Without doubt the most significant recent response was the promulgation on November 18, 1965, of the *Dogmatic Constitution on Divine Revelation* also known as *Dei Verbum*, one of the major documents to be issued from the Second Vatican Council.[1] This document was, above all, a reaffirmation of the significance of the role of scripture in the life of the church and the individual Catholic.

The first chapter of *Dei Verbum* (DV) discusses revelation itself. The object of divine revelation is God's self-revelation of the mystery of the divine will regarding human salvation through Jesus Christ (DV, 2). History is a principal forum where a revelatory interaction takes place between deeds and words (DV, 2). The council admits that God can be known in creation and through reason (DV, 3,6), but is known specifically through scripture. The Christian economy focuses on Jesus Christ as "the mediator and the sum total of Revelation" (DV, 2). As Jesus is explicitly mentioned in the New Testament and is implied by the New Testament authors in the Old Testament, this revelation in Jesus "will never pass away; and no new public revelation is to be expected before the glorious manifestation of Our Lord, Jesus Christ" (DV, 4). God's self-revelation is thus an incarnational revelation—made manifest through history, creation, and above all, through Jesus Christ as known through the scriptures. The content of revelation is the message of salvation, what Catholics would call the deposit of faith.

The second chapter deals with the transmission of divine revelation— that is, the specifics of how divine revelation is made known to all. Even though the council bishops are specific about the direction taken by revelation's transmission—namely, from God to Jesus to the apostles and institutions they founded to bishops (DV, 7)—nonetheless they allow for the broader concept of church-based "People of God" (DV, 8), to serve as the recipient and interpreter of revelation as well. What is astonishing in the rigidly hierarchical view of the transmission of revelation is the council's apparent openness to the development of revelation and the variety of interpretive fonts. For example, the document states:

The Tradition that comes from the apostles makes progress in the Church with the help of the Holy Spirit. There is *a growth in insight* into the realities and words that are being passed on. . . . Thus, as the centuries go by, *the Church is always advancing toward the plenitude of divine truth*, until eventually the words of God are fulfilled in her. . . . Thus *God*, who spoke in the past, *continues to converse* with the spouse of his beloved Son. And the Holy Spirit . . . leads believers to the full truth. [DV, 8; italics added]

This openness by the council to the development of interpretation of revelation in the tradition must be seen in the wider context of the bishops perceived as the "official" interpreters of revelation (DV, 9,10). According to the document scripture and tradition make up the single Word of God—revelation—which is entrusted to the church (DV, 10). So it is, then, that the authentic transmitters of divine revelation are sacred tradition, sacred scripture, and the magisterium entrusted to the church, as authentic recipient, which is called the people of God. These elements work interdependently. "Sacred tradition" is the apostolic preaching expressed in a special way in the inspired books maintained by the church as people of God, and includes that which helps the people of God live in holiness and grow in faith (DV, 8). Thus the entire people of God—hierarchy, clergy, and laity—working in harmonious relationship are to be considered authentic recipients and interpreters of divine revelation. This is further developed in chapter 3 of the document.

Another valuable document to consider regarding the notion of a wider yet dependent revelation is the Vatican Council's *Decree on the Church's Missionary Activity*, also known as *Ad Gentes*.[2] The key paragraph is number 11, where the council, speaking of the need for missionary witness, requires of missioners:

They should acknowledge themselves as members of the group in which they live, and through the various undertakings and affairs of human life they should share in their social and cultural life. They should be familiar with their national and *religious traditions* and uncover with gladness and respect those *seeds of the Word which lie hidden* among them. [italics added]

The recognition by the council that revelation, which is what is meant by "Seeds of the Word," is present to some extent in the religious traditions of a people is a tremendous affirmation of the validity of those very traditions and cultures from which they spring. It is but a small jump to affirm the validity of the religious traditions of U.S. Hispanics as a potential source for dependent revelation.[3] The religious traditions under consideration are those devotions I have referred to above as the devotional practices of *religiosidad popular*.

In order to understand the relationship between scripture and devotional piety, it is first necessary to probe the significance of "culture." One of the most prominent cultural anthropologists, Clifford Geertz, has given us the following definition of culture:

It [culture] denotes an historically transmitted pattern of meanings embodied in symbols, a system of inherited conceptions expressed in symbolic forms by means of which men communicate, perpetuate, and develop their knowledge about attitudes toward life.[4]

If we accept this definition of culture, then two of its constitutive elements, symbols and tradition, become means of transmitting those historical patterns of meaning.

## U.S. Hispanics and the Bible

Not only the Catholic in general but the Hispanic Catholic in particular has a special relationship with the Bible. In addition to the reasons stated above for the affiliation between the Catholic and the Bible, the Hispanic Catholic feels a strong attraction to the Word of God as expression of ongoing dialogue. I suspect that people who have experienced poverty and struggle, and can find parallels to their own lives in a sacred literature, will be drawn to that sacred literature as a source of comfort and hope.

U.S. Hispanics, for example, have more than a notional knowledge of what it means to be an immigrant people. This knowledge in turn can attract them to an image such as the exodus, reflecting their historical experience. A more concrete connection between the Bible and *religiosidad popular* is suggested by Mexican theologian Raul Vidales. He says that Mexicans, and we might imply other Hispanics as well, have a religious age equal to that of the Old Testament—that is, the age of Abraham and Israel. By that he means that Abraham and Israel in their search for deepening their relationship with Yahweh were bound to a culture, a rudimentary language and an incipient ritualistic and symbolic world. In effect, "the religious practice of our [Mexican] people is characterized by Old Testament traits."[5] Another perception of the relationship between *religiosidad popular* and the Old Testament is that offered by Herman Vorländer who sees *religiosidad popular* in the Old Testament as a popular perception of God's direct involvement in the lives of the individual, the community, and in nature, apart from or beyond what official religion prescribes.[6] Yet a stronger connection between the Bible and *religiosidad popular* is noted by the significant role of traditions in both as collective memory experiences, the predisposition in both for anthropomorphisms and personification, and the frequent utilization in both of a rich symbolism. Indeed, to distinguish biblical teaching from the people's popular religiosity is often difficult because of the symbiotic relationship between the two regarding divine causality and personal experience.

Given the fact that two of the constitutive elements of *religiosidad popular* are tradition and symbol, it is well to mention them now in connection with the Bible.

## Tradition

Traditions are very important to a people. They are the collective memories of positive and negative experiences that have significantly affected their ongoing understanding of themselves. Traditions in the Bible have been the means by which a people passed on its story from one generation to another. To understand the nature of revelation through tradition one must first grasp the distinction between *traditio* and *traditum*. The former is the process of handing down and the latter is the content of what is handed down.[7] In an article on revelation through tradition, Douglas Knight speaks of tradition as being produced by the people engaged in many aspects of life, a kind of interaction between the *traditio* and the *traditum*. The process of tradition involves people actively. He says, "for while the tradition preserved the memory of the past it is also subject to growth and change at the hands of new generations who face new situations that require reconsideration of their heritage."[8]

Thus we see that in the tradition process both *memory* and *interpretation* are crucial elements in the dynamics of revelation, because revelation is more than just a theological matter—it touches upon the phenomenological aspects of a people's view of reality, which conditions their perception of God and their interaction with God. People tend to remember in their traditions significant (positive or negative) experiences. The significance of that memory has new and reinforced meaning for later generations. Each generation reinterprets for itself the contemporary significance of its collective memory of the tradition. As illustration, we can document this process in the Old Testament prophetic tradition. Amos (5:18–20) speaks of the *yôm YHWH*, the Day of the Lord, as being a time of negative judgment for Israel. In the earlier stages of the tradition, the *yôm YHWH* signified a day of hope and prosperity. Amos took an existing tradition and reinterpreted it—to the point of reversing its original meaning—in order that the tradition have significance for his generation.

The traditions of a people include both a process and a content, the former being reinterpretation and the latter being memory. What is remembered as revelatory content is Yahweh's message. Thus revelation through tradition is seen as ongoing experience, or in Knight's phrase a "durative confrontation" between Yahweh and the people. That is to say, the memory of a meaningful experience, positive or negative, keeps alive the manifested expression of God's revelation in a particular point in time and is reinterpreted by succeeding generations for its own significance.

One possible difficulty with the revelation-in-tradition concept as discussed above is the question regarding the content of the tradition. How accurate is the memory of what is remembered in order to be handed down? Because of the memory's inherent linkage to experience, which is variable, and a people's need to share in that experience, the revelatory aspect of memory's content must be flexible, since it is reinterpreted by succeeding generations, thus making revelation patently confessional in character. Perhaps the most obvious expression of this phenomenon is memory as *Vergegenwärtigung*, or "re-presentation," "actualization" of a significant event usually within a cultic context.[9] Douglas Knight explains:

> The essence of "Vergegenwärtigung" . . . is rather to create a situation in which the people of a new generation can feel affected by the past events, can realize the implications for their own lives, can open themselves to the continued impact of previous revelation. But for this to be effected, interpretation geared to the new situation was mandatory, and through accumulation of such interpretations the tradition itself grew.[10]

Finally, as Knight points out,[11] it is important to bear in mind that revelation occurs not "as" tradition in a sense identified with it, not "in" tradition as though it is some ready commodity, but rather "through" tradition. This prepositional precision is necessary in order to underscore the complexity surrounding the nature of revelation with reference to tradition. The significance of the preposition "through" indicates three things. First, tradition provides the structures necessary to understand revelation as revelation. Second, tradition is the significant life experience which becomes revelatory. Third, tradition is the channel by which the *traditum* is made available to subsequent generations. Consequently, we see revelation "through" tradition as a dynamic, reciprocal, ongoing interaction between Yahweh and the people.

In *religiosidad popular* there is both *tradition* and *traditum*, a process/content and an interaction between the two. The content of the traditions can be the specific devotions of a community—for example, the patronal feasts of a village and memories of what the patron saint has done or not done for the community. The process of the traditions can be the goal-implementation of the specific devotion—for example, the recitation of certain prayers, the performance of a definite task as part of the devotion, such as pilgrimage to a specific shrine. The content and process are complementary to one another as two parts of the one tradition.

In addition, the context of the tradition is important for its understanding, particularly its geographic context. Quite often a certain devotion is bound to a specific locale giving that place an aura of sacrality. The traditions connected with a sacral locus usually assume paradigmatic status within *religiosidad popular*. A prime example of this is the shrine of Our

Lady of Guadalupe in Mexico City. Virtually all devotion to Our Lady of Guadalupe in the United States and Mexico has the shrine of Mexico as its prime referent[12] and all traditions—memory experiences—of Hispanic people concerning Our Lady of Guadalupe are related somehow to that shrine. The recipient of the Marian vision, the Indian Juan Diego, becomes the prototype for the Mexican—or devotee, usually mestizo poor—seeking special favor from Our Lady of Guadalupe. The place of vision was Mount Tepeyac. In both the Old Testament and the ancient Near East in general, the mountain was considered sacred space, the place of encounter between the divine and the human. For example, Moses had his encounter with Yahweh who gave him the decalogue on Mount Sinai. Also the *tilma*, the shawl of Juan Diego where the Virgin Mary is believed to have left her imprint as a result of the encounter on Mount Tepeyac, is given a reverence that is equalled only by the shroud of Turin where Jesus is believed to have left his imprint from the encounter with the divine on Mount Calvary.

As do the traditions of the Bible, so the traditions of *religiosidad popular* have a revelatory dimension.[13] The revelatory dimension in the traditions of *religiosidad popular* is the interaction between memory and reinterpretation. A community may undergo significant positive or negative experiences—for example, a bountiful harvest, flood, epidemic, and so forth. The experiences have an impact on the community, and the memory of these events preserves their meaning for the community. A case in point is the celebration of the feast of San Ysidro (May 15), patron saint of tillage. In farming communities where the particular ritual includes a procession into the fields with an image/statue of the saint, the priest in the name of the community blesses the fields, either in gratitude for a successful harvest or in further petition in case of unsuccessful harvest. The harvest may be a success or failure—reasons are found to explain, understand, and expect either result. These results together with their reasons are given an interpretation that becomes part of the community tradition. The memory of the harvest's outcome is interpreted as revelatory of God's will and is expressed in ritual for subsequent retelling in the tradition. The important thing about devotion is to ask for the intercession of San Ysidro as someone who has intercessory influence with God.

In a faith community these events are given a religious meaning, which is determined by the nature of the community's relationship with God. The challenge becomes one of fathoming God's will in a meaningful event. The event may have one meaning for one generation and another meaning for a subsequent generation. What is significant here is to see the reinterpretation of memory in the context of the prayerful devotion as revelatory of God's will. That is to say, each generation taps into the collective memory of the faith community, represented by its religious traditions, in order to see what "God's will" (revelation) was for a particular generation at a given time. It then reevaluates the traditions for itself.

The devotional practices of *religiosidad popular* allow for this process in the traditions in the sense that the tradition is basically the memory of a collective experience which in its "passing on" *(traditum)* incorporates the dynamic of self-involvement, so that there is something of each generation in subsequent interpretations of the tradition. In other words, "God's will" (revelation) has as its nucleus the primary interpretation of the experience that is evaluated and appropriated accordingly by later generations. This is how revelation occurs in the tradition.

*Symbol*

Revelation through symbol presents more of a problem because of the multifaceted dimensions of symbolic understanding. Avery Dulles offers a keen insight into the revelatory aspect of symbol that could be translated directly into the biblical context and indirectly into the ambience of *religiosidad popular*. Acknowledging the work of his predecessors in the field of symbolism and revelation, Dulles begins by clarifying his terms. For him, "a symbol is a sign pregnant with a plenitude of meaning which is evoked rather than explicitly stated."[14] This means, first of all, that there is a whole field of semantic energy surrounding a symbol whose meaning can be tapped into. The "tapping into" this semantic energy is the function of hermeneutics. Second, the evocation of meaning means that knowledge of the symbol itself demands some kind of involvement by the participant. No passive observation is possible.

Although the usual linkage is between symbol and language, Dulles is correct in not limiting symbolism to the literary sphere as far as revelation is concerned. For him historical personages, natural objects, visible artifacts, and dreams can all be symbolic. It is significant to note that these nonliterary potentially revelatory elements are also present in *religiosidad popular*.[15]

As mentioned above, one of the elements of symbol, and in my judgment one of the most crucial, is the participatory dimension of its knowledge. That is to say, a symbol is self-involving. "It [symbol] speaks to us only insofar as it lures us to situate ourselves mentally within the universe of meaning and value which it opens up to us."[16] Because of the involvement of the knower as a person, a transformation takes place in the sense that it shifts our awareness and changes our values. In addition, the symbol has a strong influence on behavior in that it can appeal to hidden energy resources of activity and response — for example, a country's flag, which can mobilize the energy of a nation. Finally, a symbol involves greater participation by opening up the horizon of possibilities that precipitate one into different kinds of action whether for good or for evil, depending upon the motivational impact of the symbol itself. This process of involvement, influence on values, transformation, and opening up further horizons is the revelatory dimension of symbol.

Revelation through symbol in *religiosidad popular* is most apparent in the various devotional practices that rely heavily on imagery. In these images the focus is on symbolic value and the impact it has on the devotee. I follow Dulles's definition and understanding of symbol as explained above.

Every devotional practice in *religiosidad popular* has a certain amount of symbolism, which can include a significant event, gesture, object, place, and the like. And it is these symbols that have a revelatory dimension. Dulles mentions four properties common to symbolism and revelation that, in my judgment, are applicable to the symbolism in the devotional practices of *religiosidad popular.*[17]

First, symbolism gives a participatory knowledge which is self-involving. That is to say, the symbol speaks to us only insofar as it draws us into its world of meaning. In the devotional practices of *religiosidad popular* this would mean that the specific symbol such as the pilgrimage or home altar becomes revelatory to the extent that the individual is drawn into the world of that specific symbolism—for example, pilgrimage as sacred journey, home altar as sacred space.

Second, symbol, insofar as it involves the knower as a person, has a transforming effect. The very "drawing into" the world of the symbol effects a certain transformation in the participant. Dulles mentions the healing capacity of symbolism as a fundamental effect.[18] In the devotional practices of *religiosidad popular* this would mean that once drawn into the symbolic world of a specific practice, the participant has no choice but to respond, and the response itself becomes the transforming element. This transforming effect is usually a deepening of faith or a religious conversion, or could be one of several other possibilities including the possibility of spiritual or physical healing. Often, when there is some sort of "exchange" in the devotion—for example, a cure for a penitential pilgrimage—the transformation is more obvious.

Third, symbolism has a powerful influence on commitments and behavior. Symbols stir the imagination and release untapped resources of energy. Significantly, almost every social movement in history has galvanized its adherents behind some meaningful symbol. In the devotional practices of *religiosidad popular* this would mean that whatever symbols were invoked in a specific devotion, the involvement in and response to the symbolic world by the participant would result in some action. For example, in the devotion known as the *manda* a promise is made, generally to some saint, in exchange for a special favor—usually physical healing. The promise is often a pilgrimage to a sacred place undergone with some hardship. A dominant symbol in this devotion would be promise as pact, a sort of quid pro quo. The granting of the favor would necessitate a strict obligation on the part of the participant to complete the promise of pilgrimage. The response here is expected because of the nature of the symbol.

Fourth, symbol introduces us into realms of awareness not normally accessible to discursive thought. Because symbolism inhabits a world beyond empirical verification, it can put us in touch with deeper realities, such as the realm of the transcendent. In the devotional practices of *religiosidad popular* this would mean nothing more than that the symbols of a particular devotion, because of their evocative and participatory aspects, bring the devotee into a world where faith and mystery are the common modes of discourse.

What has been said above concerning tradition and symbol in *religiosidad popular* can also be said concerning tradition and symbol in the Bible. The key link between the Bible and *religiosidad popular* with regard to tradition and symbol is the cultural base in both, within which revelation occurs and self-affirmation takes place. Imagery in the Bible corresponding to the experiences of Hispanics becomes the basis for the meaningful analogues in devotional practices. It is the function of hermeneutics to provide a valid interpretation of the resultant analogues.

## HERMENEUTIC FOR HISPANICS

For well over a century the predominant method for biblical criticism has been the historical-critical method with its focus on the biblical text. It tended to ask questions of the text, such as: How accurate is this manuscript reading in light of other text traditions? Which reading is the more authentic? What is the literary form, style, context of this particular text? What changes have occurred, if any, in the development of the traditions, and what have redactors added throughout the redactional process? The disciplines of textual criticism, literary criticism, form criticism, tradition criticism, and redaction criticism as constitutive of the historical-critical method developed in order to deal with these questions. Though these basic questions regarding the text were being answered by the historical-critical method, there was a whole new avenue of inquiry left unexplored until recently—namely, the *affective* dimension of the biblical text. The question here is: How does the biblical text *affect* the reader who helps give it meaning? After all, the biblical texts were written in order to be read, so the presupposition is that the reader is to have some interpretive role with regard to the text.

It is a basic datum that no one method is completely inclusive in interpretation. The rise of new methodologies is an attempt on the part of biblical scholarship to deepen the understanding of the biblical message by first making us aware of the complexities surrounding the communication of that message. As rhetorical criticism[19] emerged to refine the understanding provided by the existing historical-critical method, with its focus on the text, so other newer methodologies arose to further expand that understanding by taking into account the involvement of the reader/hearer in interpretation. All the differing methodologies work in conjunction with each other to reach a fuller understanding, for only then can there be an integrity in interpretation.

Two of the new methodologies that supplement the historical-critical method with its focus on the text and serve well as a hermeneutic for *religiosidad popular* are structuralism and reader-response criticism, which focus on the reader as interpreter.[20]

Structuralism as method analyzes human social phenomena initially from an anthropological perspective, and from there it moves on to other disciplines, including biblical hermeneutics. The presuppositions of structuralism for biblical hermeneutics are basically two, as set forth by Terence Keegan:

> A fundamental presupposition that is basic to all structuralist research is the existence of fixed sets of abstract rules which govern all forms of social activity. . . . For structuralists, all forms of social activity are forms of communication. . . . Language is simply one of the many forms of communication. . . . The work of structuralists to date has been largely the establishment of these fixed sets of laws according to which a variety of forms of social activity takes place. . . . A second presupposition for structuralists, which is usually more basic than the first, is that human beings as such have an innate, genetically transmitted and determined mechanism that acts as a structuring force.[21]

These presuppositions tell us that there are "deep structures" often not realized that are behind all social interactions, and these structures have their fixed rules that are applicable anytime and anywhere. The idea is that, according to structuralists, authors actually utilize "deep structures," which, rather than the text, communicate meaning to the reader. Keegan further comments:

> Most people who write are not the least bit aware of these deep structures that make their writing meaningful, any more than the people who receive them are aware of these deep structures. These deep structures, nevertheless, are operative both in the work of the writer and in the work of the reader.[22]

There are generally three levels of structure. The first level is called "structures of enunciation"—that is, the issues that deal with the author's concrete living situation and the purpose for writing. When dealing with a biblical text, this level is usually addressed by the historical critic through form-criticism, or whatever branch of the method is called for. The second level of structure is generally called "cultural structures" or the cultural codes of the author's culture—namely, those values and systems that explain the author's background and frame of reference. This level is what cultural anthropology would address. The third level of structure, and that proper to structural exegesis, is the level of "deep structures"—that is to say, fixed structures which are constitutive of human beings everywhere, such as the way stories are told and the existence of certain myths.

These "deep structures" of narrative and myth function primarily and effectively in the world of symbolism where meaning is frequently more connotative than denotive—that is, they are referential rather than explicit. The narrative and mythic structures, which are putatively common to all humanity, are part of the symbolic world (referential meaning) of semantics which the structuralists seek to explain.

First, there is the question of the "deep structure" of narrative. The initial presupposition is that all narrative follows essentially the identical structure—namely, the disruption of order, the attempt to reestablish order with occasional hindrance, and the reestablishment of order. Structuralists say that all narrative, including biblical narrative, follows this pattern. Thus a relatively unsophisticated person reading/hearing a biblical narrative would be able to identify with, if not fully understand, that narrative because of this dynamic of "deep structure."

Second, the "deep structure" of myth is said to be even more profound than the narrative structure, because myths are paradigmatic while narratives are sequential. For example, narratives have sequence or logic, while myths operate with a symbolism which establishes paradigms for thought and action. As Keegan points out:

> Quite frequently in biblical narratives one can find mythic structures. What a myth basically does is resolve oppositions. A myth is a way of coping with the fundamental oppositions that one constantly saves in the course of human living. ... The meaning of the myth is to be found entirely in the manner in which the oppositions, the fundamental oppositions, are overcome, fundamental oppositions like life and death, or heaven and earth, or God and man. These are fundamental oppositions that are so radically opposed that there is no middle ground, there is no way logical minds can bring the two together. Myths overcome these oppositions by providing corresponding oppositions, that can be overcome, that do admit of mediation.[23]

In the mythic structure it is important to recognize the proportionality between various pairs of opposites—namely, whether or not opposites can be mediated. For example, the opposites of life and death have no mediation. The structuring of myth attempts to make nonmediated opposition tolerable. That is to say, it would provide a corresponding opposition that can be mediated—for example, a special act of healing, a "miracle."

In the life of the average, simple person there are many pairs of oppositions functioning, especially the forces of good and evil interacting with him or her. According to deep mythic structure, the seemingly irreconcilable opposition between good and evil is overcome through a special mediation—namely, a divine intervention.

The way structuralist hermeneutics could be useful in understanding *religiosidad popular*'s reaction to the Bible would be twofold. First, with regard to the "deep structure" of narrative, the practitioner of *religiosidad popular*, with an already established link to the Bible, would be able to identify with the dynamics of the narrative because of the "deep structure," if there are any clear biblical analogues to the specific practice of *religiosidad popular* in the first place. Second, with regard to the "deep structure" of myth, there is first the paradigmatic world of symbolism which is common to both *religiosidad popular* and mythic structures. The interpretive function is consequently inferential.

In the Hispanic (as well as any other) world of experience, there are many opposites functioning within the person, especially the struggle between good and evil manifested in various forms. In a particular practice of *religiosidad popular*, often the opposites which are apparently irreconcilable in the current context—for example, suffering-joy, tension-tranquility, sickness-health—are resolved through mediation, through direct appeal either to God or the saints. The mythic structures in the Bible, again if there are analogues in *religiosidad popular*, serve as models.

## READER-RESPONSE CRITICISM

A second recent methodology that focuses on the reader rather than the biblical text and can be useful for understanding the relationship between *religiosidad popular* and the Bible is called reader-response criticism.[24] Reader-response criticism arose ironically, in response to the rigid objectivity of the new criticism that was obviously influenced by scientific positivism.[25] One of the principal postulates of reader-response criticism is that "literature deals with human attitudes, with feelings. The result of a literary endeavor is in no way objectifiable."[26] It is impossible, say reader-response critics, to have an absolutely objective interpretation, since all explanations are interpretations. The issue then becomes one of choosing the data and the method from which to make interpretations. And since the historical-critical method, in its striving toward objectivity, has neglected the reader in the hermeneutical process, reader-response criticism seeks to fill the void. Reader-response critics hold that there is no single objective meaning to the biblical text that is available to all. The biblical text has potentialities, a sort of "semantic universe" surrounding it, which make various interpretations possible. Thus the author provides a meaning for one generation, and readers of the same and subsequent generations can provide others.

Another basic presupposition of reader-response criticism is that a literary work is a bipolar "virtual entity." As Keegan puts it:

A literary work is a bi-polar virtual entity. A virtual entity is something which is capable of existing but which does not yet exist. Only when the two poles of a literary work are both operative does a literary work come into being. Every truly literary work has both an artistic pole and an aesthetic pole. The artistic pole is the artistic creation of the author. . . . The other pole, the aesthetic pole, is the work of the reader. Both these poles are necessary. Without both of them operating, the literary work is simply a potentiality. Its potentiality becomes an actuality when both these poles are operating, when a reader picks up the work of an author and actually reads it. In actually reading it, it comes into being. It is real, it has meaning, and it does something.[27]

The key factor in this scenario is that the reader's imagination is thereby activated, and from the semantic universe of the words in the text the reader as artist draws and gives meaning to the text. The potentiality is thus reduced to actuality. This process is used, above all, in narrative where the author often leaves gaps supplied by the reader, which results in the dynamic interchange of assumptions made by the reader, which are challenged by the text, which results in further assumptions, and so on. The reader thus actually becomes involved in the interpretation of the text.[28]

How does this brief glimpse into reader-response criticism help us to understand the relationship between *religiosidad popular* and the Bible? First of all, in reader-response criticism, literature deals with human attitudes and feelings. The Hispanic practitioner of *religiosidad popular* is basically an affective person and would thus respond to literature, particularly biblical literature, in that fashion. Second, in reader-response criticism the literary work, in this case the Bible, is a bipolar entity which must have its two poles interacting simultaneously in order to exist. In the context of *religiosidad popular* and the Bible, these poles are: the biblical author and the Hispanic reader-hearer who is also a practitioner of *religiosidad popular*. In the reading-hearing of a particular biblical text, especially narrative, the already predisposed imagination of the Hispanic practitioner of *religiosidad popular* is activated into entering and interacting with a symbolic, semantic world of the text, and filling in gaps in meaning through assumptions which are made and challenged.

A similar argument from a different perspective may be made by referring to the discussion of Raul Vidales who speaks of the function of sacraments among Mexicans by showing parallels to the Old Testament. He says that the "sacramental signs," such as salvation, messianism, and so forth, though functional in the present, have a future orientation, and indicate possibilities for the messianic future because they have "polyvalent meaning" (*significado plurivalente*)[29] in the sense that with the experience of the sacrament, the recipient can draw one of many possible meanings that are particularly applicable to one's personal life.

Another connection between *religiosidad popular* and the Bible, with possible inferences for the hermeneutical methods of structuralism and reader-response criticism, is made by the Mexican theologian Raul Duarte Castillo. He states that there is a certain adaptation of religious world imagery that occurs between the Bible and other cultures that share the religious world imagery of the Bible—for example, the Hispanic culture. Some examples of this would be: the image of God as father because the God of Israel/ Hispanics is seen in familiar terms; the image of the Sinai covenant because it is bilateral and conditional, and has the implication of mutual obligation.[30]

Yet a third observation by Javier Lozano Barragán, a Mexican theologian, with regard to *religiosidad popular* from which we can infer a link to reader-response criticism and the structuralist approach to biblical hermeneutics, is that religious expressions in general and Mexican *religiosidad popular* in particular have their fundamental expressions in myth, legend, and the narrative.[31]

Given the importance of structuralism and reader-response criticism as valid methods of biblical hermeneutics regarding practices of *religiosidad popular* within the Catholic Church, there is yet one more link that affirms the bond between the Bible and *religiosidad popular*—namely, the ecumenical link. Divine communication through revelation is not the sole province of a single religious group, be it Catholic, Protestant, or Jewish. The Second Vatican Council documents *Dei Verbum* and *Ad Gentes* make that clear. Hence for U.S. Catholic Hispanics to have a fuller sense of the revelatory dimension of the devotions of *religiosidad popular* it is important that they have some awareness of what Hispanic Protestants are doing with respect to interpretation of the Bible within the context of their own devotional practices.

I do not refer here to the simplistic, subjective, and usually erroneous biblical interpretations of fundamentalists or Pentecostal groups, but rather to the responsible Protestants who encounter the Bible on its own terms and listen to what it says. What I hope is emerging as a biblical hermeneutic representative of Hispanic Protestants is the perspective provided by Justo L. González in his recent book *Mañana: Christian Theology from a Hispanic Perspective.*[32] The hermeneutic that González proposes is called "reading the Bible in Spanish." By this he means reading the Bible not necessarily in Spanish translation but rather from a Hispanic perspective, and with a political dimension. He says:

> When the people read the Bible, and read it from their own perspective rather than from the perspective of the powerful, the Bible becomes a mighty political book. This is what I mean by "reading the bible in Spanish": a reading that includes the realization that the Bible is a political book; a reading in the "vernacular," not only in the cultural, linguistic sense but also in the sociopolitical sense.[33]

González then offers his four rules of grammar in order to read properly the Bible "in Spanish." These rules are:

> 1. To say that the Bible is a political book means, first of all, that it deals with issues of power and powerlessness. . . . Read it "in Span-

ish," that is, as exiles, as members of a powerless group, as those who are excluded from the "innocent" history of the dominant group. . . . In this approach to Scripture lies the beginning of a Hispanic-American theology. . . .

2. We must remember that only a small portion of Scripture was originally written to be read in private. . . . The "grammar" for a new reading of Scripture "in Spanish" . . . must be aware that even when we read Scripture in private, God is addressing all of us as a community of faith.

3. We must remember that the core principle of scriptural "grammar" is its availability to children, to the simple, to the poor . . . to read the Bible "in Spanish" means to give attention to what the "babes" find in it.

4. Above all, however, we must learn to read Scripture in the vocative. The purpose of our common study of Scripture is not so much to interpret it as to allow it to interpret us and our situation.[34]

The rules of grammar that Gonzalez postulates for a Protestant Hispanic reading of Scripture are not unlike the methods of structuralism and reader-response criticism utilized within the framework of tradition and symbol suggested for Catholic Hispanics who are practitioners of *religiosidad popular*. Nevertheless, ongoing dialogue is needed between Gonzalez's rules of grammar for "reading the Bible in Spanish" and Catholic biblical scholarship.

## TRADITION AND SYMBOL AS KEYS

To illustrate the hermeneutical method suggested above, I have chosen the example of the home altar. The Hispanic devotion of the home altar transports the devotee into the realm of sacred space. It is, above all, a sort of theophanic manifestation of the divine presence in one's home. Church and home share the sacredness of space with regard to the divine presence. In both home and church the threshold is of extreme importance, because it is the passageway between the sacred and profane worlds. The threshold has its guardians—spirits that protect the sacred space from profanation.[35] The altar in the church is the focal point of sacredness, the space where the divine presence is manifested in ritual. So it is in the Hispanic household. The primary "altar" in the Hispanic household is, from a phenomenological point of view, the hearth, fireplace, kitchen as the central place of power. Gerhardus van der Leeuw puts it this way:

The possibility of eating and drinking is experienced precisely as a divine possibility, and its position estimated as holy. This also is the basis of the sacredness of that most important spot of all in the house, the hearth: it is its central point, the totality of its power. . . . Even today the common people have preserved some of the correct feeling that the power of the house accumulates in the kitchen, on the hearth; the "best parlour" usually remains empty.[36]

It is interesting that in Hispanic homes, at least in the villages of northern New Mexico where my family roots are, the kitchen is indeed the most important room of the house. One enters a Hispanic home through the kitchen and visits in it. All visitors are received first in the kitchen, and then may or may not be ushered into another "parlor." This centrality of the kitchen in the Hispanic household reflects a vestigial awareness of the sense of the sacred in the home, which is why hospitality is considered by the Hispanics to be a test of their closeness to God. All visitors to the Hispanic household are first offered some refreshment upon entering. Since the hearth/kitchen is the entryway into the Hispanic home, the focal point of the house as sacred space, the meal then seems to function as a sort of bonding ritual.

The secondary "altar" in the Hispanic home is a more determinative and conscious attempt at localizing the divine presence—namely, the home altar itself. It is usually a simple affair—an altar set up in a nook in the family room or master bedroom. There is usually a statue of Mary or Christ as predominant, and frequently other saints in attendance. More often than not, there are flowers and votive candles on the altar. The dynamics of encounter in the devotion take the form of prayer, usually of petition or thanksgiving. Favors are requested and gratitude is expressed for favors granted. The sense of sacred space and ritual activity is quite evident. The overriding sense of the existence of the home altar is the manifestation of the divine presence in the home. God is there for the people.

Since the central concept of the Hispanic home altar is manifestation of the divine presence in one's home, one of the most suitable biblical analogues would be the theme in the Old Testament of God's presence among the people. In the Old Testament there are two principal theological traditions that deal with Yahweh's presence among the people, and both have political implications. The one is the theological tradition of God's *transcendence*, symbolized principally by the tent of meeting (for example: Ex. 29:42; 25:22; 30:36; 33:7–11). The tent of meeting was usually placed outside the people's encampment, where Moses would go to seek divine communication. This fact implies apartness from the deity, and therefore a need for structure and mediation in order for the people to have access to God. The other is the theological tradition of *immanence*, symbolized principally by the ark of the covenant (for example: Num. 10:35–36; 1 Sam. 6:3, 8, 20; 1 Sam. 4:3). The ark of the covenant was usually placed amid the people when engaged in battle. This fact implied direct relationship with God, and thus no need for a mediator. Because of their political implications, these two theological traditions have been in tension not only throughout Israel's history, but also throughout the history of those institutions, ancient or modern, that base their relationship to God on one or the other tradition.[37]

In both the Old Testament and *religiosidad popular* God's presence is effective power. Whoever "controls" God's presence has great power. Hence, any political legitimation of power must have some connection with the powerful and effective presence of God. Since transcendence and immanence as two forms of divine presence reflected two different political styles, there was always and continues to be a struggle for dominance of that symbolism and, therefore, legitimation. Assurance of divine presence legitimizes activities and decisions by those claiming that special presence. Is that presence direct and permanent, or is it mediated and occasional?

One of the two theological traditions dealing with God's effective presence — the one that best suits the Hispanic devotion of the home altar — is the tradition of immanence symbolized by the ark of the covenant. The theological tradition of immanence in the Old Testament allows for God's direct and effective presence among the people. In the Hispanic home the home altar is the equivalent of the sacred shrine/holy mountain where God's presence is invoked. The ark of the covenant is related to the Sinai covenant theology. The home altar is like a surrogate Sinai where a covenantal relationship is established between God and the people, where there is a mutuality of responsibility and commitment. It is at the home altar where, on occasion, the pact or "bargain" is struck — for example, in exchange for a favor — usually healing — granted by God, often reinforced through the instrumentality of a favorite saint, the petitioner will generally perform some penitential act. The direct mutuality of responsibility and commitment is effected here at the home altar as it was on Sinai. Or, as is more often the case, the home altar as surrogate Sinai is the sacred meeting ground where a meaningful encounter between God and the people takes place through the ritual of prayer.

The traditions of a Hispanic family who are practitioners of the home altar devotion are brought into the presence of the devotion itself. The memory of positive or negative experiences — that is, family traditions — is recalled and the divine presence is invoked for purposes of entering into dialogue with God — petition or thanksgiving, depending upon what mood is invoked by the memory of the tradition. The symbols enumerated above regarding the home altar also bring the devotee into the world of the sacred where participation is encouraged. The traditions of the family brought for consideration into the devotion of the home altar and the symbols of the devotion itself are the keys for its interpretation.

Structuralism is the first of our hermeneutical tools. In the devotion of the home altar, a deep structure narrative is functioning. By the very existence of the home altar, and the ritual connected with it, the effective presence of God is presupposed. The petitionary aspect of the prayers, together with the quid pro quo element between God and the practitioner, presupposes a probable alienation of God's presence, due, for example, to the petitioner's sense of unworthiness, or to God's simple refusal to accede if the petition is not granted within a specified time. The effective presence of God is finally reestablished either when the petition is granted or when the petitioner comes to accept the result.

Reader-response criticism likewise concerns itself with the affective dimension of biblical interpretation. Attitudes and feelings are what are communicated, and the semantic universe of the text permits applicability to the reader/hearer's environment. The biblical texts applicable to the home altar devotion are those connected with the ark of the covenant tradition and the theology of immanence. God's effective presence is experienced by the devotee, an experience which then opens up a world of possibilities.

Both structuralism and reader-response criticism as ways of understanding scripture offer the Hispanic an opportunity for this much needed sense of self-affirmation. The God who is effectively present in the home altar devotion will confront and conquer the devotee's enemies, be it illness, bad habits, exploitation, or any other forms of chaos. Attitudes of hope and expectation, coupled with feelings of confidence, anxiety, and love are experienced in relationship to God as encountered in the home altar devotion.

Second, there is the question of attitudes and feelings connected with a covenant relationship. The most suitable covenant relationship model from scripture applicable to the home altar devotion is the Sinai covenant relationship, with its mutuality of responsibility and commitment. There are feelings of self-affirmation expressed in a relationship where there exists a mutuality of responsibility and commitment. In addition, the theology of the ark tradition provides for an applicability in the devotee's environment within the framework of the home altar devotion. For example, when the practitioner reads or hears any of the biblical passages related to the ark tradition within the context of home altar devotion, the semantic world of the text's meanings is opened up so that there can be applicability to personal life of any relevant part of the text. If such occurs, then there is an effective interaction between text and reader, the bipolar reality, and understanding takes place which thus gives the biblical text meaning.

As a conclusion it is well to keep in mind that *religiosidad popular* with its traditions and symbols as biblical keys can open up the treasure trove of scriptural understanding. With the methodology proposed above, I suggest that this approach has one of the best chances of serving as the basis for a U.S. Hispanic theology in the decade of the 1990s.

## NOTES

1. This council document may be found in Austin Flannery, ed., *Vatican Council II. The Conciliar and Post-Conciliar Documents* (Collegeville: Liturgical Press, 1984), pp. 750–65.

2. Ibid., pp. 813–56.

60    *C. GILBERT ROMERO*

3. The term "dependent" revelation, as a wider form of revelation, is here used in opposition to "foundational" revelation, which is constitutive of the Catholic belief system and what Catholics have in credal formulas.

4. Clifford Geertz, *The Interpretation of Cultures* (New York: Basic Books, 1973), p. 89.

5. Raul Vidales, "Sacramentos y Religiosidad Popular," *Servir*, vol. 4, no. 52 (1972), p. 368.

6. Herman Vorländer, "Aspects of Popular Religion in the Old Testament," *Popular Religion; Concilium*, no. 186, N. Greinacher and N. Mette, eds. (Edinburgh: Clark, 1986), pp. 63–70. Vorländer, despite some negative criticism of popular religion, has an overall positive view of it: "Popular religion emphasizes the aspect of nearness to human existence by closely linking the experience of God and the experiences of life. Faith in Yahweh becomes remote from life, theoretical, unless it is continually enriched by the influence of popular religion" (p. 70).

7. This distinction is important in order to appreciate the contribution of both "process" and "content" in tradition. Also, an analysis of tradition as probable locus of revelation is necessary to broaden the scope of understanding beyond the biblical text itself. The evangelist John seemed to hint at this. See John 21:25.

8. Douglas A. Knight, "Revelation Through Tradition," in *Tradition and Theology in the Old Testament*, Douglas A. Knight, ed. (Philadelphia: Fortress, 1977), p. 144.

9. An important article on the subject was written by Martin Noth, "The Re-Presentation of the Old Testament in Proclamation," in Claus Westermann, ed., *Essays on Old Testament Hermeneutics* (Richmond: John Knox, 1966), pp. 76–88.

10. Knight, "Revelation," p. 167, note 41.

11. Ibid., p. 179. This whole paragraph reflects Knight.

12. Except those devotions connected with Guadalupe in Spain, which are antecedent to and independent of Guadalupe in Mexico.

13. The methodology and argument for this are presented and developed in my book *Hispanic Devotional Piety: Tracing the Biblical Roots* (Maryknoll, N.Y.: Orbis, 1991).

14. Avery Dulles, *Models of Revelation* (Garden City, N.Y.: Doubleday Image, 1985), p. 132.

15. On the subject of nonliterary revelation, see the useful article by René Latourelle, "La Révélation comme Parole, Témoinage, et Recontre," *Gregorianum* 43 (1962), pp. 39–54. Dulles also speaks to the revelatory aspect of ritual in his quote of John Macquarrie, *Models*, pp. 134, 140.

16. Dulles, *Models.*, p. 135.

17. Ibid., pp. 136–39

18. Ibid., pp. 136–37. He quotes Victor White, a Jungian disciple, on the beneficial and therapeutic effect of healing through symbol.

19. First suggested by James Muilenburg in his presidential address to the Society of Biblical Literature in 1968. See "Form Criticism and Beyond," *Journal of Biblical Literature* 88 (1969), pp. 1–18.

20. An excellent work which discusses these new methods in detail is that by Terence J. Keegan, *Interpreting the Bible. A Popular Introduction to Biblical Hermeneutics* (NY: Paulist, 1985). A more comprehensive discussion of reader-response criticism may be found in Edgar V. McKnight, *Post-Modern Use of the Bible. The Emergence of Reader-Oriented Criticism* (Nashville: Abingdon, 1988). For a more

extensive treatment of biblical structuralism complete with bibliography, see Robert M. Polzin, *Biblical Structuralism. Method and Subjectivity in the Study of Ancient Texts* (Philadelphia: Fortress, 1977).

21. Keegan, *Interpreting*, pp. 41–43.

22. Ibid., p.45.

23. Ibid., p. 61.

24. This method is discussed at length by Keegan, ibid., pp. 73–90.

25. Ibid., pp. 75, 76.

26. Ibid., p. 77.

27. Ibid., p. 82.

28. Keegan develops the reader-response method by discussing narrative-criticism as the logical outcome of reader-response, with particular reference to narratives in the Bible. See chapter 6 of Keegan's work.

29. Raul Vidales, "Sacramentos y Religiosidad Popular," *Servir*, vol 4, no. 52 (1974), p. 373.

30. Raul Duarte Castillo, "Utilización de Ciertas Formas Populares en la Religiosidad Biblica," *La Religiosidad Popular en México,* Mexican Theological Society, ed. (Mexico City: Ediciones Paulinas, 1975), pp. 165–72.

31. Javier Lozano Barragán, "Religiosidad Popular y Sentido de la Fe del Pueblo de Dios, *La Religiosidad Popular en México*, pp. 177–79.

32. Justo L. González, *Mañana: Christian Theology from a Hispanic Perspective* (Nashville: Abingdon, 1990).

33. Ibid., p. 84.

34. Ibid., pp. 85–86.

35. Mircea Eliade, *The Sacred and the Profane* (New York: Harcourt, Brace and World, 1958), p. 25.

36. G. van der Leeuw, *Religion in Essence and Manifestation*, vol. 2 (New York: Harper and Row, 1963), p. 397.

37. A more comprehensive treatment of the ark and tent theologies reflecting immanence and transcendence vis-à-vis the home altar devotion can be found in chapter 6 of Romero, *Hispanic Devotional Piety: Tracing the Biblical Roots.*

*Chapter Four*

# Tradition and Popular Religion:
# An Understanding of the *Sensus Fidelium*

## ORLANDO O. ESPÍN

It is practically impossible to study any Hispanic community in the United States, regardless of disciplinary point of departure or methodology, without encountering popular religion. Whether it be to denigrate it or lament its omnipresence in the Hispanic milieu, or to encourage and defend it as a sign of cultural affirmation, scholars sooner or later have to take a stand vis-à-vis popular religious beliefs, practices, and worldviews.

Popular religion (or "religiosity")[1] is indeed omnipresent in the Hispanic universe. And it is one of the few core elements shared by all Hispanic cultural communities in the country. Variations do exist, depending on the specific cultural history of each of the communities,[2] but some basic structures and symbols seem to appear as constants from coast to coast.

Popular religion has all too frequently been considered an embarrassment to Catholicism. It has been derided as the superstitious result of religious ignorance, a product of syncretism, a vestige of the rural past, and an ideologically[3] manipulated tool in the hands of those who would abuse simple folk. These accusations (and many others) do point to real issues and do express serious concerns. But when popular religion is viewed only or mainly through the prism of these accusations, the result can only be prejudiced and distorted.

Theologians have usually avoided the study of popular religion, preferring to leave the field to anthropologists and other social scientists. Even liberation theologies have tended to downplay popular religion's role in the church.[4] It is no exaggeration to say that, in Catholic theological circles, popular religion is either treated as an example of what should not be, or it is simply ignored as of no value for the serious theological enterprise.

It will be argued in this chapter that popular religion can be theologically understood as a cultural expression of the *sensus fidelium*, with all that this understanding would imply for the theology of tradition in the Roman Catholic context. To this end (and as an extended example) I will show how two core symbols of Hispanic popular religion in fact convey essential contents of Christian tradition. I will also insist that—since these symbols do no more than act as vehicles for the people's "faith-full" intuitions— the broader issue of the *sensus fidelium* must be paid closer attention in theology. I start, however, with more general but pertinent observations on tradition that will help us set the context for our argument.

## TRADITION AND *SENSUS FIDELIUM*

The study of tradition[5] lies within the overall theological discussion of revelation and the development of doctrine, with many ramifications into other theological areas. Though this is not the place for an exhaustive reflection on the meaning, importance and role of tradition in Roman Catholicism, some basic observations must be made on the subject.

In the past some authors considered tradition, together with but distinct from the scriptures, as a "source" of revelation.[6] This "two-fonts theory," however, was discarded as the theology of revelation correctly came to emphasize that Jesus Christ is *the* revelation of God, and that this revelation is not primarily the "communication of doctrinal truths" but rather the outpouring of God's love and self in human history.

The two-fonts theory also failed when the relation between the biblical text and tradition was carefully examined. It is evident that the scriptures have a privileged position as the inspired and normative witness to God's revelation. Tradition is correctly valued as the context within which the biblical texts came to be written and within which the very canon of the scriptures came to be fixed and accepted as inspired.[7] Tradition is also the ecclesial (and sometimes normative) interpretation of the scriptures. The fixed texts of the Bible are proclaimed, explained, applied to life, and correctly interpreted by tradition for every Christian generation. This role of tradition is guided and protected from error by the Spirit of God who also inspired the biblical texts.[8]

Scripture is the normative, written expression of a preceding tradition that proclaims and witnesses to the revelation of God to Israel and in Christ, and from him through the apostolic community for the universal, postapostolic church. Scripture, therefore, communicates all the essential contents (gathered in the biblical canon and received by the church) necessary for complete, true and saving faith. Scripture, which must always be interpreted in the light of the tradition that precedes and accompanies it, is the norm for the church's preaching and faith.[9]

Postapostolic tradition, on the other hand, is essentially interpretation and reception of the one gospel of God, which has found its concrete, written expression in scripture. The common content of scripture and tradition is, simply put, their normative witness to the God revealed in Jesus Christ. The Bible and tradition share the same content in the sense that tradition, *through postapostolic expressions, symbols, and language*, recognizes and confesses (creed), refines correct meaning against falsehood (dogmas), and witnesses to that same truth which scripture communicates *through the language, expressions, and symbols of Israel and the apostolic church*. Scripture has been received and its canon fixed forever, while tradition is necessarily living in and through history.

One could speak of tradition exemplified in the definitions of the great ecumenical councils of antiquity, as expounded by the fathers of the church, and as communicated and witnessed to by the ecclesial magisterium and by theologians throughout history.[10] Tradition is certainly expressed in and through all these means. Theologians studying tradition usually concentrate on *written* conciliar documents, patristic texts, episcopal or papal declarations, and the like. Quite correctly, this written material (as also the text of Scripture) is very carefully examined and the methods of textual interpretation applied to it. Most theologians are aware of the need to properly understand a written document within its linguistic, cultural, political, historical, and doctrinal contexts. Without this careful study, the interpretation of the text could be prejudiced or inaccurate. As a consequence, it can yield wrong conclusions that could mislead other theological research dependent on the proper interpretation of tradition's texts.

Just as important as the written texts of tradition (or, in fact, more important), however, is the *living witness and faith* of the Christian people.[11] This living witness and faith do not seem to be taken as seriously by those who study tradition.[12] It is difficult to limit the object of one's study when it is supposed to be found mainly at the experiential level in every faith community. Cultural differences, diversity of languages, and all sorts of other variations make the actual theological study and interpretation of the life and faith of real Christian people a very difficult task indeed. And to complicate things even further, the object of the study (though expressed through cultural categories, languages, and so forth, that run the gamut of human diversity) is found at the level of *intuition*. It is this "faith-full" intuition that makes real Christian people *sense* that something is true or not vis-à-vis the gospel, or that someone is acting in accordance with the Christian gospel or not, or that something important for Christianity is not being heard.[13] This intuition in turn allows for and encourages a belief and a style of life and prayer that express and witness to the fundamental Christian message: God as revealed in Jesus Christ. This "faith-full" intuition is called the *sensus fidelium* (or *sensus fidei*).[14]

The whole church has received the revelation of God and accepted it in faith. And, as a consequence, the whole church is charged with proclaiming, living, and transmitting the fullness of revelation. Therefore, the necessary task of expressing the contents of scripture and tradition are not and cannot be limited to the ordained ministers of the church. The whole church has this mission, and the Spirit was promised to the whole church for this task.[15] Christian laity, consequently, are indispensable witnesses and bearers of the gospel—as indispensable as the magisterium of the church. Furthermore, because the foundational origin of the *sensus fidelium* is the Holy Spirit, it can be said that this "sense of the faithful" is infallible, preserved by the Spirit from error in matters necessary to revelation.[16] In other words, the "faith-full" intuition (*sensus fidei*) of real Christian lay persons infallibly transmits the contents of tradition, and thus infallibly senses the proper interpretation and application of scripture.

The main problem with the study of the *sensus fidelium* as a necessary component in any adequate reflection on tradition, is, precisely, its being a "sense," an intuition. This sense is never discovered in some kind of pure state. The *sensus fidelium* is *always* expressed through the symbols, language, and culture of the faithful and, therefore, is in need of intense interpretive processes and methods similar to those called for by the written texts of tradition and scripture. Without this careful examination and interpretation of its means of expression, the true "faith-full" intuition of the Christian people could be inadequately understood or even falsified. This is where theology and the magisterium must play their indispensable hermeneutic roles, though, as we shall see, this process is not without its limitations and problems.

The means through which the *sensus fidelium* expresses itself are extremely varied, showing the cultural wealth of the Christian people. Given the global demographics of today's church, the means tend to be what they have been throughout most of Christian history: *oral, experiential, and symbolic.* These expressions also show (because of their origin in human culture) the wound of sinfulness capable of obscuring (but never destroying) the "faith-full" and infallible intuitions of the Christian people. The interpretation and discernment needed in the study of the *sensus fidelium* must, therefore, try to ascertain the authenticity of the intuitions (their coherence and fundamental agreement with the other witnesses of revelation) and the appropriateness of the expressions (their validity as vehicles for the communication of revelation, realizing that no human expression is ever totally transparent to God and the gospel). This process calls for at least three confrontations.

The first of these confrontations must be with the Bible, because whatever claims to be a necessary component of Christian revelation must prove itself to be in fundamental coherence with the scriptures. Although not everything that Christians hold to be truly revealed is expressly stated in the text of scripture,[17] nothing held to be revealed can ever be against scripture or incapable of showing its authentic development from a legitimate interpretation of scripture.

The second confrontation must be with the written texts of tradition. By these I mean conciliar definitions of doctrine (dogmas), the teachings of the fathers of the church, the documents of the magisterium of the church, the history of the development of doctrines, the various theological traditions, and so forth. Throughout twenty centuries of Christian history, the church has reflected on God's revelation, come to a number of fundamental decisions on the proper understanding of some dimensions or elements of that revelation, and has made decisions normative for itself and for all following generations of Christians.[18] Consequently, all intuitions that claim to be "faith-full" (as well as all means of expression of those intuitions) must be in basic agreement with those normative decisions of the church, and must also show some degree of coherence with the general doctrinal and spiritual thrust of the church's history.

The third confrontation must be with the historical and sociological contexts within which these "faith-full" intuitions and their means of expression appear. If a "sense" of the faith is to be discerned as a true or false bearer of tradition, it must be capable of promoting the *results expected* of the Christian message and of Christian living.[19] In the same way, the vehicles through which the intuition of faith expresses itself (given the fact that all these means are cultural, historical, and sociological) must somehow be coherent with Christianity's necessary proclamation and practice of justice, peace, liberation, reconciliation, as indispensable dimensions of a world according to God's will. The expressions of the *sensus fidelium* must facilitate and not hinder the people's participation in the construction of God's reign.[20]

This third confrontation, evidently, will demand of the theologian an awareness of culture and of economic and political reality, as well as awareness of one's hidden (but certainly present) class and ethno-cultural biases and interests, which may blind one to dimensions of revelation present precisely in the "faith-full" intuitions being studied. This latter danger seems most evident among theologians trained in the North Atlantic presupposition that European or Euro-American theologies are the truly profound, systematic, real, and normative theologies, the ones—they claim— which effectively dialogue with the truest and most fundamental issues of human existence.[21] Of course, these North Atlantic theologies presume (often implicitly) that their cultural, political, and economic contexts *define* what is truest and most fundamental for the human race, while considering that definitions from other contexts are either inconsequential or merely tangential to the tasks of their presumed "real" theologies. This third confrontation, obviously, calls on the theologian to become aware of the cultural and ideological limits and biases of the very theological tools employed in the study of the *sensus fidelium*.

If the infallible, "faith-full" intuitions of the Christian people can only be expressed through culturally given means, then it is possible that the *same* intuition could be communicated by different Christian communities through *different* cultural means. It is in this context, and as a consequence of what we have been discussing, that I believe Hispanic popular religion is the culturally possible expression of some fundamental intuitions of the

Christian faith. Popular religion is indeed a means for the communication of many Hispanic Christians' *sensus fidei.*

## THE ROOTS OF HISPANIC EVANGELIZATION

The Hispanic peoples of the United States have diverse origins, both ethnically and historically. Many of the communities are the result of immigration (some recent and others dating from the nineteenth century), while large numbers of Hispanics were already in present-day U.S. territory when American armies invaded and captured the populations together with their lands.[22] It is important to remember that the Hispanic Catholic Church was well established in today's United States two hundred years before John Carroll was elected first bishop of Baltimore.[23]

Hispanic communities with roots in the northeast, Florida, or the Spanish-speaking Caribbean tend to be the result of *mestizaje*[24] between Spaniards and Africans. Those communities with roots in the West and Southwest or in Mexico and Central America tend to be the outcome of *mestizaje* between Spaniards and Native Amerindian populations. In other words, U.S. Hispanics are culturally (and very often racially as well) mestizos at their origin. In fact, it is this very *mestizaje* which precisely distinguishes them from both the Spaniards and the Amerindian and African peoples. It is what binds them together as a people distinct from all other segments of the U.S. population.

The very presence of Amerindian or African elements in all U.S. Hispanic communities points to another important fact which has serious consequences for the subject of this chapter: Hispanic origins are profoundly marked by slavery, plunder, oppression, and suffering. Were it not for the African slave trade, with all its horrors, or for the cruel system of the *encomiendas*[25] (Indian forced-labor), the Hispanic peoples would not have come into existence. True, Hispanics did receive from Spain many elements which provided the offspring of *mestizaje* with a cultural richness they still cherish. Spain's greatest contribution, however, was evangelization.

Christianity came to the Americas at the end of the fifteenth century. In a few decades, numerous dioceses had been established, schools and even more than one university had been opened, parishes and scores of mission stations appeared, and holiness and martyrdom accompanied the entire effort.[26] The missionary efforts of Franciscans, Dominicans, Augustinians, and Jesuits cannot be underestimated. They began the massive evangelization of the continent and were, in general terms, quite successful.[27] So successful, indeed, that today's Catholicism in Latin America and among U.S. Hispanics is very much the direct result of the one proclaimed and planted by the early missionaries.

Historical facts, however, remind us that together with these heroic efforts at evangelization, there were enormous sins of injustice committed. As people of their times, the Spaniards who came to the Americas believed themselves to be superior to all other peoples, and their religion the only one worth professing. The same intransigent attitude that led to devastating wars of religion in Europe became the common attitude of Europeans confronted with Amerindian or African populations and their cultures and religions. The European invasion and conquest of the Americas did not take place for purely humanitarian or Christian reasons. The conquerors came in search of material rewards. Yet they never totally disavowed their specifically religious, even "humane," motives.[28]

The Christianity that was proclaimed in this continent, and that stands at the origin of U.S. Hispanic Catholicism, was the complex result of several distinct, historical elements. First of all, Spain had conquered the last Muslim-held territories in the Iberian peninsula the same year (1492) that Columbus arrived in the Americas. The process of driving the Muslims out of the Iberian peninsula had taken over seven centuries, and had made Muslims and Christians profoundly influence each other's culture. These Christians, who for hundreds of years had fought non-Christians, had developed a style of Christianity that was militant and attracted to the heroic, and was not known for its tolerance of religious or ethnic diversity. National self-definition, indeed, had depended on the conquest and expulsion of those who were different. Not surprisingly the same militant, heroic, and intolerant attitudes were brought to the Americas by the Spaniards and made present in the process of evangelization and colonization.

Another element to keep in mind is the medieval fascination with saints, shrines, relics, images, miracles, and religious storytelling.[29] The Spaniards of the late fifteenth and early sixteenth centuries were still medieval in their approach to religion. Theirs was a Christianity that communicated the gospel by means of graphic symbols (verbal or otherwise).

Though there had been much scholarly and theological learning in Spain's Muslim and Christian lands, this learning seldom filtered down to the majority, rural populations. The united Spain of the sixteenth century, though continuing the tradition of high scholarship, did not go beyond the best medieval models of education.[30] The Christian catechesis available to the rural majority tended to emphasize religious storytelling (often Bible stories or lives of saints) and religious dramas (autos de fe).[31] The observance of the liturgical seasons and the arrival of occasional itinerant preachers gave the rural poor a necessary sense and knowledge of the fundamentals of Christianity. Social and religious traditions among the people of the villages also communicated some fundamental expectations of Christian living.

I am in no way implying that Iberian Catholicism was free of the very serious limitations of the pre-Reformation church. What I am implying, however, is that in spite of the difficulties, Spanish Catholics were certainly not ignorant of the gospel. In other words, the Catholicism that came to the Americas was one used to catechizing through symbols, stories, and dramas, a Christianity that bore the mark of the European Middle Ages and of Spain's long and recent militant anti-infidel past. And it was also a Christianity that, in spite of misconceptions to the contrary, depended mostly on lay leadership at the local level.

Once the Protestant and Catholic Reformations began,[32] most of Spain's religious efforts in the colonies were devoted to keeping Lutheran and Calvinist ideas out. The Catholic Reformation in the Americas was in practice reduced to the creation of seminaries and schools (mainly for Spaniards or the white *criollo* elite), and to stopping some major abuses.[33] But for most of the population on this side of the Atlantic, the Catholic Reformation meant the affirmation (and thus the *continuation*) of that which was held to be the Catholic tradition of the continent: the Iberian fifteenth- and sixteenth-century Catholicism I have just very briefly summarized.

One last point must be added to this summary. Though many members of religious orders came to the Americas as missionaries, I believe that most of the actual communication of Christianity was done by the lay Spaniards who came to this continent (and these were, by and large, Spain's poor). As time went on, it was done by the Amerindian, African, and mestizo laity who entered the church.

The end result of the combination of elements mentioned in this brief summary of the background of Hispanic evangelization is a type of Catholicism that can be called "popular," because it truly reflects the faith and practice of the majority of people. It does not show the sophistication of the educated elites, and it shows little awareness of the issues brought to center stage of all Christian theology by the Protestant and Catholic Reformations. This popular Catholicism evinced the medieval predilection for the visual, the oral, and the dramatic. It was emphatic about certain dimensions of Christianity that tend to be overlooked or pushed aside by post-Reformation North Atlantic theologies, both Catholic and Protesant.

## BEARERS OF THE CHRISTIAN GOSPEL: SYMBOLS OF POPULAR RELIGION

The Christian gospel preached in the Spanish-speaking Americas had been previously "filtered" and interpreted by Spain's peoples. The preached gospel was in turn interpreted, understood, and accepted in faith by these Latin Americans, ancestors of today's U.S. Hispanics. This was as it should have been, since the gospel is either inculturated and thus internalized and allowed to transform a people's worldview from within, or it becomes a foreign, sterile message. And, evidently, in order to inculturate one must interpret, understand, and then accept, allowing oneself (and one's culture and previous worldview) to be challenged by the very gospel one is interpreting, understanding, and accepting. This entire process, leading from proclamation to acceptance, can only occur by means of symbols and other cultural categories in order to be a truly human process. Even under the guidance of the Spirit, the hearer of the Word remains human and thus bound by all the normal processes of humanness. It is, therefore, very pertinent to remember here the distinction recalled earlier between the *sensus fidelium* as intuition and the various cultural expressions historically employed to communicate and witness to that "faith-full" intuition. It is also important to remember that what is the infallible bearer of revelation is the discerned, intuitive sense of the faith, and not the many symbolic and historical ways employed as its inculturated expressions.

There are many symbols employed in Hispanic popular Catholicism. Most of them had their origin in the church's liturgies (including late medieval Iberian sacramental rites, and the sixteenth-century Pius V—or Tridentine—eucharistic rite).[34] Other symbols were borrowed from Spanish medieval or mendicant piety, and still more were contributed (with totally or partially modified meaning) by Amerindian and African peoples.

As can be expected, not all symbols have the same importance within the popular religious universe. For our purposes, I have chosen two that appear to be central and organizing symbols in Hispanic popular Catholicism: the crucified Christ and Mary. These two symbols are present in every Catholic Hispanic community in the United States with very similar functions and meaning, giving us a religious connecting link amid Hispanic diversity. Finally, as can also be expected, discussion of these two symbols can only be done in general strokes that in themselves summarize a much more detailed study of each of the symbols.

If these two devotions, so central to Hispanic Catholicism, are capable of communicating true elements of Christian tradition, they may justifiably be called bearers of the *sensus fidelium*. Furthermore, since these two devotions are so important, they might offer us an entrance to the gospel preached in the Spanish-speaking Americas since the late fifteenth century. I will be devoting more space to the symbol of Our Lady of Guadalupe than to the crucified Christ, because the latter's link with tradition is so much more evident.

### The Crucified Christ

Hispanics give the iconography[35] of the crucifixion a very realistic quality. The crucified Jesus is painted or sculpted to appear in horrible pain. The crown of thorns, the nails, the blood, are all made to communicate real suffering, real torture, and real death. The dying Jesus, however, is not represented only as nailed to a cross. The entire passion is expressed through numerous and well-known sculptures and paintings of the flagellation, of the crowning with thorns, of the descent from the cross. Though many of these images or paintings may have true artistic value in themselves, the religious value is usually conveyed not by beauty itself but by the work's ability to elicit feelings of solidarity and compassion.

The passion is also enacted through religious drama, not within the confines of a theater building or a church, but out in the streets. The *Santo*

*Entierro*,[36] with its *Virgen Dolorosa* and its *Jesús Nazareno*, is one of the oldest traditions of Hispanic Good Friday. Some communities are known to accompany *La Dolorosa* as the procession moves through the streets, comforting her with their *pésames* at the death of her son. Needless to say, Good Friday is very important in the Hispanic liturgical year. There are many other popular devotions to numerous *Cristos* that, in one or another graphic way, portray some scene of the passion story.

The Christ of Hispanic passion symbolism is a tortured, suffering human being. The images leave no room for doubt. This dying Jesus, however, is so special because he is not just another human who suffers unfairly at the hands of evil humans. He is the divine Christ, and that makes his innocent suffering all the more dramatic. He is prayed to as one speaks with a living person, and not merely mourned or remembered as some dead hero of the past. His passion and death express his solidarity with all men and women throughout history who have also innocently suffered at the hands of evil-doers. In other words, it seems that Hispanic faith intuitively sensed the true humanness of Jesus, like ours in all things except sinful guilt. It sensed his resurrection as an intuition that he is alive now (and forever). And it also sensed that Jesus' innocent death speaks of compassionate solidarity with suffering men and women. The expressions used to convey these faith intuitions are culturally authentic, though they could conceivably be modified as Hispanic cultures develop and adapt to new contexts in the future.[37] However, is there any doubt as to the truth of the intuitions or their infallible character?

Christian preaching in the Spanish-speaking Americas used the available catechizing tools and cultural symbols to convey the centrality of the cross. It emphasized the entire passion narrative, and not merely the actual death. It underlined Jesus' innocence as well as his compassionate solidarity with all those who suffer. The people understood, they believed and interpreted, and among the results were the inculturated expressions of popular religion mentioned above.

These expressions are not part of the normative tradition of the church. But the faith intuitions behind them most certainly are. Iconography has adequately communicated revelation, with contents authentically coherent with the text of the Bible and with other written documents of tradition. Furthermore, the passion symbols of Hispanic popular Catholicism not only do not hinder the building up of God's reign but, in fact, preach solidarity and compassion as attitudes of the crucified God, also expected from Christians. Thus, when confronted with scripture, other texts of tradition and with socio-historical contexts, the passion symbols of Hispanic popular religion can claim to witness to revelation and, therefore, to communicate the "faith-full" intuitions of the *sensus fidelium*.

## Mary

Hispanic popular Catholicism frequently stresses the figure and role of Mary. It is difficult to find, besides the crucified Christ, another more powerful religious symbol. While it is not hard to discover "faith-full" intuitions behind devotions to the dying Jesus, it does appear that Marian beliefs and practices, especially as they are expressed in popular Hispanic contexts, are farthest away from the Christian gospel (and, as a consequence, suspect as bearers of the *sensus fidelium*).

I have chosen to look more closely at only one Marian title and story, because practically every Hispanic cultural community has (at least) one title and story for Mary. These titles and stories (similarly structured accounts of apparitions of the virgin or of discovery of her statue, connected to a confirmatory miracle) are foundations of the Marian devotions of specific cultural communities.[38] The devotion I have chosen to address is the one to Our Lady of Guadalupe, which is probably the most widespread in the U.S. Hispanic universe.

The title *de Guadalupe* is a Spanish mispronunciation (and transference of an older Iberian toponym)[39] of the ancient Nahuatl term *Tecoatlaxope*, which means "she will crush the serpent of stone." The story tells of a recently converted Amerindian called Juan Diego who, in December 1531, saw and was addressed by a Nahuatl-speaking, indigenous woman on the hill of Tepeyac. It also mentions that the woman wanted a temple built on that sight and that the Spanish church authorities in sixteenth-century Mexico did not believe him until a miracle occurred.[40]

That is the title and that is the story, but this brief recounting does not communicate the context and symbols understood by Juan Diego, by his conquered fellow Amerindians, or by the Spaniards who had invaded Mexico. It was the context and symbols, not just the historical outline, that created one of the most powerful Marian devotions in the history of the Catholic Church.

The context of early sixteenth-century Mexico pitched a multitude of native peoples against a smaller number of Spanish soldiers, administrators, colonizers, and missionaries. The ancient Mexican religion and most ancient native ways were seen by the Spaniards as unacceptable creations of ignorance, superstition, and demonic powers.[41] Though there were indeed some very forceful defenders of the native populations among the Spaniards (especially among the missionaries), none of the defenders believed that the native religion was worth preserving. The missionary *cronistas* described for posterity the ancient Mexican religious universe that they knew and hoped to be disappearing.[42]

Among the important ancient deities there was a certain Tonantzin, "our mother," as she was called by the Mexican natives.[43] She was frequently said to be pregnant, or to be carrying a small child on her back or arms. When depicted as pregnant, the religious symbol representing the fundamental reconciliation of opposites was placed over her womb. Her sacred place had been precisely on the hill of Tepeyac. She dressed in a particular type of tunic and wore a mantle, and was connected in myth to the serpent-high god. The woman who spoke with Juan Diego (in his native Nahuatl) did so on the hill of Tepeyac, wore that particular style of dress with a mantle, appeared to be pregnant, and had the symbol of the reconciliation of opposites over her womb.

I am in no way implying that Juan Diego saw the goddess Tonantzin, however. Though the similarities are too striking to be dismissed, the differences are also too evident to be ignored. Tonantzin had a large enough mythology stressing her inclination to inflict cruel punishment on her worshipers. The goddess was quite capable of sending all kinds of diseases and disgraces on her people, and often did. She was not, in any sense, a loving parent who could easily symbolize divine tenderness or warm affection. Tonantzin was also, under the title of Cihuacóatl, the wife of the serpent-god.

The woman seen by Juan Diego was very pointedly kind and tender, with no trace of cruelty or anger. Her gestures were explicitly those of peacefulness. And the very title used (*Tecoatlaxope*) clearly indicated opposition to the serpent. These and other religious symbols present in Juan Diego's apparition do not allow us to identify Mary with Tonantzin. How do we explain the similarities and the differences?

Juan Diego, a recent convert to Christianity, interpreted what he believed himself to have experienced and seen through cultural categories available to him. He was now a Christian, but his cultural milieu—of which he remained a part—was still in the process of assimilating the shock of the conquest. As was and is common among many peoples, reality in sixteenth-century Mexico was understood in religious terms. And the conquest, followed by the arrival of Christianity, was a part of Juan Diego's reality that had to be explained, understood, and assimilated in *his people's* religious terms. Many were Christians now, but the traditional Christian religious symbols the natives received from the missionaries were Spanish, foreign to them.[44] Guadalupe seems to be the birth of Christianity's inculturation in colonial Mexico. In other words, precisely *because* Juan Diego claimed to have seen Mary *the way* he did, we can say today that this is a sign that the Christian gospel was in fact announced and accepted in early colonial Mexico, and this in spite of all the betrayals of the gospel that can also be documented.

Mary is seen through religious symbols of motherhood and of the reconciliation of opposites, and for this Tonantzin's symbols were used, but without Tonantzin. Mary is also perceived as opposed to the serpent-high god, without whom there could be no native Mexican religion. She is pointedly tender and kind, a behavior not expected of Tonantzin. Juan Diego's Mary assumes the symbols that are useful for Christianity but certainly rejects those that could identify her with the old religion or that appear to at least condone it (and in this the Virgin of Guadalupe followed a long history of Christian appropriation and use of symbols from newly converted peoples).[45]

The devotion to Our Lady of Guadalupe, especially among Mexicans and Mexican-Americans, has remained central throughout the centuries since Juan Diego's visions. The Guadalupe symbol was immediately judged to belong to the poor, since the educated and the wealthy had their Virgin of Remedies. And for over four centuries Guadalupe has belonged to the vast majority of the people.[46]

The inculturation of Mary through the religious symbols of ancient Mexicans does not alone justify our calling it an inculturated *Christian* symbol. Mary herself must in turn be the symbol. Catholic pneumatology and ecclesiology should have today little difficulty in affirming this role for Mary.[47] But can we say the same thing of pre- and post-Tridentine Mexico? Were the Marian symbols of sixteenth-century Mexico capable of communicating, to the native peoples of that period and place, the meaning of Christ and his unique role in salvation, as well as other indispensable contents of the gospel?

To answer these questions one first needs to ask other more fundamental ones. Can analogy (semantic and cultural, *not* ontological) legitimately help us speak (in the manner of the semantic, cultural analogy) of God and his Christ?[48] Could Mary be considered, in that sense, an analogy of *some* dimensions or attributes that Christians have discovered—as a gift of the Spirit—in the one they call God? If Mary can be a semantic, cultural analogy of the church in Catholic theology, could she be the same in reference to God? These are issues, it seems to me, at the core of all mariology. And also at the heart of our questions about sixteenth-century Mexican popular mariology.

But just as important are other issues about development in the understanding of Christian revelation. Obviously, the core of the gospel (its most indispensable content, upon which all others rest) is God's self-revelation and self-donation in Jesus Christ. But it is more than evident that the complete meaning of this revelation was not fully understood and explicitated at the beginning of the church. The history of doctrine is clear proof of development in Christian perception and progressive acceptance of the revelation of God.[49] What might be *clearly* true or accepted at a given age or place in church history might not have been so at an earlier period or at a different place in that same history. This sometimes provokes a confrontation about a certain understanding of truth or about the way the truth is being expressed.

Could it be possible that sixteenth-century Mexican natives, recently converted to Christianity, intended to say something very true but (given their particular cultural and sociological context and Spain's style of Catholicism) could only express it through the symbols that surrounded Juan Diego's Marian visions? Could the Virgin of Guadalupe be understood as a step—albeit an extremely important one—in the inculturation of the tradition in Mexican (and later Mexican-American) history? Need all Christian communities share the same synchronized steps and moments in the development of doctrine in order to perceive each other as orthodox?

Is Mary of Guadalupe the cultural, historical expression of "faith-full" intuitions of the *sensus fidelium*? I believe she is and, as a consequence, she is also open to "doctrinal development" that might or might not reaffirm all the Guadalupe-related symbols. All development, it should be understood, must be culturally authentic for those who historically have employed these Marian expressions in order to witness to tradition. Cultural inauthenticity would disqualify as bearer of tradition any development of doctrine or of expression.

*If* it could be shown that Mary may be perceived as a semantic, cultural (never ontological) analogy of some divine attributes—which is another way of asking if she could be interpreted as a culturally legitimate means to express some content of the Christian gospel—which of these contents would the Virgin of Guadalupe be communicating and witnessing to?

To answer the question we must look at the history of this devotion, and especially at two key aspects of it. First of all, Mary of Guadalupe has always been perceived by the people as a tender mother, always compassionate, accepting, supportive and forgiving. And secondly, she is seen as protector, identified with her people but most specially with the weakest and neediest. She procures justice for the oppressed and takes up their cause.

Is it possible to truthfully refer to the Christian God as tender, compassionate, accepting, supportive, and forgiving? Is it possible to experience God as protector, committed to the liberation and defense of the weak and oppressed?[50] Is God really incarnate ("inculturated," therefore)? Can a Christian also refer to God as "mother," using in private devotion, liturgy, and theology the language and symbols of motherhood as validly as those of fatherhood?[51] But more to our point, must the revelation of these attributes of God be communicated *exclusively* through Jesus? Scripture does *not* allow us to answer this last question affirmatively. Though Jesus Christ is the final and unique revelation of God—*the* revelation in the strict sense of the term—nowhere is it affirmed that only through Christ has God been revealed. As a matter of fact, the exact opposite has been a constant in orthodox Christian tradition.[52] What one must affirm with the tradition is the uniqueness and finality of the revelation in and through Christ, and the impossibility of its being repeated. But these affirmations do not exclude other means of revelation, only that these must never appear to compete with or add something *new* to the fullness of Christ's revelation.

This being the case, we can now ask whether it is impossible to understand that, in a given cultural and historical context, certain contents of revelation may be expressed through Marian symbols? As long as what is expressed through Mary is consonant with the gospel (and it is, as we have just seen), is there any theological difficulty in seeing the truth of the "faith-full" intuitions communicated through the devotion of the Virgin of Guadalupe as cultural *embodiments* of the *sensus fidelium*?

## Elements of Christian Tradition

If we tried to briefly explicitate through words (as distinct from devotional symbols) the elements of the tradition (elements of revelation) communicated through these two popular Hispanic devotions, what would we find?[53] From the first of these symbols we discover these "faith-full" intuitions: (1) Jesus' true humanness, (2) his compassionate solidarity with the poor and suffering, (3) his innocent death caused by human sin, and (4) his (implied) resurrection and divinity. Through the Guadalupe devotion we find these other "faith-full" intuitions: (5) God's compassion and solidarity with the oppressed and vanquished, and (6) God's maternal affirmation and protection of the weakest. From both devotional symbols we can retrieve a clear sense that (7) if God and the gospel are to be heard and accepted, they must be inculturated ("incarnated"), as they have been, in the world and through the symbols of the poor and the disregarded (Jesus as a tortured Galilean outsider, and Mary as a member of a conquered race). And finally, (8) implied in both stories we might also discover that a lack of faith and a rejection of the truth and of God results where the symbols of the poor (*and* the poor of the symbols) are rejected.

But could we find the same eight or similar elements present in other Hispanic contexts and in other expressions of popular religion? I believe we can.[54] Even though a complete and thorough theological examination of Hispanic popular religion is yet to be done, the few studies that have appeared and those in progress all seem to confirm this thesis.

Much more important, however, is to question whether these eight affirmations, which may be retrieved from the two core devotions of Hispanic popular religion, are in fact contained in tradition. It is necessary to know if these affirmations (which are linguistic transpositions of symbolized or experienced intuitions of faith) can be said to be an integral part of the Christian gospel. If we brought these affirmations, retrieved from the symbols of the crucified Christ and of the Virgin of Guadalupe, to the threefold confrontation with scripture, with the texts of tradition, and with the sociohistorical context (as suggested above), we would have to conclude that within contemporary Roman Catholic theology no one, in good conscience, can deny that the eight faith intuitions are, without doubt, elements of Christian revelation, clearly and universally taught by the magisterium, and more importantly witnessed by the texts of scripture and tradition.

And still, in contemporary theology, as witnessed by seminary, university, and theological center curricula and by bibliographical research, there is an evident reticence in the acceptance of popular religion as a valid field for study and for theological reflection on tradition.

## THE LIMITATIONS OF POPULAR RELIGION AS *SENSUS FIDELIUM*

I have been arguing in favor of the study of popular religion as an authentic bearer of the *sensus fidelium*, and for that purpose I have reviewed the roots of Hispanic popular Catholicism and attempted to interpret and retrieve doctrinal contents from its two main symbols. Given the importance that the Spirit-given "faith-full" sense of the Christian people has for theology (especially in Catholicism), and given the appeals to it at the hour of justifying theological, dogmatic, or even disciplinary statements in the church, it will be important to look a little closer at the fundamental limitations of the expressions of the *sensus fidelium* as transmitted in popular religion. Our discussion, though prompted by and applicable to Hispanic popular Catholicism, will not be limited to it.[55]

*All* expressions of the "faith-full" intuitions of the Christian people are, of necessity, not equal to the intuitions they communicate. The expressions are *human* means through which the Spirit leads the whole church to a deeper and clearer understanding of revelation. As human means these vehicles of understanding are subject to the same conditioning limitations all things human bear. The limitations I am referring to can be grouped in two categories.

### Human, Contextual Limitations

There are those limitations, in the first place, that come from the cultural, socio-political, linguistic, and even economic contexts within which the Christian gospel is proclaimed, understood, and lived.[56] The Spirit-suggested "faith-full" intuitions, when expressed, will evidently employ the means made available through the people's cultural and linguistic codes. But the Christians who communicate their sense of faith will also exhibit in their expressions the privilege or the oppression to which they are subjected in society. Their faith will be *their* response to the gospel, and this means that their history, their struggles, failures, and victories, their social class, will *necessarily* act as vehicles (or as contributors to the vehicles) of God-inspired affirmations of Christian truth. The whole of their social, human reality becomes involved as a filter, offering means of expression to the gospel. But if the Christian people's reality is mainly a wounded and invaded context, the truth that the Spirit stirs within them will then express itself in a wounded and invaded manner. It is certainly the function of the entire church (and more specifically of theologians and of the magisterium) to discern the truth amid its wounded expressions. However, it is crucial that this discernment not be guided by or based on the presupposition that the poor's expressions of faith are of a lesser Christian quality than those of intellectual, ecclesiastical, or political elites. Were this evidently false presupposition to be operative in the discernment, the latter would be vitiated as a vehicle for discerning revelation's truth.[57]

In the universe of popular religion, socio-historical and cultural reality has offered opportunities and also created limitations. The experience of poverty and injustice, for example, seems to have inclined Hispanic religious imagery to symbols and devotions that have explicitly to do with compassion and suffering. The same can be said of the Hispanic emphasis on the extended family and on other social networks. These moved the people to conceive symbols and devotions that stress solidarity, community, and even familylike networks with the living and the dead. Many features of the Hispanic family have been projected into the religious realm.[58]

The active presence of these socio-historical and cultural dimensions among U.S. Hispanics has indeed created adequate vehicles for the *sensus fidelium*, as we have been seeing. But—when not properly understood and received, or when wounded by an unjust reality—their presence could also produce doctrinal exaggerations and deviations. However, the only discernment that can help avoid doctrinal deviation (as I mentioned before) is the threefold confrontation with scripture, the texts of tradition, and with the socio-historical context itself.[59] And, one must add, this discernment must also confront the implied racist or class ideologies (frequently expressed through theological or pastoral categories) of those who either by training or ecclesial function might be conducting the discernment.

### Limitations of Any Bearer of the Sensus Fidelium

The second group of limitations facing popular religious expressions of the *sensus fidelium* are those inherent in the very idea and reality of the *sensus fidelium*.

As I have pointed out several times, the *sensus fidelium*, strictly speaking, is not the expressions or vehicles through which it makes itself known. It is the "faith-full" *intuition* of the Christian people, moved by the Spirit, that senses, adheres to, and interprets the Word of God.

It is evident that no intuition may be had or may be expressed in human reality without somehow being mediated. This mediation, as we have seen above, will involve the reality of the ones experiencing the intuition. This is just as true of Hispanic popular religion as it is of the expressions of all the other bearers of the *sensus fidelium* in the church. Even if difficult to discern in actual practice, it is theoretically possible (and even necessary) to affirm that the "faith-full" intuitions of Christians are not coextensive or equal to the expressions they employ as vehicles for the former. However, what is left of the intuition after distinguishing and discerning it from its expression? What is an intuition without some mediation to make it understandable or, indeed, even perceivable even at the preconceptual stage?[60]

Evidently, when discerning the truth behind the expression, we must use some kind of symbolic means in order to understand. But the instant a symbolic code is appealed to as mediation (as expression), is this still considered an intuition in the strict sense of the *sensus fidelium*? Are then the mediating expressions of the *sensus fidelium* also granted the gift of infallibility?[61] The seriousness of these questions should be obvious, since so many culturally given, ideologically tainted, and socially wounded mediations are considered to be vehicles of the intuitions of *sensus fidelium*.

These issues cannot be addressed here, but sooner or later professional theology will have to address them, because the days when the *sensus fidelium* was an academic appendix to studies of tradition seem to be coming to an end. The social sciences and non-European theologies have begun to uncover for us the complex and socio-culturally bound structures and functions of religion and theology (and of the ideological "uses" of tradition).[62] They have also begun to uncover the limitations of *all* bearers of tradition, including the *sensus fidelium* and its popular religious expressions.

## AN OPEN-ENDED CONCLUSION

Within the church some seem to be arguing that the faithful need their faith "protected." But if the Christian people's "faith-full" intuitions are infallible, Spirit-given witness to the gospel, it seems rather strange to claim that they are practically defenseless against error. On the other hand, to deride the use of the people's defense as a mere political ploy is not to face the issue directly. Can the people's *sensus fidelium* or its expressions be misled? Why? What is the theologically adequate understanding of the relationship between faith intuition and mediation, given the results of the social sciences? Does the *sensus fidelium* witness to all of revelation? Do *any* of the bearers of tradition ever witness to the whole of revelation?

And even more importantly, do the Christian people *actually* play a role in *today's* transmission of tradition, beyond being paid lip service for their "reception" of truth? What is their actual, real-life role in that transmission in the real-life church? Are they supposed to be mere mouthpieces or mirrors for the expressions of the faith of the intellectually sophisticated (whether these be theologians or bishops)? Do they in fact contribute (what and how) to the ongoing process of deepening the church's understanding of revelation?[63] Obviously, to claim that only the theologians or the bishops really understand revelation and, as a consequence, that only they should speak and express the faith in order to avoid deviations and error is to dismiss the *sensus fidelium* outright, to ignore too many facts in the actual history of the development of doctrine, and especially to come uncomfortably close to disregarding the incarnation of the one who is at the heart of the Christian gospel. There is need for a systematic, historically factual, intellectually honest, and detailed study of the relationship between the bearers of tradition and their indispensable interdependence.

This chapter has not been the place to enter into some of the questions that I have been raising throughout. I have also tried to avoid comparing the limitations and contributions of the *sensus fidelium* with those of the magisterium, theologians, and other bearers of tradition (liturgy, for example). This would have led us too far from our subject. Instead I have insisted on the legitimacy of popular religion as one vehicle for the *sensus fidelium* and, as a consequence, as a valid (and necessary) area of theological reflection.

80    *ORLANDO O. ESPÍN*

The presence of limitations in the expressions of popular religion (insofar as they express the contents of tradition) cannot be an acceptable argument against popular religion's role as bearer of tradition. Limitations apparently have not challenged the fundamental legitimacy of the other witnesses to Christian tradition.

Perhaps one contribution Hispanics can make to the North American church is to bear prophetic witness—in the name of God—to those elements of tradition essential to Hispanic faith intuition that are not taken seriously by the Euro-American church, starting with the very legitimacy of popular religion itself.

NOTES

1. For a comprehensive review of different approaches to and definitions of popular religion, see O. Espín, "Religiosidad popular: un aporte para su definición y hermenéutica," *Estudios Sociales* 58 (1984), pp. 41–56. Popular religion is not necessarily co-extensive with popular Catholicism in the U.S. Hispanic context. In fact, a number of Hispanic communities in Florida and the Northeast would recognize as theirs religious expressions that are certainly not Catholic (e.g., Santería, etc.). In this chapter I will use "popular religion" as synonymous with "popular Catholicism." In my aforementioned article there is an extensive bibliography on the subject, but it needs to be complemented by P.W. Williams, *Popular Religion in America: Symbolic Change and the Modernization Process in Historical Perspective* (Urbana: University of Illinois Press, 1989).

2. The distinctiveness of each Hispanic (or Latino) community in the U.S.A. is more than evident. The different cultural groups cannot be naively grouped together or thought of as having the same basic history, culture, etc. However, there are some fundamental similarities that allow for valid generalizations. The best example is probably the common structures, function and features of popular Catholicism. The *mestizaje* of all Hispanic cultures is also a binding force. See, for example, R.J. Cortina and A. Moncada, eds., *Hispanos en los Estados Unidos* (Madrid: Ediciones de Cultura Hispánica, 1988).

3. By "ideology" I mean the theoretical (conscious or not) explanation or justification of a held option or position, previously chosen (again, consciously or not) for other reasons which cannot be openly acknowledged. Ideology is created and held by social classes or groups as a tool to promote their interests in the context of their interaction with other social classes or groups. A particular ideology is disseminated in society according to the number, extension, and pervasiveness of the means of socialization (schools, mass media, churches, etc.) available to the social class or group that created the ideology in question. See A. Gramsci, *Il materialismo storico e la filosofia di Benedetto Croce* (Rome: G. Einaudi Editore, 1955), pp. 868–73, 1319–20.

4. See S. Galilea, "The Theology of Liberation and the Place of Folk Religion," *Concilium* 136 (1980), pp. 40–45; and J.C. Scannone, "Enfoques teológico-pastorales latinoamericanos de la religiosidad popular," *Stromata* 40 (1985), pp. 33–47. M.R. Candelaria, *Popular Religion and Liberation: The Dilemma of Liberation Theology* (Albany: State University of New York Press, 1990) presents an interesting and suggestive study of the views of popular religion taken by two highly represen-

tative liberation theologians: Juan C. Scannone and Juan L. Segundo.

5. See P. Lengsfeld, "La Tradición en el período constitutivo de la revelación," in J. Feiner and M. Lohrer, eds., *Mysterium Salutis: Manual de teología como historia de la salvación* (Madrid: Ed. Cristiandad, 1974), I, pp. 287–337; J. Feiner, "Revelación e Iglesia. Iglesia y revelación," ibid., I, pp. 559–603; M. Lohrer, "Sujetos de la transmisión de la Tradición," ibid., I, pp. 607–68; K. Rahner and K. Lehmann, "Historicidad de la transmisión," ibid., I, pp. 794–851; K. Rahner and J. Ratzinger, *Revelación y Tradición* (Barcelona: Ed. Herder, 1971); Y. Congar, *Tradition and Traditions* (London: Burns and Oates, 1966); J. Geiselmann, *The Meaning of Tradition* (New York: Herder and Herder, 1966); R.P.C. Hanson, *Tradition in the Early Church* (London: SCM Press, 1962); J. Walgrave, *Unfolding Revelation* (Philadelphia: Westminster, 1972).

6. The "two-fonts theory" seems to have resulted from a misunderstanding of Trent. See P. Lengsfeld, "Tradición y Sagrada Escritura: su relación," in J. Feiner and M. Lohrer, eds., *Mysterium Salutis*, I, pp. 527–35.

7. Ibid, I, pp. 535–55.

8. See the Vatican II *Dei Verbum*, nn. 7–11.

9. See *Dei Verbum*, nn. 9, 12. Also G. O'Collins, "Revelation Past and Present," in R. Latourelle, ed., *Vatican II: Assessment and Perspectives* (New York: Paulist Press, 1988), I, pp. 125–37.

10. It is common in contemporary theology to include other less "ecclesiastical" means as legitimate transmitters of tradition. For example, the arts. See H.U. von Balthasar, "Arte cristiano y predicación," in J. Feiner and M. Lohrer, eds., *Mysterium Salutis*, I, pp. 774–92.

11. I think that the discussion on the relationship between "literality" and "orality" is pertinent to the study of the *sensus fidelium* as distinct from the written texts of tradition. See J. Goody, *The Interface Between the Written and the Oral* (Cambridge: Cambridge University Press, 1987); idem, *The Logic of Writing and the Organization of Society* (Cambridge: Cambridge University Press, 1986); M. Vovelle, *Ideologies and Mentalities* (Chicago: University of Chicago Press, 1990).

12. As will be stated immediately in the main text, the reluctance to study that which is transmitted orally or through popular symbols is partly due to the difficulty in limiting the object of study. This is why the oral or symbolic communication of tradition (with the exception of the official liturgies) has not received the attention it deserves in theology. And this might have also contributed to the often superficial view of popular religion held by many theologians. In interpreting popular religion one needs to appeal to the interdisciplinary approach, just as it is the accepted procedure in the study of scripture and of the other texts of tradition. Popular religion is a very complex reality that cannot be reduced to any one category such as "devotionalism," and cannot be explained by the simplistic appeal to ignorance or syncretism caused by social conditions of poverty. See O. Espín, "Religiosidad popular," pp. 44–52.

13. As we will see later, popular religion insists on the solidarity and compassion of God, and it emphasizes the reality of the incarnation of the Son and his true humanness. Popular Catholicism expects God's affection and care for humans to be maternal and engaged. It sees Christianity as "familial" and it stresses justice, freedom, and equality as part of God's plan for humankind. Evidently, the texts of the magisterium of the church and of much of Catholic scholarship clearly agree with these emphases of popular religion. But since the agreements are mostly set

out in written texts and are all too often watered down in practice, they do not appear as bearers of true tradition in the eyes of very many of those whose sincere faith is expressed through popular Catholicism. The permanence and vigor of Hispanic popular religion for close to five centuries in the United States, in spite of frequent efforts to "educate" or eradicate it, might be partially due to the people's Spirit-led insistence that the fullness of tradition be heeded and *put to practice* (and not just in written texts). Relatively recent events and divisions among Catholic African-Americans hinted at the frightening depth of racism in the U.S. church. Hispanics all across the country are well aware of the prevalence of anti-Hispanic racism and discrimination at the diocesan and (specially) the parish levels, often couched in religious or pastoral language. Justice and equality are paid lip service in chanceries and rectories, but reality tells a different story in most places. Popular Catholicism, it seems, will continue insisting on some gospel values being ignored or pushed aside by so many of the ordained ministers of the North American church.

14. These two expressions are practically equal in their use and meaning in the church. See K. Rahner and K. Lehmann, "Historicidad de la transmisión," in J. Feiner and M. Lohrer, eds., *Mysterium Salutis*, I, p. 843.

15. See the Vatican II *Lumen Gentium*, nn. 3–4, 12.

16. See *Lumen Gentium*, n. 12.

17. See J. Pelikan, *Development of Christian Doctrine* (New Haven: Yale University Press, 1969); G.A. Lindbeck, *The Nature of Doctrine: Religion and Theology in a Postliberal Age* (Philadelphia: Westminster, 1984). Also, *Dei Verbum*, n. 9.

18. See T. Citrini, "Tradición," in L. Pacomio et al., eds., *Diccionario teológico interdisciplinar* (Salamanca: Ed. Sígueme, 1983), IV, pp. 523–42; J.H. Leith, "Creeds," in A. Richardson and J. Bowden, eds., *Westminster Dictionary of Christian Theology* (Philadelphia: Westminster, 1983), pp. 131–32. Also, *Dei Verbum*, n. 8.

19. See Third General Conference of Latin American Bishops (1979), *Puebla Document*, nn. 388, 476, and passim.

20. It seems contradictory to profess belief in the indispensable nature and value of the *sensus fidelium* and then use its intuitive character as a reason to dispense with it in theology or in official church statements. Unfortunately this line of thought appeals to the fear of error in order to justify its mistaken position. Equally contradictory is the admission of the *sensus fidelium* while actually disregarding the people's "faith-full" sense in pastoral practice.

21. See R. Goizueta's chapter in this book (chap. 1).

22. See, for example, M. Sandoval, ed., *Fronteras: A History of the Latin American Church in the United States since 1513* (San Antonio: MACC, 1983); M.V. Gannon, *The Cross in the Sand: The Early Catholic Church in Florida, 1513–1870* (Gainesville: University Presses of Florida, 1965); P. Castañeda Delgado, E. Alexander, and J. Marchena Fernández, eds., *Fuentes para una historia social de la Florida española* (Madrid: Fundación España en USA, 1987); W. Moquin and C. van Doren, eds., *A Documentary History of the Mexican Americans* (New York: Bantam Books, 1972); R. Acuña, *Occupied America: A History of Chicanos* (New York: Harper & Row, 1981).

23. After several failed attempts dating back to 1513, the first permanent (and still functioning) settlement of Spanish Catholics occurred at St. Augustine, Florida, on September 8, 1565. See M.V. Gannon's *The Cross in the Sand* for the history of Hispanic Catholicism in Florida during the entire colonial period and well into the

ninteenth century. Missionaries and settlers began penetrating today's American Southwest from Mexico as far back as the 1530s.

24. *Mestizaje* is the condition of being a mestizo, a person of mixed races. During the colonial period, and perhaps still today, persons of exclusive European ancestry looked down on the mestizo as a half-breed. So did the Amerindian or African groups that tried to reject everything from the oppressor. The mestizo among them was a living reminder of the rape and violence that accompanied their condition. Colonial legislation often denied civil rights to mestizos, and the ordained ministry was closed to them. In many places there is still a strong sense of prejudice against these persons of mixed blood. (The mestizo of Spaniard and African is usually called *mulato* in Spanish.) I am using the term mestizaje here more in reference to cultural mixing than to biological mixture, though the latter evidently happened and in some places very much so. For a theological and pastoral use of *mestizaje* in the United States, see the works of V. Elizondo: *Galilean Journey: The Mexican-American Promise* (Maryknoll, N.Y.: Orbis Books, 1983) and *The Future is Mestizo* (Bloomington: Meyer Stone Books, 1988).

25. The *encomiendas* were groups of Amerindians "entrusted" (i.e., *encomendados*) to a Spanish settler. The latter was supposed to evangelize them, teach them a trade, and some rudimentary arithmetic and writing. In return for these benefits the Amerindians were to show their gratitude by working (for only lodging and food) for the Spaniard. The system was, in fact, a way of theoretically preserving the natives' freedom while in fact subjecting them to slavery. Very few Spanish settlers carried out their commitment to evangelize and teach, while most were eager to put the natives to work in the mines and fields. See translations of some pertinent original documents in H.M. Goodpasture, *Cross and Sword: An Eyewitness History of Christianity in Latin America* (Maryknoll, N.Y.: Orbis Books, 1989). Also B. de Las Casas, *En defensa de los indios. Colección de documentos* (Seville: Editoriales Andaluzas Unidas, 1985); O.K. Uya, *Historia de la esclavitud negra en las Américas y el Caribe* (Buenos Aires: Ed. Claridad, 1989).

26. Besides the work by H. Goodpasture mentioned in the preceding note, see the following: M. Sandoval, ed., *Fronteras* (note 22, above); E. Dussel, *Historia general de la Iglesia en América Latina* (Salamanca: Ed. Sígueme-CEHILA, 1983), vol. 1; L. Lopetegui and F. Zubillaga, *Historia de la Iglesia en la América española. Desde el descubrimiento hasta comienzos del siglo XIX* (Madrid: BAC, 1965), vols. 1 and 2. Florida was the first place, in today's United States, to see Christians martyred. See M.V. Gannon, *Cross in the Sand*, pp. 10–14.

27. See, for example, R. Ricard, *The Spiritual Conquest of Mexico* (Berkeley: University of California Press, 1966). For the lands that now are part of the United States, see, among others, M. Sandoval's *Fronteras* and M. Gannon's *Cross in the Sand*.

28. For translation of the early colonial documents, see H. M. Goodpasture, *Cross and Sword*.

29. See B. Ward, *Miracles and the Medieval Mind* (Philadelphia: University of Pennsylvania Press, 1982); R. and C. Brooke, *Popular Religion in the Middle Ages* (London: Thames and Hudson, 1984).

30. See M. Andrés, *La teología española en el siglo XVI* (Madrid: BAC, 1976), vols. 1–2. As Andrés clearly explains, the contents of Spanish theology and philosophy did develop (remember the Dominican scholars in Salamanca and Alcalá, for example), but the educational methods were still medieval.

84    ORLANDO O. ESPÍN

31. *Autos de fe* were free dramatizations of Bible scenes, performed in the atrium in front of the church building or, less frequently, inside. The laity acted in these dramatizations, which were often quite elaborate. The *autos de fe* were commonly used in the evangelization of the Americas. For example, see R. Ricard, *The Spiritual Conquest of Mexico*, pp. 194–206. For Spain's popular religion at that time, see W.A. Christian, *Local Religion in Sixteenth-Century Spain* (Princeton: Princeton University Press, 1981); and idem, *Apparitions in Late Medieval and Renaissance Spain* (Princeton: Princeton University Press, 1981).

32. It is usual to refer to the Catholic Church's activities in the sixteenth century (and beyond) as the "Counter-Reformation." I think the "counter" dimension, which was certainly there too, does not fully explain what was actually happening in and through the church. See F. Martín Hernández, *La Iglesia en la historia* (Madrid: Ed. Atenas, 1984), vol. 2, pp. 83–170.

33. See E. Dussel, *Historia de la Iglesia en América Latina* (Mexico: Mundo Negro-Esquila Misional, 1983), pp. 91–115. The *Patronato Real* (i.e., "Royal Patronage") had the colonial church firmly under control. No Tridentine or pontifical document could be executed in any of Spain's territories without the royal *exequatur*. This system, which determined even minutiae of church government and customs, ended either with Latin American independence (though some of the new republics attempted for a while to continue the colonial control of the church) or with incorporation into the United States (as was the case of Florida).

34. See L. Maldonado, *Génesis del catolicismo popular* (Madrid: Ed. Cristiandad, 1979). See also C. Dehne, "Devotion and Devotions," in J.A. Komonchak, M. Collins, and D.A. Lane, eds., *The New Dictionary of Theology* (Wilmington: Michael Glazier, 1987), pp. 283–88.

35. By "iconography" I mean the sculptures, paintings, dramatizations, and stories used in the Hispanic context to graphically communicate or symbolize a biblical scene, a doctrine, or a religious disposition or feeling. It is thus only vaguely related to the Eastern Orthodox meaning of the word.

36. The *Santo Entierro* is a Good Friday public procession wherein statues of a grieving Mary (*La Dolorosa* or sorrowful one) and of a dead Jesus are carried about. Sometimes there are other statues of passion scenes included in the procession, such as one of Jesus being flagellated. The *pésames* are words of sympathy offered to the grieving Mary, and they are either set phrases sanctioned by custom or spontaneous ones. The *Cristos* are either crucifixes or statues of Jesus suffering other torments.

37. There has been some discussion as to the future of Hispanic popular Catholicism in the United States. It is argued that the forces of secularizing modernity will extinguish the need for it and the worldview upon which it depends. It seems to me, however, that indications of the effect of secularization on popular religion (in other cultural areas as well as among Hispanics) do not allow us to forecast its early demise. The symbols might be transformed or reinterpreted, as has already happened in the past, but this would be a sign of health and not of impending death. See Candelaria, *Popular Religion and Liberation*. The *Puebla Document*, nn. 460–49, addresses this issue.

38. For example, the story of the discovery of the statue of Our Lady of Charity (for Cubans and Cuban-Americans) and the legend of the origins of the painting of Our Lady of Altagracia (for Dominicans and Dominican-Americans) have the same function as the one involving Our Lady of Guadalupe. The names, geography,

and other details are different, of course, but there seems to be a certain *structure* that is *culturally set* to convey precisely the religious meaning intended and to elicit the desired faith response. See Christian, *Apparitions in Late Medieval and Renaissance Spain*, pp. 10–25, 203–14; and also V. and E. Turner, *Image and Pilgrimage in Christian Culture* (New York: Columbia University Press, 1978).

39. See J. Lafaye, *Quetzalcóatl and Guadalupe: The Formation of Mexican National Consciousness, 1531–1813* (Chicago: University of Chicago Press, 1976), pp. 217–24.

40. See F.J. Perea, *El mundo de Juan Diego* (Mexico: Ed. Diana, 1988); and Lafaye, *Quetzalcóatl and Guadalupe*, pp. 211–300.

41. See Ricard, *The Spiritual Conquest of Mexico*, pp. 35–38.

42. Well-known are the chronicles (i.e., *crónicas*, hence *cronistas*) of the Franciscans Toribio de Benavente (a.k.a. "Motolinía") and Bernardino de Sahagún, and of the Dominican Bartolomé de Las Casas.

43. See Lafaye, *Quetzalcóatl and Guadalupe*, pp. 211–37. Also L. Sejourne, "La antigua religión mexicana," in C.J. Bleeker and G. Widengren, eds., *Historia Religionum. Manual de historia de las religiones* (Madrid: Ed. Cristiandad, 1973), vol. 1, pp. 645–58.

44. See Ricard, *The Spiritual Conquest of Mexico*, pp. 83–96, 264–83.

45. Brown, *The Cult of the Saints: Its Rise and Function in Latin Christianity* (Chicago: University of Chicago Press, 1981); J. LeGoff, *The Medieval Imagination* (Chicago: University of Chicago Press, 1988); C. Saldanha, *Divine Pedagogy: A Patristic View of Non-Christian Religions* (Rome: Ateneo Salesiano, 1984).

46. Lafaye, *Quetzalcóatl and Guadalupe*, pp. 238–300; Ricard, *The Spiritual Conquest of Mexico*, p. 188. As Lafaye points out, the Virgin of Guadalupe became the symbol of Mexican nationality and independence. Ricard explains the devotion of the Spaniards to Our Lady of Remedies almost as in conscious opposition to the natives' and mestizos' devotion to Our Lady of Guadalupe. In the United States today César Chávez and his followers have explicitly evoked the symbol of Guadalupe in their struggle for farm workers' rights.

47. From a growing body of literature, see, as examples, L. Boff, *O rosto materno de Deus. Ensaio interdisciplinar sobre o feminino e suas formas religiosas* (Petrópolis: Ed. Vozes, 1979); P.D. Young, *Feminist Theology/Christian Theology. In Search of Method* (Minneapolis: Fortress, 1990).

48. D.B. Burrell, "Analogy," in Komonchak, Collins, and Lane, eds., *The New Dictionary of Theology*, pp. 14–16; idem, *Analogy and Philosophical Language* (New Haven: Yale University Press, 1973); J.S. Martin, *Metaphor and Religious Language* (New York: Oxford University Press, 1986); P.A. Sequeri, "Analogía," in L. Pacomio et al., eds., *Diccionario teológico interdisciplinar*, vol. 1, pp. 400–12.

49. Alszeghy, "The *Sensus Fidei* and the Development of Dogma," in R. Latourelle, ed., *Vatican II: Assessment and Perspectives*, vol. 1, pp. 138–56. See also the works mentioned in note 17, above.

50. The references to the Bible, to texts of tradition and of the magisterium, and to the works of spiritual writers and theologians could be countless. The point is that all agree in affirming this possible way of experiencing and imaging God. Merely as a recent and good example, see M.K. Taylor, *Remembering Esperanza: A Cultural-Political Theology for North American Praxis* (Maryknoll, N.Y.: Orbis Books, 1990).

51. After the contributions of feminist theology, it is very difficult to deny this.

52. It is interesting to remember the church's reaction to the Marcionites'

attempt to reject the Hebrew scriptures, because these too were considered a vehicle of God's revelation. It is also pertinent to recall that the church has always believed that, though intimately connected to Christ, the apostles and other authors of the New Testament were inspired when writing their texts. The modern exegetical sciences do not allow us to think that the New Testament authors were literally reporting events or words. See the very nuanced article by G. O'Collins, "Revelation Past and Present," in Latourelle, ed., *Vatican II: Assessment and Perspectives*, vol. 1, pp. 125–37. On Marcionites, see R.B. Eno, "Marcionism," in Komonchak, Collins, and Lane, eds., *The New Dictionary of Theology*, pp. 623–24.

53. For background on a method of retrieval of content from popular religion, see O. Espín and S. García, "Hispanic-American Theology," *Proceedings of the Catholic Theological Society of America*, 42 (1987), pp. 114–19; idem, "The Sources of Hispanic Theology," *Proceedings of the Catholic Theological Society of America*, 43 (1988), pp. 122–25.

54. Each devotion or symbol will have its uniqueness, as can be expected, but a systematic retrieval of contents across cultural communities would yield similar results. As an example of the work done with other symbols, see O. Espín and S. García, "Lilies of the Field: A Hispanic Theology of Providence and Human Responsibility," *Proceedings of the Catholic Theological Society of America*, 44 (1989), pp. 70–90.

55. Given the demographics of present and future Catholic population growth in the U.S.A. and in the world at large, and also given that popular religion is very much present and alive among U.S. Hispanics and in Latin America, Africa, and Asia (where the largest number of Catholics live), one is led to wonder if popular Catholicism is not in fact the *real* faith of the majority of Catholics.

56. Pertinent here is a careful consideration of P.L. Berger and T. Luckmann, *The Social Construction of Reality* (Garden City, N.Y.: Doubleday, 1966). Suggestive also are H. Portelli, *Gramsci y la cuestión religiosa* (Barcelona: Ed. Laia, 1977); P. Bourdieu, *A economia das trocas simbólicas* (São Paulo: Ed. Perspectiva, 1974); R. Ortiz, *A consciencia fragmentada. Ensaios de cultura popular e religiao* (Rio de Janeiro: Ed. Paz e Terra, 1980).

57. The magisterium and the theologians must also look at *their* own stereotypes, their biases and prejudices, perhaps even their own racism. Without a clear awareness of these limitations, bishops and theologians run the risk of blocking within them the voice of the Spirit speaking through the poor. What would result, then, from their discernment if they are deaf to the Spirit?

58. See O. Espín and S. García, "Lilies of the Field: A Hispanic Theology of Providence and Human Responsibility," pp. 76–79; O. Espín, "Hacia una teología de Palma Sola," *Estudios Sociales*, 50 (1980), pp. 53–68; idem, "Religiosidad popular: un aporte para su definición y hermenéutica," pp. 41–56.

59. This also means that there is an urgent need, among the people, for a culturally respectful biblical catechesis, for promoting awareness of and critical reflection on church history and socio-historical reality. This will evidently require a socially "engaged" church to grant this process real credibility.

60. See P.L. Berger and T. Luckmann, *The Social Construction of Reality*; and also S.J. Hekman, *Hermeneutics and the Sociology of Knowledge* (Notre Dame: University of Notre Dame Press, 1986). The sociology of knowledge is a pertinent contributor to this discussion.

61. Do the racism, biases, and prejudices embedded in the mediating code affect

the intuition or the perception of the intuition being mediated by the code?

62. Perhaps more theological dialogue should be conducted with the social sciences, especially those that directly deal with studies of culture.

63. The theological answers to these questions might at first appear evident. But it is difficult to have these theological answers actually fit the practices that they, in the first place, are supposed to be describing and explaining. There is a gap here that needs to be addressed.

# Chapter Five

# United States Hispanic and Mainstream
# Trinitarian Theologies

## SIXTO J. GARCÍA

The systematic trinitarian theological reflections born in European and North American cradles—what I refer to as "mainstream"—have traditionally drawn from biblical, patristic, scholastic, and contemporary sources mediated by the philosophical and historical categories of each age. With the advent of political theology in Europe and liberation theologies in the Third World within the last three decades, contemporary trinitarian theologies now address questions formerly regarded by theologians and non-theologians alike as the exclusive domain of the socio-political sciences.[1] Along with perennially debated issues such as "trinitarian persons," processions, perichoresis, economic-immanent relation, theologians discuss the trinitarian impact on social issues, and on the trinitarian structures present in human existence and society.[2]

Within this broad range of trinitarian issues, there is, as we should expect, a diversity of emphases. Here we shall look at three European approaches, those of Johann Baptist Metz, Karl Rahner, and Walter Kaspar.

Metz, in his *Faith in History and Society*, looks at the socio-political impact of trinitarian faith in terms of narrative theology. He retrieves the concept of the "dangerous memory" of Jesus which summons the believer to a more apocalyptic ("here and now") perspective on social praxis, over against a more bourgeois eschatological flow that dilutes social sensibilities and social reform.[3]

Karl Rahner and Walter Kaspar, through different methodological considerations, look at the Trinity as the (real, tripersonal) manifestation of God's *ad intra* and *ad extra* act of love. Rahner's incarnational emphasis affirms the humanity of Christ as the insuperable act of God's love, as God becomes, in the inexhaustible ocean of divine love, the totally other in the person of Jesus Christ.[4] Given the contemporary, more relational shift in the concept of "person," Rahner offers alternatives to the use of this term to designate the triune reality of God. Although reluctant to jettison from the trinitarian vocabulary the word "person," Rahner feels that, in contemporary philosophical terms, the expression "relations of subsistence" would be more accurate and intelligible.[5]

Walter Kaspar reformulates the "opposition of relations" by focusing on the dimension of such relations as a dialogue of love eternally spoken between Father, Son, and Holy Spirit. For Kaspar, this dialogue finds its foundational reality in the term "perichoresis" already formulated by Gregory of Nazianzus in the fourth century. The interpenetration (without confusion) of the three persons constitutes the theological articulation of this dialogue of love, which supports both diversity and unity, or better yet, the diversity in the unity.[6] Kaspar criticizes Rahner's alternative to the term "person" on pastoral grounds: however foreign the original trinitarian use of "person" may be to men and women today, the word may still evoke, from a contemporary homiletic-theological point of view, a relational and dialogical reality that is more pastorally coherent than Rahner's heavily abstract term "relations of subsistence."[7]

*Brief Remarks on the Relationship of First-World and Hispanic Trinitarian Theologies*

The preceding are syntheses of certain aspects of Metz's, Rahner's, and Kaspar's systems. They are representative of mainstream trinitarian theologies in the First World. Quite obviously thinkers like Karl Barth, Wolfhart Pannenberg, and others could easily be added. These brief profiles should suffice, however, as an introduction to the question of correlation between first-world, or, if the reader wishes, non-Hispanic trinitarian theologies, and those trinitarian theological efforts made within Hispanic cultures. What follows here is a discussion of what a Hispanic perspective on trinitarian theology may be. I speak as a Hispanic vitally interested in developing such a theological perspective.

The Hispanic theologian may retrieve and reformulate into his or her own theological milieu all that is seen as true and methodologically sound. This theologian allows first-world theological systems to stand critically before his or her system, but becomes acutely aware that one's theology must also stand before the dominant theologies and be an even sharper critic of their often fatigued, bourgeois, and so-called neutral qualities.

The Hispanic theologian, moreover, knows that one's own system has many seminal insights forgotten by or utterly unknown to first-world, Western colleagues. Although some of these elements which I will treat further on are common to all theological latitudes, they all are uniquely and intensely lived and reflected upon within the Hispanic religious domain.

This applies, quite obviously, to Hispanic trinitarian theologies, which constitute the core of this essay.

The reader will gain a better understanding—or so I hope—of my Hispanic trinitarian reflections only if I offer some foundations of Hispanic theology in general. I begin with a brief analysis of a fundamental Hispanic theological method.

## A Foundational Matter: Popular Religiosity

In our joint workshop presentations at the Forty-Second and Forty-Third Annual Conventions of the Catholic Theological Society of America, as well as in our joint plenary address at the Forty-Fourth Convention, Orlando Espín and I discussed structure, sources, and providential-human themes within Hispanic theology.[8] The central concept upon which we built our presentations was popular religiosity. We defined it as:

> the set of experiences, beliefs and rituals which more-or-less peripheral human groups create, assume and develop (within concrete socio-cultural and historical contexts and as a response to these contexts) and which to a greater or lesser degree distance themselves (superficially or substantively) from what is recognized as normative by church and society, striving (through rituals, experiences and beliefs) to find an access to God and salvation which they feel they cannot find in what the church and society present as normative.[9]

We also distinguished between two general Hispanic-American religious universes: "popular Catholicism," closer to, if not rooted in, mainstream Catholicism, and "marginal religions," substantially further from the doctrine, liturgy and praxis of normative Catholic life.[10]

Given the key hermeneutical role of Hispanic popular religiosity, O. Espín and I developed the theme of "Sources of Hispanic Theology" at the 1988 convention by analyzing how popular religious tradition deepens and enriches mainstream tradition.[11] I offered a "test case" for this theory: Hispanic popular "passion plays" (which I will retrieve later on as I develop a trinitarian theology). These paraliturgical celebrations unveil (in the Heideggerian sense of the *Enthüllung*—again, a concept which will surface again in this trinitarian analysis) the implicit christologies (antimonophysitic, centered on the salvific, human suffering of Jesus who is in solidarity with others) and ecclesiologies (the entire community participates in, rather, celebrates the paschal event of Jesus) of the Hispanic faith communities. The same "test case" proved useful in our plenary address at the 1989 convention as we developed a Hispanic approach to divine providence and human responsibility.[12]

Popular religiosity conjures up the notion of praxis. This word is often associated with the debate on orthopraxis versus orthodoxy.[13] Here I would like to offer some remarks that will again prove useful for our trinitarian theology.

Praxis does not exclude theological reflection (or theoretical/academic theology). One presupposes the other. A truly correct meaning of "praxis" conveys the notion of "correct practice." This presupposes a reflection on correct and incorrect modes of acting, on good and evil, and so on. The notion of "doing the truth," quite obviously, needs qualification. The truth about a proposition, a system, does not emerge as if created out of nothing, from praxis itself. This would be a philosophical contraction in terms. But the explicit reflection or the intuition of a community, responding to its popular religious perception of God's salvific action in history, remains open to theological reflection simply because it is rooted on a theological reality and an (often nonthematic) theological response from the community.[14]

My own personal reflections offered at a presentation before the CTSA 1990 seminar on trinitarian theology led me to develop my own notion of "popular hermeneutics." The popular religious celebration, reflection, belief, and praxis of the community, insofar as they reflect the community's understanding of their relation with God, constitute "popular hermeneutics." Through their liturgy, their prayer, their thematic or nonthematic articulations of God, Jesus, Mary, and the church, the community expresses its understanding, its grasp, ultimately, its exegesis of its faith experience. A celebration such as a passion play, for instance, is nothing less than the popular hermeneutics of the Christ-event—that is, the popular understanding and articulation of its christology.

### The Hispanic Theologian as the Thinker, Actor, Poet, and Prophet of the Community

The preceding reflections on popular religiosity require the Hispanic theologian to correlate these popular religious elements with scholarly, biblical, foundational, and systematic reflections. Hispanic theologians, as it were, have the task of providing a "language" for the faith-experience of the community. Here the reader will surely object that this is the task of theologians everywhere, that this role is not exclusive to the Hispanic theologian. In principle, such an objection is well-founded. There is, however, a seminal difference: the Hispanic theologian's interpretive language consciously tries not to *replace* the language of the community: it helps deepen the understanding of its faith experience through dialogue with and within the community. It tends not to flow from the "computer-heavy" comfort of first-world air-conditioned offices, often peripheral to a community's language, but rather from the living contact with the community's experience.

These considerations underscore the unavoidable commitment of the Hispanic theologian as *an acting member of the community*. If popular religiosity is a central hermeneutical element to the Hispanic theologian, he or she must be thoroughly involved in the dynamics of the community's popular faith-experience. Here we may well apply (with the necessary reformulations and adaptations) Hans-Georg Gadamer's notion of *Zugehörigkeit*: "belonging-ness."[15] Gadamer applies this notion to the hermeneutics in the language proper to the tradition and heritage of the interpreter. It is the task of the Hispanic theologian to decide how this can be assimilated in terms of his or her "belonging-ness" to the tradition and faith experience of the community.

The idea of "belonging-ness" finds full meaning within the perspective of the oft-mentioned "hermeneutical circle" (or "horizon"). The Hispanic theologian functions within critically and responsibly accepted tradition and heritage — hermeneutical parameters of the community. This acceptance of the hermeneutical context is what allows the theologian to open up, in dialogue and understanding, to other traditions and modes of interpretation.

The idea of the Hispanic theologian as the poet of the community may easily evoke the wrong images: a Hispanic theologian as the community's Emily Dickinson, Robert Frost, or Gabriela Mistral. The notion as such requires explanation.[16] First, theologians and poets have a certain commonality of roles: their use of language as the bearers of meaning for a community, a social group, a group of theologians or poets, or more unlikely, for themselves. Second, the language theologians and poets use is never descriptive, never observes a one-to-one correspondence. Heidegger and Gadamer have reminded us that the poets give life to the specific form of being that their verses bear within themselves. We have but to remember Heidegger's dictum in his *Brief an Humanismus*: "Language is the house of being and the residence of humanity."[17] The theologian tries to approximate, as Rahner never wearied of repeating, the inexpressible God as mystery of love, through the ongoing reflection on God's revelation through the prism of the cultural (philosophical, historical) categories of the age.[18] One theologizes fully aware that language will not "capture," or define, that ineffable God of love. Not even the sacramental approximation of Jesus of Nazareth can fully unveil the one who is mystery; those who have seen Jesus, have seen, definitively, but still mysteriously, the Father (John 14: 9b).

Both theologian and poet use, often enough, similar language. The theologian relies traditionally on philosophical language such as analogy of attribution (or proportion), but also resorts to metaphor, symbol, and occasionally myth. But are not these different forms of language, on many occasions at least, interwoven with one another? Dave Burrell has argued that all analogy contains metaphor; analogy itself may stand as a symbol for whatever we say of God, since, as Thomas Aquinas has so emphatically affirmed, nothing we predicate of the triune godhead is synonymous with it.[19] The poet also appeals to symbol and myth, to metaphor and even to analogy, with the freedom (license) proper to his trade. We may say, then, that theological language is, in one certain and specific sense, poetic language, even the most dense and difficult to decode. Hence the theologian is not only the interpreter of the faith experience of a community of which he or she is an active member, but also its poet with unlimited possibilities for liberative and redemptive creativity.

Is this poetic role, however, exclusive of the Hispanic theologian? I answer that it is not exclusive. Indeed, by definition it cannot be so, but at the same time it is an especially indispensable role, a much more intensive role in the Hispanic faith groups than is generally so in first-world communities, for example. For the Hispanic mind, especially the religious-theological mind, performs in deep contact with myths, stories, traditions, and nature. This contact, this dialogue, requires a poetic framework for its theological formulations.[20] In expressing the trinitarian concept of perichoresis, for example, the Hispanic theologian must formulate it through the analogies of family love, of nature's interpenetration of being, of the metaphors of conjugal intimacies, of the beauty of human conversation and dialogue, using the words and story frameworks known to, and constitutive of, the tradition and heritage of his or her particular community. Thinker, actor, poet, the Hispanic theologian must also bring together speculative capacity with a gift for storytelling. The story, after all, is salvation history, with the promise of healing, integration, and enrichment to the broken Hispanic world to which the theologian belongs.

The Hispanic theologian must be a prophet if he or she is going to theologize at all. This prophetic element probably will have become evident to the reader from a reflection on the preceding roles of the Hispanic theologian. The interpreter, actor, poet-storyteller of a community must unavoidably sing of the glory of the saving God as well as bewail the injustice, oppression, and brokenness of the community. Theology must point out the way to conversion, commitment, involvement with the poorest members of the community, with the sorrows and frustrations of the people. As an interpreter and poet who is also a living member of the community, the Hispanic theologian will probably be one of the oppressed, of the suffering, of the marginalized. He or she must share the fate of the community, lest theology become something foreign to the experience, especially the faith experience, of the people. Indeed, the hermeneutical circle or horizon of the Hispanic theologian will be the circle or horizon of those who hope against all hope, who hunger and thirst, who cringe under the oppressing boot, who have only the burning sun or the distant stars for an abode. This is "belonging-ness" to a suffering tradition rooted in hope, and to a despised and trampled people enduring in love. From within this wounded but hope-filled world, the theological roar of the prophetic lion must be heard.

## TOWARD A HISPANIC TRINITARIAN THEOLOGY

I have devoted the first part of this essay to the elucidation of the profile, method, and role of Hispanic theologians. I proceed now to developing a trinitarian theology from a Hispanic theological milieu. In doing so I will elaborate on three key aspects of such a theology: (1) the christocentric dimension of all Hispanic trinitarian formulas; (2) the difficulties in profiling and imaging the Spirit in them; (3) the seminal hermeneutical datum represented by the Marian dimension in Hispanic theology and prayer. Finally I will attempt to articulate the experience of the Trinity in Hispanic faith-communities and societies.

The construction of a Hispanic trinitarian system begins, like any other Hispanic theological project, with the popular, religious faith experiences of the community. Here I retrieve the practice of the passion plays that I have used before as somehow foundational.

I have already mentioned that Hispanic popular christologies are basically antimonophysitic (for that matter, antidocetist). To quote the 1989 CTSA plenary session address, "There are few monophysites in the Hispanic faith communities."[21] The practice and iconography of the passion plays and the Good Friday processions provide the reason why: the bleeding images of Christ bearing the cross or nailed to it, the red-tinted tears flowing from the grief-stricken eyes of the Dolorosa, the mother of sorrows, convey a dimension of very real suffering. The broken humanity of Jesus stands as a sacrament of the brokenness of the body of the Hispanic communities. Jesus the Christ is our brother in sorrow and oppression, and we can touch him, mourn with him, die with him, and yes, also hope with him.

This kenotic Hispanic christology, however, does not stand in a vacuum. Most passion plays utter the words, taken from the beginning of Psalm 22, that Matthew and Mark place in the mouth of Jesus: "My God, my God, why have you forsaken me?" (Mark 15:34; Matthew 27:46). Jesus fulfills God's mysterious but efficacious will of salvation. The Hispanic passion plays reflect, almost universally, this conviction.

I remember watching, as a child, the passion play staged by the small and very old parish church about three blocks from my maternal grandfather's home. As the bleeding icons paraded before the iron grate of my grandfather's front yard, followed by the parish men (chosen from among the tallest and strongest) dressed in imposing Roman legionnaire's garb, wielding what seemed to be very threatening spears, I experienced the slow but certain growth of the "sacred" all about me. I became totally immersed in the Pasch of the Lord being played out before my eyes. For a few short hours I lived within sacred space and sacred time, and experienced God's own penetration of time in the person of the suffering Son. Father and Son were there. And the Spirit? It was much later, at an age when theological reflection became possible for me, that I realized that my experience of sacred space and time was the work of the Spirit of holiness and truth, the Spirit who confirms what Jesus had taught, the Spirit sent by the Father through the historic-salvific paschal mystery of the Son. The experience *was* very real, and it continues to be, in slightly changed fashion, as I celebrate every year the paschal triduum with my community.

The kenotic Jesus symbolizes the presence of God the Father in the communities of faith. The christocentric dimension of Hispanic trinitarian theology utters this reality unequivocally, in celebration, prayer, and belief. There is no Jesus, crucified and risen, without the Father who sent him. But again, what about the Spirit? I have just said how the presence of the Spirit became a reality in my reflection and experience only after I pursued my trinitarian reflections further. How about before the reflective stage? How is the experience of the Spirit, often unthematic, manifested in the praxis of celebration and prayer in Hispanic communities?

## Mary as the Hermeneutical Key to the Trinitarian Experience of the Spirit

The following remarks on the role of the Marian dimension for a Hispanic trinitarian theology are not intended to restore an obsolete Marian pietism as untenable to Catholics as it is to other Christian traditions. I intend to offer theological ruminations on the five-centuries-old reality of the Marian presence in Hispanic-American faith experience, prayer, and liturgy. Most of all, I want to argue how this Marian dimension can help the Hispanic theologian formulate the pneumatological dimension within the context of a Hispanic trinitarian theology. After all, theologians from different Christian traditions agree that the biblical role of Mary as disciple, as hearer of the Word, as the receptor of the Holy Spirit, can offer common points of ecumenical discussion and theologizing.[22]

In his work *Trinity and Society*, Leonardo Boff offers an interesting thought: he argues that the Spirit "pneumatizes" Mary; the Spirit brings about, in the context of God's invitation and Mary's assent in faithful discipleship, the incarnation of the Son, and thereby becomes personified in the person of Mary, just as the Word took presence *(shekinah)* in the tent of the covenant where the *dabarin* (the words or commandments of the covenant) were kept. Boff adds that the Spirit became personified in Mary just as the Son became personified in Jesus of Nazareth.[23]

A theologian can dialogue with Boff in this particular text as to his intended meaning. His wording comes close to connoting a hypostasis of the Spirit with Mary. Taken in a literal, ontological sense, this would convert Mary into a divine person, indeed, the fourth person of the Trinity. Boff actually uses the word "divinization" to refer to the action and presence of the Holy Spirit in Mary.[24] This expression, however, should not be taken literally, since "divinization" has been used since the age of the fathers to signify many things: conversion, growth in divine grace, reshaping of the "image and likeness of God," and so on. Maximus the Confessor refers to the incarnation and its trinitarian implications as divinizing human beings.[25] It would be somewhat difficult to imagine that such an accomplished theologian as Boff would not advert to the theological (and philosophical) problems resulting from an ontological hypostatization of the Spirit in Mary.

This particular discussion underscores the role of Mary in the Hispanic perception of the unity and trinity in God. It is superfluous to remind the reader of the traditionally seminal role that Mary has played through the centuries in Hispanic prayer and liturgy. This reality did not spring from an old tradition that associates Mary with the salvific activity of Jesus, and through Jesus with the Father and the Spirit. This Hispanic tradition can claim a foundational New Testament background, especially, though not exclusively, in the Gospel of Luke.

Critics in non-Catholic Christian traditions, and also within the Catholic tradition itself, have lamented what they perceive to be pure and simple mariolatry in the Hispanic communities. While it is undeniable that exaggerations, at least in form and style, have occurred and continue to occur regarding the proper, biblically and theologically founded role of Mary in salvation history and Christian worship, I should like to point out that in most cases this perception of mariolatry is a misperception. Hispanic faith communities have, as I have said before, a deeply kenotic and incarnational christology. Jesus is the Son of God, but also a very real and very vulnerable human being (indeed, going along with recent discussions by Walter Kaspar and William M. Thompson, he is a human person, precisely because he is a divine person).[26] He is a member of the Hispanic larger family of saints, indeed the head of the family.

The same can be said of Mary: she is unequivocally perceived as the interceding mother, as the ultimate symbol, given to us by God, of feminine strength and loving concern for her own. She is one of us, a creature like us; and yet, Hispanics see her as the one among us closest to the ineffable mystery of love sacramentalized in Jesus, her Son. She is the holiest among us, and that holiness results from the action of the Spirit within her. In this sense Boff is right in saying that the Spirit "pneumatizes" Mary and becomes personified in her, for in no other created being has the Spirit acted so decisively and definitively. Within this framework the Hispanic theologian can discover the clue to the role of the Spirit in a Hispanic trinitarian approach. Hispanic Marian spirituality can become a *locus theologicus* for a theology of the Spirit; Mary becomes the sign of the Spirit of holiness and healing for suffering and marginalized Hispanic faith communities. She points away from herself to the Spirit, who has made her its privileged indwelling in salvation history.

The Hispanic theologian can argue that a genuine Hispanic ("economic") trinitarian theology begins with the suffering Son who reflects the mysterious salvific, loving will of the Father, as it points to the Spirit dwelling in the community, of which Mary is the type. From a historico-salvific point of view, however, the fullness of salvation history begins with Jesus. Given this, it could be argued that, from an economic trinitarian standpoint, the Spirit is the beginning of the economic Trinity, since its active, Jesus-begetting inherence in Mary initiates the Jesus event, which ultimately delivers, through his paschal reality of death and resurrection, a redeemed creation to the Father.

Recently, Allan Figueroa Deck has reminded us about the liberating symbol that Mary of Guadalupe has conveyed for centuries to Mexicans and Mexican-Americans.[27] The story of the epiphany to the Aztec catechumen Juan Diego on the slopes of Tepeyac hill in 1531 began a process of intimacy in trust and love between the Virgin of Guadalupe (whose image, imprinted in Juan Diego's *tilma*, crowns the altar of the basilica dedicated to her in Mexico City) and the Mexican people. It is noteworthy to remember, as Deck has pointed out, that, as prayer and devotion to Mary of Guadalupe began to spread a short time after Juan Diego reported his encounters, the Spanish clergy tried to root it out from the Mexican Indians they were evangelizing.[28] They regarded it as superstition and pagan syncretism (the epiphanies took place not far from the former shrine of Tonantzin, an Aztec feminine deity). Above all, the Spaniards felt threatened by the symbol of hope and redemption she conveyed for the oppressed native Mexicans. This hope assumed concrete social and political form in 1810, when the Mexican priest Miguel Hidalgo raised the image of Guadalupe as a standard of Mexican independence against Spanish colonial rule.

The Hispanic trinitarian tradition and experience—again, not always thematically expressed—may also be described through the (adapted and rethought) concept of unveiling, to which I have alluded earlier in this essay. I have said that one of the roles of the Hispanic theologian is to thematize, to provide in communitarian dialogue, a language for the faith experiences, celebrations, sufferings, brokenness, joys and sorrows of the community. I have attempted to show this process of "unveiling" the trinitarian tradition in Hispanic theology by reflecting on the kenotic christology of the passion plays and the pneumatological symbol reality of Mary. The passion plays and the Hispanic emphasis on the kenotic dimension of the Jesus-event, as elements of Hispanic popular religious hermeneutics, unveil the particular modes of the presence of Jesus the Christ in the faith communities. In similar fashion, the Marian dimension in prayer, liturgy, and faith-life experience unveils the presence of the Holy Spirit within the same communities.

In personal conversation with this writer, Virgil Elizondo criticized Boff's notion of the pneumatization of Mary on the grounds that the people do not conceptualize their relationship with either Mary or the Spirit in such a fashion. The question here, however, is *not only* to ascertain how the people explicitly manifest their relationships to God, Jesus, Mary, and the Spirit (that indeed should always be the starting point), but how a Hispanic theologian can correlate such popular religious manifestations to the biblical and systematic theological data on the trinitarian God. In Hispanic communities, the parenthood of God, the redemptive solidarity in the suffering of Jesus, and the strong tenderness of Mary are fairly evident. The Spirit, however, needs to be unveiled, and this is the task proper to the theologian who reflects on the Hispanic experience.

A Hispanic trinitarian theology must establish the grounds for an "experience" of the Trinity conceptually accessible to the community as a necessary complement to the thematically formulated systems and catecheses. For indeed, if the Trinity has entered the economy of salvation, it has become experiential and this experience demands from the theologian a language to give it being.

The community experiences God as Father when it recognizes itself as "coming from" someone or something—specifically, from the loving, creating will of God. When we become aware that we have been "sent" with a purpose, however dim this may be, we identify ourselves as begotten and sent (not projected or thrown, in the sense of Heidegger's *Entwurf* of being) by God the Father.

When the Hispanic community unveils its identity and thematizes its meaning, even in the midst of oppression and brokenness, and can name this meaning as agape, love, it has experienced the Son as logos, as wisdom, as loving redemption.

When the Hispanic community goes a step further and identifies itself as a living spark of God's love and discovers its foundations as love itself, then it experiences the Holy Spirit. When the community experiences that love in self-renewal, in daring to hope for liberation from structures of oppression, then it experiences the Holy Spirit. Finally, when the Hispanic communities interpret their ultimate reality as love sacramentalized in Jesus the Christ, the Son sent by the Father to loosen the unpredictable Spirit of love, healing, and sanctification in the world, then it experiences the Holy Spirit.

### The Trinity as a Unifying Dialogue of Love

Walter Kaspar, Leonardo Boff, and others have pointed to the trinitarian structure of creation, history, and society. Boff even proposes looking at the trinitarian profile of social structures to avoid the ontological, individualistic pitfalls facing those who engage in a discussion of the trinitarian notion of "person." Kaspar asks whether the socio-political impact of trinitarian theology does not constitute the "end of political theology," since a society whose heartbeat echoes the trinitarian dialogue of love has fulfilled the ultimate categories of a theology of the human polis.[29]

These reflections have powerful theological grounds. It is fair to say that Kaspar, Boff, Rahner, and others perceive the existential (pastoral, spiritual) impact of trinitarian theology in similar ways, albeit coming from different methodologies: the trinitarian God is a dynamic of loving dialogue, a perichoretic relationship comprising the Word which the Father utters in the Son, which the Son loosens in the world as the Spirit, who in turn constitutes the response in dialogue of God's word to God's own self.

The trinitarian God has, biblically and analogically speaking, an immanent and an economic dimension. Rahner holds for an equation of equality between the two. Kaspar fears creeping modalism in Rahner's notion and offers that the biblically and tradition-manifested mystery of the immanent Trinity finds new (not different!) expression in the theological formulas which speak of the economic Trinity.[30]

The debate surrounding the relation between immanent economic Trinity, although present in much of what I say in this essay, does not constitute a main point. Suffice it to say that this author has suggested to his students possible ways to partially reconcile Rahner's and Kaspar's theories. The important concept for our purposes here is the economic-trinitarian dialogue of love which penetrates human history, offering liberation, renewal, hominization. The Trinity thus stamps its profile on every human being's personal reality and by extension on every human society and political structure. There is a perichoretic activity in society in whose structures the trinitarian God images godself.[31] The original source of this imaging is the trinitarian dialogue of love which grounds the divine oneness in its tripersonality.

The trinitarian image of a God engaged in a salvific dialogue of love with God's own self and overflowing into human history provides the Hispanic theologian with a working trinitarian model. The intensely personalistic dimension of Hispanic faith-life, as exemplified by its popular celebrations, can readily identify itself with a personal God whose tripersonal dialogue empowers human existence with the promise of liberation, redemption from oppression, and inexhaustible love flowing endlessly in the midst of suffering and absurdity.

### The Present, Dysfunctional Social Image of the Trinity

Karl Rahner spent a lifetime arguing against "hidden" or "implicit" monophysitism, practiced by many sincere and well-meaning Christians. He constantly emphasized, in a number of essays in his *Schriften zur Theologie*, as well as in chapter (or section) six of his "little *Summa*" entitled *Foundations of Christian Faith*, that the humanity of Jesus *is* the humanity of the Son; the sonship of Jesus is constituted by his humanity, and conversely, his humanity is fully affirmed by his sonship lived in full openness and obedience to his Father.

But the humanity of Jesus, sacrament of a healing and redeeming love, has been distorted by social structures which sacrifice human dignity in its pantheons, decorated with the icons of our day: money, power, prestige, racial supremacy, and religious intolerance. Our society is sick, as Paul VI remarked in *Populorum Progressio*.[32] The implicit christology of our society is accordingly, and for the most part, comfortably docetistic or monophysitic. The privatized Christian experience of the priests of first-world consumerism and supremacy divinizes Jesus in order to keep him away from them at a safe, noninterfering distance. Jesus' "dangerous voice" becomes dim. His "dangerous memory" fades away. Society tucks itself safely away from him within the four walls of a building they call "church," as they ignore the larger, dangerous walls of the *koinonia* that is the true church, sacrament of Christ, where one may expect to hear a few but powerful prophetic voices demanding justice and love.

This kind of societal praxis contradicts the fundamental notion of incarnation discussed here: that in Jesus of Nazareth the Holy Spirit has actualized God's mystery of unfathomable love as a true human being whose sonship does not distance him from us, but rather brings us, through his filial death and resurrection, renewal and liberation from sin and its sinful personal and social structures. If we allow society to place the incarnate love of God, the human person Jesus of Nazareth, inside the golden cage of undisturbing, bourgeois docetism and monophysitism, then the presence of the creating God, the parental God who wishes to enter our history in the person of Jesus, is practically negated. In the face of this, any language about the action and presence of the Holy Spirit becomes contradictory. Our society thus defaces the image of the Trinity in and through its oppressive structures. The image of the Trinity in society becomes, as it were, dysfunctional.

### A Theologically and Socially Functional Image of the Trinity

The Hispanic theologian, then, has an urgent summons to articulate a functional correlation between immanent/economic theological profiles of the Trinity and its social images. At the risk of sounding repetitious, the Hispanic theologian must turn first to the difficult task of retrieving the true biblical and theological dimension of the incarnation. This implies not so much a dedivinization of Jesus the Christ (avoiding here the discussion on the "divinity" of Jesus), but rather a true affirmation of his human reality and its implications and demands for an authentic, Christian faith experience. This retrieval and reformulation of the true face of Jesus Christ presents dangers to our society's conventional wisdom and comfort. This danger is nothing less than actualizing God's demand for a renewal of the covenant, given in personal and communitarian justice and love. John Meier has argued that the historical Jesus always transcends any attempts to co-opt him as standard for any given ideology. Meier thinks in particular of liberation theology.[33] In our society, however, the danger has an opposite sign. Society would love to co-opt Jesus the Christ as the silent, passive guarantor of its greed, selfishness, and oppression of the economically weak. It would like this bland, smiling Jesus not to reawaken their dulled sensibilities as they practice racial discrimination, rejection of the destitute migrant, sexism, and the almost infinite number of sins of which human creativity turned demonic is capable. Granting the difference in specific cruelties and horrors as well as in numbers of victims, Hispanic communities, more often than not broken by economic injustice of various kinds, may well question, impulsively perhaps, the providence of the God of the *anawim*.

A soundly formulated christology, however, will reflect the loving face of God expressed in the text of John 14:9b and a U.S. Hispanic theology will echo it: "Whoever has seen me, has seen the Father." Only the face of a Jesus, the Christ of God, who communicates God's transcendental, ultimate victory over the structures of oppression through the paschal pathway of the cross and the radically new humanity of the resurrection, can affirm the permanent presence of God the Father in community.

But this Father-Son relationship, expressed in terms of mission, obedience, death, and resurrection, begins economically, as I have said, with the action of the Spirit, who enters in a personalistic fashion into salvation history through the committed yes of Mary. This is the same Spirit whom Jesus promised as he stands at the threshold of his Pasch (John 14:26; 15:16; 16:13), and who, in a sense, goes back to God the Father bearing a renewed humankind sacramentalized in the community of forgiveness and proclamation which it has constituted through the breath of the risen Lord (John 20:19ff.). The Spirit can sanctify the human polis only when the economic fruits of his action, the incarnation and paschal mystery of Jesus, as well as the mission of the church, receive substance and formulation, and become concrete through theological activity and the experience of the community.

## CONCLUSION: SYNTHESIS OF A HISPANIC TRINITARIAN THEOLOGY

I maintain that a Hispanic trinitarian theology must begin with a sound reflection, born of Hispanic popular religious faith experiences and liturgies, of christology, and in particular of the kenotic and paschal dimensions of Jesus the Christ.

This kenotic approach, however, cannot ignore the best theological insights into the incarnation. A docetist or monophysite Jesus offers neither healing nor liberation. This is true, of course, of all responsible christological systems, Hispanic and otherwise. It bears, however, a special meaning in Hispanic communities, where the true humanity of Jesus, the victim of suffering, discrimination, rejection, and oppression is essential to the whole of the communities' faith life. In this context the Hispanic theologian can emphasize the resurrection as the proleptic liberation from structures of oppression and the actualization of the new human being. This is the new creation, the dawn of the (never complete, but very much in progress) new age of justice and love for the Hispanic groups within church and society.

The Marian dimension remains the privileged locus for the Hispanic theologian out of which the pneumatological dimension of his trinitarian system emerges. Mary becomes the symbol of the personal indwelling of the Holy Spirit among humankind as she points away from herself to the action of the Spirit who brings the fullness of the Father's love into this, our broken society, through the sacrament of Jesus' true humanity, the true (and never separable) humanity *of the Son.*

A Hispanic trinitarian theology, therefore, follows the initial economic action of the Spirit, indwelling the person of Mary, actualizing the salvific humanity of Jesus of Nazareth, Son and Christ of God, obedient to this God whom he calls Abba. The Son's death and resurrection ushers in the new age of salvation, healing, and renewal, releasing and sending forth the Holy Spirit, his own and the Father's, into the structures of a sinful and dehumanized world. This powerful trinitarian vision, finally, emerges with a certain originality and cogency in the lives of Hispanic communities who in their struggles and faith witness to a trinitarian love that even now sustains them with an indomitable hope.

## NOTES

1. For a discussion of this topic, see Johann Baptist Metz, *Faith in History and Society: Toward a Practical Fundamental Theology* (New York: Seabury Press, 1980), pp. 130–32. See also Leonardo Boff, *Trinity and Society* (Maryknoll, N.Y.: Orbis, 1988).

2. See note 1, above.

3. Metz, *Faith in History and Society*, pp. 88–99.

4. Karl Rahner, "Theology and Symbol," *Theological Investigations* IV (New York: Crossroad, 1982), pp. 221–52.

5. Rahner, "Esbozos de una teología de la Trinidad," *Mysterium Salutis* II/12 (Madrid: Ed. Cristiandad, 1977), pp. 328–31.

6. Walter Kaspar, *El Dios de Jesucristo* (Salamanca: Ed. Sígueme, 1988), pp. 323–24.

7. Ibid., pp. 326–30.

8. Orlando Espín and Sixto J. García, "Hispanic American Theology," Catholic Theological Society of America, *Proceedings of the 42nd Annual Convention*, vol. 42, Philadelphia pp. 114–19; Espín and García, "The Sources of Hispanic Theology," CTSA, *Proceedings of the 43rd Annual Convention*, vol. 43, Toronto pp. 122–35; Espín and García, "Lilies of the Field: A Hispanic Theology of Providence and Human Responsibility," CTSA, *Proceedings of the 44th Annual Convention*, vol. 44, St. Louis, pp. 70–90.

9. Espín and García, "Hispanic American Thology," *Proceedings* 44, pp. 84-86.

10. Ibid.

11. Espín and García, "Sources," *Proceedings* 43.

12. Espín and García, "Lilies of the Field," *Proceedings* 44, pp. 84–86.

13. Leonardo and Clodovis Boff, *Introducing Liberation Theology*, (Maryknoll, N.Y.: Orbis, 1987), pp. 6–42. See also Leonardo Boff, *Jesucristo Liberador: Ensayo de Cristología Crítica para Nuestro Tiempo* (Santander: Sal Terrae, 1972), pp. 58–62.

14. Walter Kaspar, *Theology and Church* (New York: Crossroad, 1989), pp. 136–37.

15. See Richard Palmer's discussion on Gadamer's *Zugehörigkeit* in his *Herme-*

*neutics* (Evanston: Northwestern University Press, 1969), pp. 208–9. See also Hans-Georg Gadamer, *Wahrheit und Methode: Grundzüge einer philosophischen Hermeneutik* (Tübingen: J.C. Mohr, 1960), p. 438.

16. Robert J. Schreiter, *Constructing Local Theologies* (Maryknoll, N.Y.: Orbis, 1986), pp. 18–19: "The poet has the task of capturing those symbols and metaphors which best give expression to the experience of a community."

17. Martin Heidegger, *Über den Humanismus* (Frankfurt am Mcin: Vittorio Klosterman, 1981), p. 51. Originally this was a letter from Heidegger to Jean Beaufret written in the fall of 1946.

18. I owe this definition (with my own modifications) to dissertation director and dear friend, Thomas Franklin O'Meara, Walter K. Warren Professor of Theology at the University of Notre Dame.

19. See Thomas Aquinas, *Summa Theologiae*, 1a, q. 13, a. 2–5.

20. Palmer, *Hermeneutics*, p. 140.

21. Espín and García, "Lilies," *Proceedings* 44, p. 84.

22. Bertrand Buby, *Mary: The Faithful Disciple* (Mahwah, N.J.: Paulist Press, 1985), pp. 67ff.; Raymond E. Brown, Karl P. Donfried et al., *Mary in the New Testament* (Philadelphia: Fortress Press/New York-Toronto: Paulist, 1978); Frederick M. Jelly, *Madonna: Mary in the Catholic Tradition* (Huntington, Indiana: Our Sunday Visitor, 1986).

23. Boff, *Trinity*, pp. 210–12.

24. Ibid.

25. For a detailed discussion of Maximus' notion of "divinization," see Juan Miguel Garrigues, *Maxime le Confesseur: La Charité, avenir divin de l'homme* (Paris: Editions Beauchesne, 1976).

26. Walter Kaspar, *Jesús el Cristo* (Salamanca: Sígueme, 1986), pp. 281ff. William M. Thompson, *The Jesus Debate* (Mahwah, N.J.: Paulist Press, 1985), pp. 329–33.

27. Virgil Elizondo, "Foreword," in Allan Figueroa Deck, *The Second Wave: Hispanic Ministry and the Evangelization of Cultures* (Mahwah, N.J.: Paulist Press, 1989), pp. xi–xvi.

28. See the allusion to how the *Morenita del Tepeyac* countered the stratified, programmatic catechesis of the European in Elizondo, "Prologue," in Deck, *Second Wave*. The missionary opposition I allude to was mentioned by Elizondo at a summer theological lecture series conference at the University of Notre Dame, summer 1985. Orlando Espín also reflects on the Guadalupe event in chapter 4 above.

29. Kaspar, *Dios de Jesucristo*, p. 349.

30. Kaspar, see note 6.

31. Among his numerous essays and works on the topic, K. Rahner, "On the Theology of the Incarnation," *Theological Investigations* IV (New York: Crossroad), pp. 105–25; *Grundkurs des Glaubens: Einführung in den Begriff des Christentums* (Freiburg-Basel-Vienna: Herder, 1984), pp. 278–98.

32. Paul VI, *Populorum Progressio*, nos. 62–67.

33. John P. Meier, "The Historical Jesus: Rethinking Some Concepts," in *Theological Studies*, vol. 51, no. 1, pp. 3–24.

# Chapter Six

# *Mestizaje* as a Locus of Theological Reflection

## VIRGIL P. ELIZONDO

From the perspective of the millions of Hispanics in the United States, two great events took place in 1971 which have had a tremendous impact on Hispanic ministry in the United States: the birth of the Mexican-American Cultural Center (MACC) and the first publication in Lima, Peru, of Gustavo Gutiérrez's *Teología de Liberación*. Since then, Gustavo and the work of MACC have been intimately interrelated. Both emerge out of the same situation: the need for the church to see the suffering of the poor, to hear their cries, and to enter into their quest for liberation. In a way there was nothing new. Moses had already started the way, Jesus had died for it, and others in time have dedicated their lives to it.

What was radically new about MACC and Gustavo was that at a time when the institutions of the church had, generally speaking, ignored the cries of the poor or at best had sought to feed them, clothe them, and give them minimal medical aid, this new way was beginning with the poor themselves becoming the active agents of the salvation of all! It was not for the church to go out to the poor to be of service, but for the poor themselves, in response to God's word, to become church and work for the betterment of their own situation. As long as we did it "for the poor," we would maintain them poor! But to empower them so that out of their own poverty they would dare to dream and begin something really new, would indeed be an act of the all-powerful creative Spirit of God.

It has been my privilege to know Gustavo well since 1971. I have been his student, close friend, and collaborator. He has come to MACC every summer. It was here that he learned English and was able to experience the complexities of the U.S. way of life. He formed close friendships with MACC's team, especially our scripture scholars John Linskens and Juan Alfaro, both of whom are continually feeding him good scriptural interpretations and works that can further the biblical understanding of liberation.

104

Everyone at MACC and in the archdiocese of San Antonio loves him and believes in him.

Whether eating, exchanging jokes, discussing scripture, exploring new theological insights or church practices, swimming, or speaking about the issues of the poor in Latin America, the U.S.A., or anywhere in the world, being with Gustavo has always been a memorable experience. Padric O'Hare, formerly of Boston College, says that Gustavo is the only person he has ever met who seems to consciously live in the presence of God every moment of his life. I would certainly concur with that opinion. In the summer of 1985, Archbishop Flores introduced Gustavo to an auditorium full of expectant listeners, saying: "The two people I most admire and respect in this world are Mother Teresa and Father Gustavo for they have both chosen to do the greatest work of all: dedicate their lives to the service of the poor."

### The MACC Challenge

The Hispanic Catholics of the United States have experienced a long history of neglect and oppression not only by society at large, but by the very church that is supposed to be our mother. We had somewhat been ministered to but we had never been invited to be active ministers in our own church. The church was so foreign to us that many felt that priests came only from Ireland or Spain, but it was unthinkable that we would become a priest or a religious.

Quite often we were scolded because we were not what the foreign missioners expected us to be as measured by the standards of the Catholicism of their place of origin. But hardly ever were we confirmed in our faith and helped to grow and develop in our pilgrimage of faith. Yet it was the deep faith and simple home practices of our *abuelitas* and *abuelitos* (grandparents) that sustained us in the faith and maintained us loyal to the Catholic tradition.

Church institutions had been so oppressive to us that when the radical Chicano movements started in the 1960s, the leaders often told priests and religious who tried to join them to get lost. They felt that the only way to help Hispanics get ahead was to get rid of Catholicism. It was painful to hear their insults, but as painful as their accusations were, we had to admit that they were true—if not totally, at least 95 percent of what they were saying against the church was correct. The church had kept us out and had by its silence approved the ongoing exploitation and oppression of Hispanics in the country.

The Chicano movements gave inspiration to the Chicano clergy and later on to all the Hispanic clergy in this country. We began to organize and to work for change within our own church. It was quickly evident that it was not sufficient simply to use Spanish in the liturgy, create our own music, and get more people involved in the work of the church. Much more was needed. We needed both practical know-how so that we could make the structures of our society work in favor of our people and we needed to have a new knowledge about ourselves, our social situation, and our religious beliefs. Until now, others had been telling us who we were. Nobody had bothered to ask us "Who are you?" Until now, all kinds of experts had studied us, but no one had even sought to enter into conversation with us so that they might truly understand who we see ourselves to be. This was the very root of our oppression. We were not allowed to be who we were. We were never allowed to simply say: "I am."

It was at this moment of the struggle that we met Gustavo and became aware of his method of doing theology. It was God-sent! He was conceptualizing and expressing perfectly what we felt had to be done but had no idea of how to do it or even that we were on the right track. From the documents of Vatican II and our own experience of exclusion, we pretty well sensed what had to be done, but it was not yet clear. Reading Gustavo's work was like turning on the lightswitch.

The first thing we learned from Gustavo was that theology is so important that we cannot leave it to the theologians alone . . . and much less to theologians who are foreigners. Theology cannot be imported. Neither can it be developed in isolation from the believing and practicing community. It is a joint enterprise of the believing community, which is seeking the meaning of its faith and the direction of its journey of hope lived in the context of charity. Great theologies were coming out of other parts of the world, but no one could do our theologizing for us. We had both the privilege and the responsibility! What follows is an attempt to do our own interpretation of our Christian existence.

## THE HUMAN SITUATION OF MEXICAN-AMERICANS

The ancestors of today's Mexican-Americans have been living in the present-day United States since the early 1700s. Our group did not cross the border to come to the United States; rather the United States expanded its borders and we found ourselves to be a part of the United States. Since the early beginnings, many generations have crossed the Rio Grande to come over to the other side of family lands. Yet we have always been treated as foreigners in our own countryside—exiles who never felt at home. The Mexican-Americans are a people twice conquered, twice colonized, and twice mestized. This is our socio-historical reality!

### Mestizaje: *Undefined Identity and Consequent Margination*

*Mestizaje* is simply the mixture of human groups of different makeup determining the color and shape of the eyes, skin pigmentation, and makeup of the bone structure. It is the most common phenomenon in the evolution of the human species. Scientists state that there are few, if any, truly "pure" human groups left in the world and they are the weakest, because their genetic pool has been gradually drained. Through mixture, new human groups emerge and the genetic makeup is strengthened. Biologically speaking, *mestizaje* appears to be quite easy and natural, but culturally it is usually feared and threatening. It is so feared that laws and taboos try to prevent it from taking place, for it appears as the ultimate threat to the survival of the species itself.

*Mestizaje* could certainly come in various ways, but it is a fact of history that massive *mestizaje* giving rise to a new people usually takes place through conquest and colonization. This has certainly been the case of the Mexican and the Mexican-American *mestizaje*. The first one came through the Spanish conquest of Mexico beginning in 1519, and the second one started with the Anglo-American invasion of the Mexican northwest beginning in the 1830s. The French biologist Ruffie states that, since the birth of Europe thirty-five thousand years ago when the invading Cro-Magnons mated with the native Neanderthals, no other event of similar magnitude had taken place until the birth of European-Mexico less than five hundred years ago. I would add that a similar event of equal magnitude is presently taking place in the southwest of the United States—an area larger than Western Europe and populated by several million persons.

Conquest comes through military force and is motivated by economic reasons. Yet, once it has taken place, conquest is totalitarian. It imposes not only the institutions of the powerful, but also a new worldview in conflict with the existing one. This imposition disrupts the worldview of the conquered in such a way that nothing makes sense anymore. In many ways, the ideas, the logic, the wisdom, the art, the customs, the language, and even the religion of the powerful are forced into the life of the conquered. Although the conquered try to resist, the ways and worldview of the powerful begin to penetrate their minds so that, even if political and economic independence come about, the native culture can never simply return to its preconquest ways.

Yet there is not only the obvious violence of the physical conquest, but the deeper violence of the disruption and attempts to destroy the conquered's inner worldview, which gives cohesion and meaning to existence. The conquered's fundamental core religious symbols provide the ultimate root of the group's identity, because they mediate the absolute. They are the final tangible expressions of the absolute. There is nothing beyond them that can put us in contact with God. They are the ultimate justification of the worldview of the group and the force that cements all the elements of the life of the group into a cohesive, meaningful, and tangible world order. When such symbols are discredited or destroyed, nothing makes sense anymore. The worldview moves from order to chaos, from significant mystery to meaningless confusion.

Hence, the ushering in of new religious symbols, especially when they are symbols of the dominant group, are in effect the ultimate conquest. In a nonviolent way, missioners were the agents of a deeper violence. They attempted to destroy that which even the physical violence of the conquerors could not touch—the soul of the native people. In spite of the missionary's conscious opposition to the cruel and bloody ways of the conquistador, the nonviolent introduction of religious symbols of the Spanish immigrant in effect affirmed and justified the way of the powerful, and discredited and tried to destroy the way of the powerless. This same process has taken place with the predominantly Irish-German clergy and religious, who have ministered to Mexican-American Catholics.

The most devastating thing about the conquest is that it established a relationship so concrete and so permanent that it took on the nature of a metaphysical reality. In many ways, it determines the behavior and the characteristics of the members of each group. It even influences the theological reflection as the members of the conquistador group will appeal to scripture and theology to explain and legitimate the relationship. Martin Marty in his classical book, *The Righteous Empire*, gives an excellent exposition of how theology and biblical studies can be used to legitimize oppression. The powerful now establish their own version of truth as objective truth for everyone and impose it through their various means of power.

The image of the conquistador as "superior" and of the conquered as "inferior" will be imposed and interiorized by all the media of communications: dress, food, manners, language, modes of thinking, art, music, bodily gestures, mannerisms, entertainment, and all the institutions of society, such as the family, economics, school system, politics, and church, and most of all by the religious imagery and mythology. It is now the gods of the powerful who preside over the new world order. The totalitarian image that colonizing Europe established and implanted in the colonized peoples as the universal model for everyone continues to have a determining influence around the world. This "normative image" of Western civilization continues to be reinforced and projected through television and movies, books, periodicals, universities, and the European/United States-controlled religions. Only the white Western way appears as the truly human way of life; all others continue to be relegated to an inferior status. This is not necessarily a conscious effort, but it takes place all the time.

Yet, in spite of the difficult situation of inequality, the very seeds for the destruction of this dichotomy of colonizer-superior vs. colonized-inferior are physically implanted by the conquistador himself. Through his very bodily intercourse with the women of the conquered group, a new biological-cultural race is born, a race that will be both conquistador and conquered, superior and inferior, at one and the same time: he or she will be a real blood sister/brother of both, without being exclusively either. Furthermore, because the mother is the fundamental transmitter of deep cultural traits, it is the culture of the conquered that will gradually triumph over the culture of the conquistador in providing the dominant and deepest personality characteristics of the new group.

Mestizos are born out of two histories and in them begins a new history. The symbolic and mental structures of both histories begin to intermingle so that out of the new story which begins in the mestizo new meanings, myths, and symbols will equally emerge. They will be meaningful to the mestizo as the firstborn of a new creation, but will remain incomprehensible to persons who try to understand them through the meanings, mythologies, and symbols of either of the previous histories alone. Yet from birth to maturity, there is a long period of painful search.

The deepest suffering of the mestizo comes from what we might call an "unfinished" identity, or better yet an undefined one. One of the core needs of human beings is the existential knowledge that regardless of who I am socially or morally, I am. The knowledge of fundamental belonging—that is, to be French, American, Mexican, English—is in the present world order one of the deepest needs of persons. When this need is met, it is not even thought about as a need; but when it is missing, it is so confusing and painful that we find it difficult to even conceptualize it or speak about it. We strive "to be like" but we are not sure just which one we should be like. As Mexican-Americans, we strive to find our belonging in Mexico or in the United States—only to discover that we are considered foreign by both. Our Spanish is too anglicized for the Mexicans and our English is too Mexicanized for the Anglos.

In the case of Mexico, it was the mestizo image of Our Lady of Guadalupe that provided the beginning of the new socio-cultural synthesis. It was not merely an apparition, but the perfect synthesis of the religious iconography of the Iberian peoples with that of native Mexicans into one coherent image. This marks the cultural birth of a new people. Both the parents and the child now have one common symbol of ultimate belonging. For the first time, they can begin to say "we are." As the physical birth of Mexicans had come through conquest, cultural birth came through the new image. It is only after the apparition that those who had wanted to die now wanted to live and to celebrate life. In and through Our Lady, new meanings, myths, and symbols will begin to emerge that will be truly representative and characteristic of Mexico.

## Struggles for Accepting and Belonging

In the first stages of the struggle to belong, the mestizo will try desperately to become like the dominant group, for only its members appear to be fully civilized and human. This struggle includes every aspect of life, because the whole world structure of the dominant will have been assimilated and made normative for human existence. It equally involves a violent rejection of the way of the conquered, because that now appears to be inferior. Only the scholars of the dominant group will appear as credible, only their universities are prestigious, their language is civilized, their medical practices are scientific, and their religion is true religion. The dominated will sometimes attempt to keep some of their original folklore, but, in every other way, they try to become like the dominant.

Some of the well-intentioned and kind members of the dominant group will help the brighter and more promising ones (according to their own standard of judgment) to better themselves by "becoming like us." They will privilege them with scholarships to the best universities in Europe or the United States, and help them to learn the European or American way of life and language.

Some of the marginated will make it into the world of the dominant society, only to discover that they will never be allowed to belong fully, and furthermore that down deep inside they are still somewhat "other." Yet it is this very pain of not being able to belong fully that also marks the beginning of a new search.

In the first stages of the search, the ones who choose not to join the struggle to become like the dominant ones will tend to reject the world of the dominant in a total way: absolutely nothing good can come of it. They will not only reject it but will hate it passionately. The only way to treat the dominant ones is to get rid of them. They are the ones who are guilty not only of the individual sin of homicide, but of the collective sin of ethnocide.

Throughout all these struggles, there is something radically new beginning to emerge. Even though the seeds are planted from the very beginning, and biologically this new life begins from the very start, it will take time for cultural identity to emerge as a distinct identity of its own. This new identity does not try to become like someone else, but it struggles to form its own unique individuality. It accepts from both parent cultures without seeking to be a replica of either. It is like the maturing child who no longer tries to be like the mother or like the father, nor to simply reject both of them, but is simply himself or herself. Through the pains and frustrations of trying to be what we are not, the uniqueness of our own proper identity begins to emerge. It is an exciting moment of the process and usually the most creative stage of the life of the group.

It is at this moment that the quest to know ourselves begins to emerge in a serious way. In the beginning, knowledge of ourselves will be confused because we see ourselves through a type of double image—that is, through the eyes of the two parent groups. As the group develops, its own proper image will begin to emerge and it will be easy to study ourselves more critically. It is this new and more clearly defined self-image of who we are as Mexican-Americans that is presently beginning to take shape. As usual, it is the poets, the artists, and the musicians who are beginning to point and to sing and to suggest the new identity. It is now the critical thinkers who are coming in and beginning to deepen, to conceptualize, to verbalize, and to communicate the reality of our identity. And it is only now that for the first time we begin to ask ourselves about our Christian identity, about our church, and about our religion. What does it really mean? Who are we as Mexican-American Christians?

## The Human Situation: Divisions and Collective Self-Protection

When one looks at the history of humanity, then wars, divisions, and family fights appear more natural than do peace, unity, and harmony. This is evident from the global level down to the family cell. It appears more natural for brothers and sisters to fight one another than to love one another. We struggle to protect ourselves against each other and to conquer others before they conquer us. We prepare for peace by preparing for war. Only violent means appear to be able to control or curb violence. Might makes right, because power establishes its views as objective truth so as to justify its own position of privilege. The survival of the fittest appears to be the first law of individuals and of society—the survival of the powerful at the cost of the weak.

From this struggle for survival at the cost of others, certain anthropol-ogico-sociological characteristics and behavioral laws appear. The members of the dominant group in power see themselves as pure, superior, dignified, well-developed, beautiful, and civilized. They see themselves as the model for all others. They see their natural greatness as the source of their great achievements. Even the least among them consider themselves superior to the best of the dominated group.

On the other hand, they look upon the conquered and colonized as impure, inferior, undignified, underdeveloped, ugly, uncivilized, conserva-tive, backward. Their ways are considered childish and their wisdom is looked upon as superstition. Because might is subconsciously assumed to be right, everything about the weak is considered to be wrong and unworthy of being considered human. The conquered are told that they must forget their backward ways if they are to advance and become human. Accultur-ation to the ways of the dominant, in every respect whatsoever, is equated with human development and liberation.

Even the best among the dominant group find it very difficult to truly accept the other as other: to enjoy their foods, learn from their wisdom, speak their language, dress in their styles, appreciate their art and their music, interpret life through their philosophies, live in their ways, even worship through their forms of cult. Even though many go out, even hero-ically, to be of service to the poor and the oppressed, and really love them, there is still an inner fear and rejection of their otherness. The way of the powerful as the normative human way for all persons is so deeply ingrained that it takes a dying to oneself to be able to break through the cultural enslavements that keep the dominant from appreciating the inner beauty, the values, the worth, and the dignity of the ways of the conquered.

Because of the image imposed upon them about themselves, some of the conquered will begin to think of themselves as inferior and good for nothing. This develops a type of domesticated, happy-go-lucky, subservient attitude in relation to the dominant. It is a very dehumanizing existence, but the powerless have no choice—either conform to the status assigned by the powerful or be eliminated physically. Law and order work in favor of the rich against the poor. Whereas the rich tend to be considered innocent until proven guilty, the poor are usually considered guilty until proven innocent. They are blamed for all the problems of society and are considered to be the source of all evil and crime. Thus, the very victims of the institutionalized violence of power are labeled by the establishment as the causes of this violence! The powerful can define the image and status of the oppressed as "guilty of all evil" and force them to live accordingly. The poor and the oppressed thus serve as the scapegoats of the crimes of the establishment, which can continue to think of itself as pure and immaculate. However, as long as the traditions of the oppressed continue, especially their deepest religious traditions, they may be forced to live as dirt, but they cannot be forced to perceive themselves as such. Through their traditions, perfectly understood by them but incomprehensible to foreigners, they continue to perceive themselves as they truly are: free human beings with full human dignity who, although dominated through external powers, nevertheless remain free and independent in the innermost core of their being.

The in-group will defend tradition, law, and order because its members are the privileged ones of the establishment. National and personal security will be among the top priorities of this group as it strives to maintain the status quo. For the powerful, tradition protects their position of privilege; for the powerless, their own traditions are the ultimate rejection of the status quo of the dominant—their bodies might be dominated but not their souls.

Tradition functions in a diametrically opposed way for the powerful and for the powerless. For the powerless, tradition is the affirmation of inner freedom, independence, and self-worth. It is the power for the radical transformation of the existing order. For the moment, it might appear as a tranquilizer, but we should not underestimate its power in keeping a people alive as a people. As long as their traditions are alive, they are assured of life and ultimate liberation. If their traditions disappear, they will no longer have to work for integral liberation, because they will have ceased to exist as a people.

In attempting to analyze the dynamics between the oppressor in-group and the oppressed out-group, three constants seem to function as anthropological laws of human behavior.

First, when one studies the human story across the ages, the tendency of group inclusion/exclusion—that is, to protect our own by keeping others out—appears to be one of the most consistent and fundamental anthropological laws of nature. Dominant groups will struggle to maintain outside influences in a multiplicity of ways, and weaker or dominated ones will likewise fear and resist any type of intrusion. The purity of the group must be maintained. Human barriers of race, class, language, family name, education, economic status, social position, and religion are regularly used as signals to distinguish "our own" from "the others."

The second tendency that appears as an anthropological law of nature is: others can be used and enjoyed, but a social distance must be maintained. Deep friendships might develop and even strong love relationships, but the social barriers are so deeply interiorized and assimilated that they are very difficult to do away with. There are not just laws that keep peoples apart, but the relationship of superior-inferior that is established, projected, transmitted, assimilated, and even sacralized by religion. This keeps persons from truly appreciating each other as fully equal and from seeing the true human dignity of one another. Even the best among the dominant group tend to see and treat the others as inferior and "different." We can even do good things for the lesser others, but they remain lesser. They can be exploited legitimately, because the culture and the laws of the dominant sanction the superior-inferior relationship. This gives the "master" the right and the obligation to use and "protect" the lesser ones.

This law of social distance is probably the hardest one to break through, because it is not only enforced by external laws and the economic-political mechanisms of the land, but it is interiorized in a number of ways. For example, in ordinary commercials we see blacks waiting on whites, but I have never seen a commercial with a white serving a black. Blacks, but never racially mixed families, appear in commercials. Brown skins do not even appear at all. Social barriers of separability are drilled into a people through all the media of communication and education. Even religious education material and religious images in our churches exhibit a definite racial preference, thus indirectly telling the others that they cannot be reflected in the sacred.

Finally, the third constant that appears as an anthropological law of nature is: anyone who threatens to destroy or annul the barriers of separation will be an outcast—an impure untouchable who must be eliminated.

As should be evident by now, *mestizaje* is feared by established groups because it is the deepest threat to all the humanly made barriers of separation that consecrate oppression and exploitation. It is a threat to the security of ultimate human belonging—that is, to the inherited national/cultural identity that clearly and ultimately defines who I am to myself and to the world. It is even a deeper threat to established societies because the mestizo cannot be named with clarity and precision. So much is in the mystery of a name! I am comfortable when I can name you, for, in many ways, it indicates that I am somewhat in control of the situation. I may not like what I know, but at least I have the comfort of knowing what it is. But there is a nervousness when I do not know who you are—your name and your cultural nationality are so important, for they tell me who you are personally and fundamentally. They give me your immediate and ultimate human identity.

Because of their hyphenated identity, mestizos cannot be named adequately by the categories of analysis of either group. They do not fit into the single history set of norms for testing and identifying persons. This is threatening to both groups—we can name them and even study them, but they cannot name us or even figure out how to really study us. It is threatening for anyone to be in the presence of one who knows us very well even in our innermost being, but we do not know who they are. To be an outside-insider, as the mestizo is, is to have both intimacy and objective distance at one and the same time. Insofar as we are in Mexico, we are outside the United States; but insofar as we are in the United States, we are distant from Mexico. As such we can see and appreciate the aspects of both, which neither sees of themselves or each other. In this very in-out existence lies the potential for our creativity: to pool the cultural genes and the chromosomes of both so as to create a new being!

The potential for newness will not be actualized automatically. The mestizo can simply become like one of the parent groups and continue to do unto others as they have done unto us. However, they can equally, although with more hidden difficulties than anyone suspects, choose to live out the radical meaning of their new being. This is exciting but difficult because, even though the dominant way may be rejected totally and explicitly, subconsciously the oppressed will strive to become like the oppressor, for they have already assimilated many of the characteristics of the dominant group. Will the group simply obtain power and acceptance by reverting to the ways of the parent group or will they initiate new life? That is the key question.

As a Mexican-American Christian, I am convinced that the full potential of *mestizaje* will be actualized only in and through the way of the Lord, which brings order out of chaos and new life out of death. It is in the Lord's way that the salvific and liberating role of our human mestizo way finds its ultimate identity, meaning, direction, and challenge.

## THE CONCRETE HISTORICAL MEANING OF GOD'S SAVING WAY

### The Human Identity of the Savior

The racial-cultural identity of a person is the very first and immediate revelation of who one is. We all have stereotype prejudices about certain colors, accents, languages, features, regions, and religions. There is a natural tendency to categorize persons according to our stereotypes of them and to prejudge them as to their human worth and potential even before they have said or done anything. Looks are all-important and they are the first revelation, according to the standards of the world, of the worth and dignity of the person. Persons from the outer regions of any country are usually looked down upon as rustics, whereas those from urban centers look upon themselves as sophisticated.

What was the racial-cultural identity of Jesus? What did others think of when they first saw or heard of him . . . before they even heard him speak or saw his actions? These are all-important questions, for we know from the New Testament itself that it is in the human face and heart of Jesus that God has been self-revealed to us. It is through the full humanity of Jesus that God has allowed us to see God in a human way.

There is no doubt that, during his lifetime, Jesus was regularly known as a Galilean, that most of his disciples were from Galilee, and that most of the things we remember best of his activity took place in Galilee. There is no doubt that Galilee plays a key role in the life and mission of Jesus as presented in the Gospels.

The full human signification of the kenosis of the Son of God becomes evident when we look at the image of Galilee in Jesus' time. First of all, if it had not been for Jesus, Galilee would probably remain an unknown region of the world. Jerusalem, Greece, and Rome were all important with or without Jesus, but not Galilee. It was an outer region, far from the center of Judaism in Jerusalem of Judea and a crossroads of the great caravan routes of the world. It was a region of mixed peoples and languages. In Galilee the Jews were looked down upon and despised by the others as they were in the rest of the world. They were considered to be stubborn, backward, superstitious, clannish, and all the negative stereotypes one could think of. Furthermore, the Jews of Judea looked down upon the Galilean Jews, for they considered them ignorant of the law and the rules of the temple, contaminated in many ways by their daily contacts with pagans, not capable of speaking correct Greek, for their language was being corrupted by admixture with the other languages of the region. In short, their own Jewish relatives regarded them as inferior and impure. Because of their mixture with others, they were marginated by their own people. There were not doubts about the cultural *mestizaje* that was taking place and, knowing the ordinary situation of human beings, a certain amount of biological *mestizaje* was equally taking place. Culturally and linguistically speaking, Jesus was certainly a mestizo between Judaism and the other cultures that flourished throughout Galilee. And we know from the early Jewish charges that tried to discredit Jesus that he was even accused of being the bastard son of a Roman soldier named Pantera, which could also be a colloquial term simply meaning "a Roman," which could have made of him a biological mestizo as well. I am, of course, in no way denying or even questioning that Jesus was conceived by the Holy Spirit. What I am saying is that in his human appearance, as viewed by those who knew him only in a worldly way and not through the eyes of faith, he certainly appeared to be of mixed origins. The New Testament itself gives clear evidence that nothing good was expected to come out of Galilee.

The point of bringing out all this is to appreciate the human beginnings of God's mission. God becomes not just a human being, but the marginated, shamed, and rejected of the world. He comes to initiate a new human unity, but the all-important starting point is among the most segregated and impure of the world. Among those whom the world has thrown out, God will begin the way to final unity. It is among those whom the world labels as "impure" that a new criterion for real purity will emerge.

Because the world expected nothing good to come out of Galilee, God chose it to be the starting point of God's human presence among us. The principle behind the cultural image of the Galilean identity is that God chooses what the world rejects. What is marginal to the world is central to God. It is through those whom the world has made nothing that God will reduce to nothing the power and wisdom of the world. It is through the poor and nonpersons of the world that God continues to reveal God's face and heart in a human way and among them—the Galilees and Galileans of today—salvation continues to begin for all the peoples of the world.

### The Cultural Function of His Mission

The mission of Jesus is not some sort of esoteric or esthetic truth. He comes to live out and proclaim the supreme truth about humanity, which will have immediate and long-term implications in everyday life and in the history of humanity. Those who hear his word and are converted to his way will see themselves and will equally see all others in a radically new way. This new image of self and of others will allow everyone to relate with each other as never before.

Because of his concrete human identity, Jesus had personally suffered the pains of margination and dehumanizing insults. He was concerned with the pains of hunger, sickness, bad reputation, rejection, shame, class struggles, loneliness, and all the real sufferings of humanity. His concern was not abstract, but real and immediate. He spoke with the Samaritan woman, ate with the rich, the tax collectors, and sinners alike. He did not feel repelled by the leper; he enjoyed the company of women and little children. Jesus was truly at home with everyone and it is evident that everyone felt at home with him. This is nowhere more evident than in his ability to enjoy himself in table fellowship with everyone without exception.

Out of the cultural suffering of rejection, Jesus offers a new understanding of the kingdom. He did not come to restore the kingdom of David for the Jewish people, but to initiate the reign of God who is the Father of everyone. The innermost identity of Jesus was his life of intimacy with God-Father. It is this living relationship with the absolute that cuts through and relativizes all human images of importance or nonimportance, dignified or undignified. When we know the ultimate origins of a person—that he is really the son of the king—the superficial appearances are no longer important. It is the ultimate origins and name of a person that give us his true worth. It is precisely this intimacy with God-Father which is the basis of the innermost identity of Jesus, which he offers to all others. It is not the labels that the world places on persons that count, but one's own innermost identity and image of oneself as reflective of the likeness of God.

By discovering that God is our real father we begin to see everything in a new way. No longer will I see others as superior or inferior to me, but as brothers and sisters of the same father. In this realization is the basis for a totally new value system for humanity. In fidelity to God, Jesus refuses to conform to any human law or tradition that will dehumanize and make appear as inferior any human being whatsoever. The truth of Jesus will upset humankind's criteria of judgment. Because one is, one is a child of God. But precisely because everyone can now belong, those who have set up and guarded the multiple barriers of separation, which allow them to enjoy the privileges of being "in" at the cost of keeping the so-called inferior ones "out," will not only refuse the invitation but will discredit the new way and try to prevent it from coming into existence.

But it is not sufficient to invite the rejected into the kingdom. It is not sufficient to tell the exploited and marginated of society that they are truly free human beings who are equal to all others. One must go to the roots of the human mechanisms, both to the external and the internal structures of society, to make known the segregating and dehumanizing evil that has been institutionalized and is now hidden in the various structures of the group. Jesus makes known that he must go to Jerusalem, where the sufferings of his people are highlighted. Truth in the service of love must bring out clearly the evil hidden in human structures, which passes as good. Such a confusion allows the evils of power to appear as the good of society, to even appear as the sufferings of the marginated, as the causes of all evil. Criminals appear as good; victims appear as criminals. This is the ongoing confusion of Babel, which continues to mask and confuse both the evil and the good of the world.

Jesus appears in the New Testament as the aggressive prophet of non-violent love who refuses to conform to the violence of the structures in full loyalty to the tradition of the God of his people, of the God who sees the suffering, who hears the cries of affliction, and who wills to save. He questions the human traditions that oppress or destroy a people. Jesus must go to Jerusalem, because that is the center of institutionalized power. When he arrives he goes to the very core of Judaism: the temple. In Jerusalem we see Jesus who does not hesitate to question the very legitimacy of the structures that were enslaving the masses of the people. The house of the God of compassion and justice had become the place that now legitimized and covered up the evil ways of the establishment. The same story is found in all human institutions. We need institutions in order to live in an orderly and peaceful way. Yet, all institutions have the tendency to become self-serving to the benefit of those in control. They are set up to serve persons, but persons end up serving them. It is this very tendency to absolutize that must be confronted and made known.

As institutions, customs, and traditions become absolutized, they function as the idols of the group. Whether we call them God or not, they function as the real gods of the group. To question them is the same as questioning God. And when we challenge them, we will be accused of blasphemy. Yet to the degree that these ways dehumanize or reject any human being, they must be questioned in the name of God. But Jesus does not confront the power of the world with a power of the same order. He does not give in to the ways of humanity. He confronts the power of the world and human violence with a power of an entirely different order: the power of unlimited love, which will not give in to violence to eliminate violence.

The nonviolent way of Jesus worked in a diametrically opposed way to the nonviolent way of the missioners of the power countries. First of all, he begins by assuming the way, the language, and the worldview of Galileans—the nonpersons of the world. The all-powerful God, in becoming a Galilean, converts so as to become the marginated, the rejected, and the nonperson of the world. Second, he does not only denounce the accepted practices of the powerful, as good missioners often do, but unlike the average traditional missioner, he even denounces and desacralizes their ultimate authority as enshrined in their religious symbols, for it is the religious symbols of the powerful that ultimately legitimize their way as God's way. Third, the radical difference between the missionary activity of Jesus and that of missioners who are culturally and nationally members of the powerful countries is apparent in the response of officials.

Official Judaism condemned Jesus and got rid of him. His accusers disowned him to the Romans because he questioned their ultimate authority and the ultimate legitimacy of their structures. The officials of mission-sending countries support and reinforce the missionary endeavor because it in effect affirms and perpetuates the legitimacy of their own world order. In supporting the missions, they affirm their own ultimate authority and the divine legitimacy of their ways. Let me be clear on this point; this is not necessarily done in an intentional or malicious way; in fact, I would say that quite often it is done with the best of intentions; however, the final result remains the same. The Spanish missioners did not hesitate to chastise openly and consistently the crimes and abuses of the conquest; however, they legitimized the way of the conquerors by affirming their ultimate symbol as superior and true in relation to the symbols of ultimate reality of captured peoples.

The way of Jesus to Jerusalem and the cross is the challenging task of those who are on the margins of society. Their temptation will always be to become simply the powerful themselves, as even the disciples wanted to do. But the challenge is to be willing to die so that a new way will truly be ushered in. The authorities kill Jesus but they cannot destroy him. He remains faithful to his way to the very end. He came to reject every type of human rejection and, even when all appear to have rejected him, even his God, he rejects no one. He dies in perfect communion with his people and his God. He came to tear down barriers of separation; and no matter what humans tried to do to stop him, they were not able to break him down. As he lived his life in communion with everyone—so he died. All had rejected him, but he rejects no one.

God's love in and through Jesus triumphs over all the divisive hatreds and consequent violence of humanity. Jesus passes through death to life. In resurrecting him, God rejects the rejection of humanity, destroys all the charges of illegitimacy and demolishes the idolized structures. In the resurrection, God ratified the entire way and message of Jesus. It is from the resurrection that the entire way of Jesus and every aspect of his life takes on a liberating and salvific signification.

It is in the resurrection that the new life initiated and offered to everyone by Jesus is now fully and definitively present. No human power will be able to destroy it or slow it down. Jesus is the firstborn of the new creation, and in his followers a new human group now begins. It is definitely a new human alternative now present in the history of humanity.

First of all, those who had nothing to offer now have the best thing to offer to everyone: new life. It is the rejected and marginated Galileans who have received the Spirit and, without ceasing to be Galileans, now see themselves in a new way as they begin to initiate the new humanity. Everyone is invited, but it is the very ones who had been excluded who are now doing the inviting. It is obvious from the history of the early church how quickly the new way spread to all peoples. It crossed all boundaries of separation. Persons, without ceasing to be who they were culturally, nevertheless saw themselves in such a new way that the ordinary human barriers were no longer obstacles to the new fellowship.

It is equally evident that the crossing of cultural boundaries was not easy, for each group had its own unsuspected idols, yet the miracle is that it took place. Cultural-national groups, which had been totally separated, now can come together—no longer Jew or gentile, master or slave, male or female, but all one in Christ. They continued to be who they were, but they lived their nationality and religion in a radically new way. Their identity was affirmed but their exclusiveness was destroyed. This openness led them to discover new values and criteria of judgment ... from competition to cooperation, from divisions to unity, from strangers to a common family, from a superior or inferior status to common friends and all children of the same father.

The radical all-inclusive way of Christianity started among the rejected and lowly of society. This is the starting point. In the Spirit, they struggle to build new human alternatives so that others will not have to suffer what they have had to suffer. It is they who first hear the invitation to the new universal family of God, and it is the converted poor and suffering of the world, who see themselves in a new way, who now go out to invite—by deeds and words—all others into the new society. God continues to begin where humanity would never suspect. Out of the Nazareths and Galilees of today, salvation continues to come to the entire world.

## THE GOD-MEANING OF OUR MEXICAN-AMERICAN IDENTITY AND MISSION

*"God chose those whom the world considers absurd to shame the wise"*
*(1 Cor. 1:28)*

It is in the light of our faith that we discover our ultimate identity as God's chosen people. It is in the very cultural identity of Jesus the Galilean and in his way from Galilee to Jerusalem that the real ultimate meaning of our own cultural identity and mission to society become clear.

For those who ordinarily have a good sense of belonging, the idea of being chosen is nothing special. But for one who has been consistently ignored or rejected, the idea of being noticed, accepted, and especially chosen is not only good news, but new life. For in being chosen, what was nothing now becomes something, and what was dead now comes to life. In the light of the Judeo-Christian tradition, our experience of rejection and margination is converted from human curse to the very sign of divine predilection. It is evident from the scriptures that God chooses the outcasts of the world not exclusively but definitely in a preferential way. Those whom the world ignores, God loves in a special way. But God does not choose the poor and the lowly just to keep them down and make them feel good in their misery. Such an election would be the very opposite of good news and it would truly be the opium to keep the poor quiet and domesticated. God chooses the poor and the marginated of the world to be the agents of the new creation.

The experience of being wanted as one is, of being needed and of being chosen, is a real and profound rebirth. Those who had been made to consider themselves as nothing or as inferior will now begin to appreciate the full stature of human beings. Out of the new self-image, new powers will be released, which have always been there but have not been able to surface. Through this experience, the sufferings of the past are healed though not forgotten, and they should not be forgotten. For it is precisely out of the condition of suffering that the people are chosen so as to initiate a new way of life where others will not have to suffer what the poor have suffered in the past. When people forget the experience of suffering, as has happened to many of our migrant groups in this country, such as the Irish in Boston, then they simply inflict the same insults upon others that had previously been inflicted upon them. The greater the suffering and the more vivid the memory of it, the greater the challenge will be to initiate changes so as to eliminate the root causes of the evils which cause the suffering. It is the wounded healer, who has not forgotten the pain of wounds, who can be the greatest healer of the illnesses of society.

It is in our very margination from the centers of the various establishments that we live the Galilean identity today. Because we are inside-outsiders, we appreciate more clearly the best of the traditions of both groups, while equally appreciating the worst of the situation of both. It is precisely in this double identity that we in effect have something of unique value to offer both. The very reasons for the margination are the bases of our liberating and salvific potential not only for ourselves but for the others as well. In a privileged way, God is present in the marginated, for distance from the powers of the world is closeness to God. It is consistently in the frontier regions of human belonging that God begins the new creation. The established centers seek stability, but the frontier regions can risk to be pioneers. It is the frontier people who will be the trailblazers of the new societies. "The stone which the builders rejected has become the keystone of the structure. It is the Lord who did this and we find it marvelous to behold" (Matt. 21:42).

### *"I Have Chosen You to Go and Bear Much Fruit" (John 15:16)*

God chooses people not just to make them feel good, but for a mission. "I have chosen you to go and bear much fruit" (John 15:16). To accept God's election is not empty privilege, but a challenging mission. It is a call to be prophetic both in deeds and in words. It is a call to live a new alternative in the world, to invite others into it, and to challenge with the power of truth the structures of the world that keep the new alternative from becoming a reality.

Our Mexican-American Christian challenge in the world today is not to try to become like someone else — Mexicans or Americans — but to combine both into a new way. It is through the very mechanisms of forging a new and more cosmopolitan identity that new life begins to emerge. It must be worked at critically, persistently, and creatively, for the temptation will always be there to become simply one or the other of the previous models. The temptation will always be there to restore the kingdom rather than to usher in the kingdom of God. In our present powerlessness we may think that this is stupid, but, in our faith, we know that we must take the risks and begin to initiate new ways of life that will eliminate some of the dehumanizing elements of the present one. We know that we will not eliminate them all, nor will this come about easily and without much effort, organization, and frustration, but nevertheless the efforts must be made to introduce new forms and new institutions that will continue some of the best of the past while eliminating some of the worst. We will not build the perfect society, but we must do our part to at least build a better one. We must begin with the grass roots, but we must equally go to the very roots of the problems.

This is our "divine must"! We, too, must harden our faces and go to Jerusalem. We must go to the established centers of power, whether political, economic, educational, or religious, to confront their sacred idols which prevent them from truly serving all the people. It is the idols of society which function in favor of the rich and the powerful, and against the poor and powerless. It is they which mask the hidden viciousness and manipulations of the wise of the world who find many ways of exploiting the poor and the simple of the world.

We really do not have a choice if we want to be disciples following Jesus on his way to the cross. It is this road from Galilee to Jerusalem which has to be continued if evil is to be destroyed, not with new forms of evil, but with the power of truth in the service of love. We have no choice but to speak the truth which brings tc light clearly the evil of the world, knowing full well that the powers of darkness will not stop at anything in order to put out the light.

### *"Your Grief Will Be Turned to Joy" (John 16:20)*

It is in our fiestas that our legitimate identity and destiny are experienced. They are not just parties; in fact they are the very opposite. They are the joyful, spontaneous, and collective celebrations of what has already begun in us even if it is not recognized by others or verbalized even by ourselves. It is the celebration of the beginning of the ultimate eschatological identity where there will be differences but not division. It is the celebration of what has already begun in germ but is yet to be totally fulfilled. Yet the fiesta is a foretaste and experience, even if for a brief moment, of the ultimate accomplishment. It is a result of who we are and a cause of what is yet to become. For just as it is true that the celebrations of the people can be used to drug the people and keep them in their misery, it is equally true that the fiestas can be used as rallying moments that not only give the people an experience of togetherness, but can also nourish the movements of liberation. In the fiestas, we rise above our daily living experiences of death to experience life beyond death. They are the moments of life that enable us to survive, to come together, to rally, and to begin anew. The spirit not only to survive but to bring about a new existence can be enkindled in the fiestas so as to ignite the people to action.

Fiestas without prophetic action easily degenerate into empty parties, drunken brawls, or the opium to keep the people in their misery. But prophetic action without festive celebration is equally reduced to dehumanizing hardness. Prophecy is the basis of fiesta, but the fiesta is the spirit of prophecy. It is in the combination of the two that the tradition of faith is both kept alive and transmitted to newcomers. It is through the two of them that the God of history who acts on our behalf, on behalf of the poor and the lowly, continues to be present among us bringing the project of history to completion.

Thus it is precisely through our fiestas that we are kept together as a people. It is through them that we have continued to maintain our identity and sense of belonging. They are the deepest celebrations of our existence — meaningful to those who belong and incomprehensible and folkloric to outsiders. They are the lifeline of our tradition and the life sources of our new existence.

*Chapter Seven*

# The Hispanic Woman:
# *Pasionaria* and *Pastora*
# of the Hispanic Community

## GLORIA INÉS LOYA, P.B.V.M.

In the Hispanic world the titles *pasionaria* and *pastora* have been given to outstanding women who have demonstrated a high level of leadership, commitment to justice and love for their people. Dolores Huerta, vice president of the United Farmworkers Union in Delano, California, for instance, has been called *la pasionaria de Delano* in light of her decades of commitment to the struggle of her people.[1]

It is common enough to hear the word *pastora* used with reference to the committed women and lay ministers who successfully work alongside the pastor in countless pastoral contexts. The *Velázquez Dictionary* defines *pastora* as one who nourishes the spirit of others with sound values. Her work is to *pastorear* or shepherd.[2]

In this article it is precisely this image and understanding of the woman's leadership in the life of the community that provides a basis for further discussion of a theology of and for U.S. Latina women. What follows is a modest framework and method for developing a Hispanic women's theology.

### A GENERAL FRAMEWORK

I begin, as might be expected, inductively. My intention is to do what Clodovis Boff calls a "feet-on-the-ground theology."[3] The social sciences, especially sociology, provide practical ways to gather, analyze, and interpret the rich, lived experiences of Hispanic women. The empirical reality needs to be assessed through a careful process of *listening* made possible through social science instruments and by literature. Stories of women's joys, pain, and suffering emerge through the process of interviewing women in the field and studying Latina literature. These stories, narratives, and questionnaires provide insight into the symbols and myths which are most expressive of the women's religiosity, faith, and hope. Trends and insights will emerge in the interpretive process. Not only particular symbols, but the symbols of the culture itself will emerge as well as the wisdom of the people, the *pueblo*, and their concrete concerns.

Ada María Isasi-Díaz and Yolanda Tarango stress the need for listening to the experience of women in the first book written by U.S. Latina theologians, *Hispanic Women: Prophetic Voice in the Church*.[4] Women begin to do theology by sharing insights about themselves, their lives, and their faith. They then struggle to develop a corresponding pastoral praxis.

A second moment occurs when women apply the fruit of their study of Christian sources—scripture, tradition, and the magisterium—to the reality they are discovering and revealing. God's word as found in the Bible is particularly important. The appeal of new religious movements, sects, and fundamentalism to U.S. Hispanics has much to do with the people's conviction that the Bible has something to offer, is a source of unequaled authority for elucidating life and the people's realities. Yet Hispanics feel that somehow they have been deprived of this inexhaustible source, and ardently desire to fathom its riches as best they can. Hispanics are also quite aware of the fact that they have not generally been exposed to theology beyond the simple catechetical formation of home and parish. That is why this second moment—taking the sources seriously, studying and applying them—is of such great importance especially in the contemporary Hispanic context.

A third moment occurs when the reflection leads to action. In both the Latin American and U.S. Hispanic Catholic communities it has been quite common to refer to this third step as the elaboration of a pastoral plan. What this means is that the application of the insights derived from the careful analysis of the reality in the light of the scriptures and other Christian sources is not a simple, discreet "doing this or that." Rather, it has to do with a *plan*—that is, an organic vision of the integral relationships between faith and justice, between the personal and the structural.

The carrying out of this plan, the doing of this theology, involves women in a discovery of the Word living in them and evoked by their study of the scriptures. They experience the presence of the Holy Spirit who guides them into discipleship. Women thus become familiar with the mission entrusted to God's people by Jesus himself, namely, the mission to evangelize. Hispanic women come to the task of evangelizing with the gifts at their disposal—that is, with ancestral wisdom and faith. As they have always done (as *pasionarias* and *pastoras*) they *take responsibility* for ministry. They see the need to concretize their mission in pastoral praxis, a plan that is creative, organized, and coherent. In this way Hispanic women may become the salt, the light, and the leaven for U.S. Hispanics and for the entire North American Catholic Church.

*A Survey of Hispanic Women in California*

What follows now is a more detailed instance of the relatively simple method sketched above. First, I will refer to some data gathered on Hispanic women in California. This information is a source of reflection, including theological reflection. Second, I will discuss some literary sources for gathering the experience of Hispanic women. Literature, stories, and poetry can provide a rich basis for theological reflection. The use of social science instruments in the doing of theology is a major contribution of liberation theology. Literary sources, however, can also be used to deepen and intensify the experience and understanding of the Hispanic reality.

In 1989 more than 170 Hispanic women were interviewed and asked to answer a rather detailed questionnaire.[5] They all resided in California. The questionnaires were prepared in both English and Spanish. What follows is a brief overview of the data, perceptions, and opinions generated by this cross-section of women.

1. Eighty-five (50.6 percent) of the women were U.S. born. Yet only two (1.2 percent) identified themselves as North American or American. They identified with their parents' country of origin—for example, Mexico, El Salvador, Puerto Rico. Interestingly enough, only one woman out of 170 referred to herself as Hispanic.[6]

2. Thirty-two (24.4 percent) of the women were "professionals." Closer analysis of these respondents revealed that they were catechists, service agency workers or teachers. There were no lawyers, doctors, or accountants surveyed. The largest number of the women who had full-time work outside the home were involved in clerical work or in the sales and service areas. A breakdown of the survey reveals that Hispanic women are *working* women: of the teenagers 82.9 percent had at least part-time work; of the young adults 75 percent were working; of the middle-aged women, once again, 75 percent were working outside the home; and of the older adults 43.5 percent were also working.

3. With regard to religious beliefs the survey revealed the following: the teenagers said they owed their faith to their family; 92.3 percent of the young adults said they owed it to their families; 78 percent of the middle-aged said it was due to their family; and 90.9 percent of the older adults said they owed their religious beliefs to their family. In a related area—the importance given to the faith by each woman—the results were the following: 71.7 percent of the teenagers ranked faith high; 80.0 percent of the young adults ranked it high; 97.6 percent of the middle-aged ranked it high; and 100 percent of the older adults gave it the high ranking. Another interesting statistic regarding religious attitudes is that 54.6 percent of the women said they were not satisfied with women's place in the church. This points to an area of growing concern—namely, the strong interest of these women in faith in a church that does not yet respond adequately to their expectations. The strong faith orientation of Hispanics, especially women,

is undoubtedly an aspect of the "blessing" that the Hispanic presence represents in the U.S. church as the bishops insisted in their 1983 pastoral letter *The Hispanic Presence: Challenge and Commitment*. One of the features of that blessing is the presence of some extremely gifted and dedicated women who, as this survey reveals, are dissatisfied or perhaps even frustrated with their roles in the church. This "treasure" of information needs to be respected. The questions the women raise, their strong faith, frustrations, and concerns must be heard.

The women who speak out by means of this survey are mostly working-class with lower incomes. They are quite young, the majority being between the ages of 18 and 35.

Some of the questions that emerge from the survey are: How can women be encouraged to develop their faith? Is the road of discipleship open to them? How might they assume active roles in ministry? How can their highly relational and personal faith continue to grow in the church? How can the church be a place of belonging for women and a place for their empowerment?

### Hispanic Women's Literature: A Theological Source

Literature, music, and art of U.S. Hispanics are also expressions of the experience and collective memory of women. Few Hispanic women, unfortunately, are writing and being published. Even fewer are writing in the field of theology. There is, however, a growing Latina creative literature in the form of poetry, short story, novel, and essay. Here their struggles, values, and spirituality are beautifully expressed. This literature can become a source for theology, a mirror of the lived experience of women.[7]

In the powerful character of the grandmother in Rudolfo A. Anaya's *Bless Me, Ultima*, one of the earliest Chicano novels, the *pasionaria* and the *pastora* of the family are personified in the grandmother, Ultima, who is, above all else, a healer:

"And the children?" my father asked. I knew why he expressed concern for me and my sisters. It was because Ultima was a *curandera*, a woman who knew herbs and remedies of the ancients, a miracle-worker who could heal the sick. And I had heard that Ultima could lift the curses laid by *brujas* (witches), and that she could exorcise the evil the witches planted in people to make them sick. And because a *curandera* had this power she was misunderstood and often suspected of practicing witchcraft herself.[8]

More recently Sandra Cisneros has written evocative short stories about her Chicana experiences growing up in Chicago.[9]

In addition to Chicano and other U.S. Hispanic literatures, the word of women is found in oral tradition, in popular legends and stories that abound in the Hispanic world. These are narrations that capture the experience of the Hispanic people and reflect, as well, their faith histories. The central figures of this oral tradition are the grandmothers, the *abuelitas*. Both pastoral ministers and theologians will find in this oral tradition a great deal of wisdom (*sabiduría*) and truth in the form of stories, narratives, and prayers passed down by grandmothers. Orlando Espín discusses this wisdom and truth in terms of the doctrine on the *sensus fidelium* in chapter 4 of this collection. He and Sixto García theologically reflect on popular wisdom and sayings especially cultivated by women in Hispanic cultures in their presentation at the 1989 meeting of the Catholic Theological Society of America entitled " 'Lilies of the Field': A Hispanic Theology of Providence and Human Responsibility."[10]

Within this oral tradition it is common to hear stories about women in their role as midwives. As such they are often called upon to baptize infants who are born sick. Similarly, women are the ones who accompany the sick in the last stages of death and dying. These women pray, anoint the dying, and share the Word of hope with them and those who grieve the passing of their beloved. In many places in Latin America women traditionally have assumed the role of *rezadoras* or *oradoras*. In places where the priest has historically been absent, especially in small towns and rural areas, there are certain women prepared to perform the rites associated with Christian burial. Both mother and father are expected literally "to give blessings," much like those given by priest and bishop, but it is the grandmother's blessing that is most prized in the Hispanic family. Hence Hispanic women in a multitude of ways are acknowledged as official prayer leaders. Here one finds a fertile field for reflection on the people's sense of ministry, their popular theology of ministry. Women unquestionably figure prominently in the phenomenon of ministry.

Oral traditions enshrined in stories and narratives abound in Hispanic culture. The stories of immigrants newly arrived in *el norte* speak of the hardships of women. They continue to live and endure the passion of Jesus, as these words taken in an interview with a Salvadoran refugee attest:

> Survival has been difficult. I have no legal documents, and I don't know the language. My family here hasn't given me the moral support I need. We work where we can find work. We try to give a decent life to our children. The new immigration laws of the United States make it almost impossible for us to be employed. I want to return to my country, but when there is peace and justice for all.[11]

A Hispanic women's theology, then, needs to consider these and many other sources for exploring the experiences of women. On the phenomenological and practical level as distinct from the theoretical, Hispanic women have had a decisive role to play in the religious life of their people. They are the real teachers of values and evangelizers of the people. They exercise a basic kind of leadership that often goes unrecognized. Yet that role, as depicted in social science studies and popular literary and oral traditions, has generally been ignored by theology. The words *pasionaria* and *pastora* as used in Spanish point to this primordial call and ministry of Hispanic women.

Following from this discussion about Latina women as religious leaders is the question about the image of women in general in Hispanic cultures. That image is undoubtedly complex and has tradionally been codified in powerful stories and symbols. Two examples readily come to mind: La Malinche and Our Lady of Guadalupe.

La Malinche is the name of Hernán Cortez's Indian mistress, also known as Doña Marina. She bore him some sons and thus became a prototype of the mestizo people of Mexico. Feelings toward her are ambiguous: she collaborated with the *conquistador*, but she *is* our mother. Associated with La Malinche is the legend of *La Llorona*, the "Weeping Woman," who is condemned to forever look for her children whom she murdered in a rage against the father of her children. He, being Spanish and of a higher social class, did not marry her.[12] There is obviously a darkness and ambiguity in this disturbing story. Can theology shed any light on what this powerful legend attempts to express?

In contrast to the image of the woman in the story of *La Llorona* is the Guadalupan event. More and more is being written about this vastly influential image and story. Here the woman is experienced as an intermediary of God and as the prophetic figure of the mestizo race. She is one of them and even speaks to the Indian Juan Diego in the Aztec language, not in the Spanish of the conquerors.[13]

Through the images of these two women, La Malinche (*La Llorona*) and Guadalupe, one tragic and the other thoroughly redemptive, Hispanics come to confront more than historical and anthropological realities. They speak of psychological, spiritual, and theological realities. In a U.S. Hispanic feminist theology, as well as in any Hispanic theology, these images and others like them found in the various Hispanic cultures need to be further examined. Where is God's Word present in this darkness and light, and in the salvation history of the Hispanic peoples?

In looking into the darkness I am not suggesting a fatalistic approach for the elaboration of a theology and spirituality for Hispanics. Rather, it is an invitation for Hispanics to really look into the darkness of *mestizaje*, the violence of the process of miscegenation characteristic of their life experiences. Through this darkness perhaps they can come to the light and the grace offered by the contrasting image of Mary of Guadalupe.

What is at stake here is not only what happened five hundred years ago, but also what is happening today: ongoing experiences of discrimination and domination. The darkness can continue to assert itself in the form of excluding the Word of God and its peace from one's heart. It shows itself in letting the darkness take over as *La Llorona* does in her murderous rage.

The darkness reveals itself in allowing oneself to become spiritually powerless or dead. Emblematic of this condition is the refusal to weep when it is time to do so, to feel and to have compassion when it is right to do so. Hispanic women can live through this darkness which the culture has tried to symbolize in these disturbing legends. In darkness and dryness, in the clash of values and struggles, Latina women have confronted so many intractable problems. They turn and transform the fatalistic image of La Malinche into new life.

In a Hispanic feminist theology the dialogue between the life experience of women and God's Word continues in a dynamic, dialectical exchange. One side of this dialogue is represented by the realities of women as portrayed in approaches offered by social science—surveys, questionnaires, collection of data, intepretation. This side is enhanced by popular oral traditions and the growing Latina women's literature. The myths and symbols that arise in the long history of the Hispanic cultures are expressive of the other side of this exchange: the Word, God's presence, in the very complexity, in the darkness and light, the pathos, of the culture. These images become a lens for returning to the realities in an effort to discover their deeper meaning.

In this task God's Word specifically in the sacred scriptures and especially in the gospel cannot be ignored. For example, the Gospels of Luke and John have much to offer a Hispanic feminist theology. The figures of Mary, Mary Magdalene, and the Samaritan woman have so much to offer when confronted with the realities of Hispanic women today. In the elaboration of a Hispanic feminist theology, however, there is need to stress the validity of using the cultural symbols themselves, those associated especially with women, in deciphering and discerning the theological meaning of Hispanic women's experiences.

### The Final Task: Moving Back to Praxis

The last stage in the process of elaborating a Hispanic feminist theology involves returning to pastoral praxis. The sharing among the women that often has taken place in gathering the data, the consequent analyses, the darkness and light, the spiritually powerful symbols are means by which the Spirit moves toward a transforming and creative praxis. Women committed to the gospel begin to consciously take responsibility for ministry. This is seen in various efforts to build basic ecclesial communities and small groups of women, as well as in the task of elaborating a common pastoral plan. This occurs at many levels of the church and society. For Hispanics it has occurred in the vast pastoral planning process called the Third National Hispanic Pastoral Encuentro, which resulted in the National Pastoral Plan for Hispanic Ministry.[14]

Taking these developments seriously and viewing them in the light of the information gathered in the survey and in the discussion of Latina women's literature and cultural symbols, it is possible to suggest some concrete, practical directions for a U.S. Hispanic feminist theology. What follows are areas of concern for effective pastoral planning focused on Hispanic women.

The first area of practical concern has to do with the historic role of women as promoters of Hispanic spirituality. There is a danger that this positive role will be increasingly eroded by North American secularization. The creative pastoral leadership of women, a basic, long-standing feature of Hispanic cultures, will be enhanced by somehow preserving the spirituality of women. That spirituality is fed by the cultivation of times for reflection and prayer. Together with that there must be time for research and for appropriate pastoral action. Prayer is not only the activity of women. Men too must come to see it as their need and opportunity as well. But the image of the women as *rezadora* speaks to us of the past but also of the future, of a role that women must not abandon in the process of becoming contemporary. The women of the community who were *pasionarias* and *pastoras* were, above all, women of prayer.

A second area of practical concern is the phenomenon of the basic ecclesial communities in which women may find an arena for action that is unfortunately denied them in other institutional settings. The dissatisfaction of the women in the survey discussed above revealed the need for church structures more inclusive of women and their talents. Women need to be encouraged to assume roles of leadership in these emergent communities. Here the women enjoy a more deeply communal experience of church and of their leadership potential. They find an arena for creativity in forming communities that move them beyond the limits of "serving" others, often the men, in the work that traditionally is reserved for women. In the basic ecclesial communities they often find a context for the development of their giftedness as leaders of prayer and worship, something historically denied them in the official church but cultivated in endless ways in popular Hispanic culture.

A third practical concern ought to be rather obvious: the need to cultivate Hispanic women theologians. In the United States there is only a handful of Latina theologians.[15] This is an intolerable situation for the U.S. Catholic Church, which by the year 2000 or shortly thereafter will be 50 percent Hispanic. Currently there is very little research and writing on Christian faith from a Hispanic woman's perspective. One of the hopeful signs is the participation of women in the Academy of Catholic Hispanic Theologians of the United States and their growing contributions to this theology. In addition, the voice of Latina women is fundamental for the future growth of North American feminist theology which has seldom entered into dialogue with U.S. Latinas.

The issue of Hispanic women's participation in the theological enterprise is crucial with regard to the development of effective ministry within the growing Hispanic communities. Just as women are moving beyond the passivity that characterized their role in *official* church contexts, so too they are actively entering into the reflection taking place regarding the impact of faith on life and society. There is a great need for lay women to write about their understanding of faith and its exigencies in their situations. Women have something to say, for instance, with regard to family-life issues, a topic of special concern to Hispanics given the intense family orientation of their culture. Theological insights focused on Hispanic family issues are in great demand, but there is little to point to yet.

A realistic application of theological reflection upon the situation of U.S. Hispanics requires that close attention be paid to social and political issues. The faith and spirituality of Hispanic women lead to discernment and a corresponding guidance of the Holy Spirit. These, in turn, result in compassionate and prophetic praxis. Jesus' mission of justice and compassion can be lived out and exemplified in the committed service of Hispanic women. This is being modeled throughout the U.S. church every day. Pilar Aquino in her contribution to this collection (chapter 2) mentions the essential if often unacclaimed role of women in pastoral and social ministries throughout the country. Hispanic ministry respects the achievement of women, given their influential and decisive roles at many levels of parish, movement, school, and diocese.

## CONCLUSION

The evocative terms *pasionaria* and *pastora* used in reference to Hispanic women of faith have served to point out the reality of these women in the context of the U.S. Catholic Church. A Hispanic feminist theology finds in these terms and the rich experiences behind them an apt place to begin shaping a theology of and for these women. The theology being shaped is eminently pastoral in orientation and spirit. It issues in praxis and gives great importance to effective pastoral planning.

Ivone Gebara, a leading Latin American theologian, has captured one of the key components of this emergent women's theology:

The theological work of women reflects an ability to view life as the locus of the simultaneous experience of oppression and liberation, of grace and lack of grace. Such a perception encompasses what is plural, what is different, what is other. Although this way of looking at things is not the exclusive property of women, we must say that it is found to an extraordinary extent among women. In popular struggles, in which women have played a very important role, this ability to grasp in a more unified way the oppositions and contradictions, the contrasts and the differences is seen as a way in which women live and express their faith. Such behavior enables them to avoid taking dogmatic and exclusive stances, and to perceive and intuit the real complexity of what is human.[16]

U.S. Hispanic women must follow the lead of their Latin American sisters in pursuing this kind of theological reflection. The diverse and highly pluralistic North American environment requires precisely the "woman's presence" Gebara so fittingly describes. A Hispanic feminist theology that arises from the experience of yesterday's and today's Hispanic women of faith, the *pasionaria* and *pastora*, promises to be just such a theology.

## NOTES

1. Luis Valdez, "Tribute to Dolores Huerta," *San Francisco Examiner*, pp. 9–11 of *Image Magazine*, August 12, 1990.

2. Mariano de la Cadena Velázquez, *New Revised Velázquez Spanish and English Dictionary* (New Jersey: New Century Publishers, 1985), p. 501.

3. Clodovis Boff, *Feet-on-the-Ground Theology* (Maryknoll, N.Y.: Orbis Books, 1987).

4. Ada María Isasi Díaz and Yolanda Tarango, *Hispanic Women, Prophetic Voice in the Church* (San Francisco: Harper and Row, 1988).

5. This study was part of my doctoral dissertation at the pontifical university of Salamanca. The entire work, still in process of completion, is entitled *The Presence of Hispanic Women in the Theology of Hispanics: A Significant Reality in the U.S. Church.*

6. Even though umbrella terms like "Hispanic" or "Latino" are widely used in the media, the people often prefer to use more specific terms, such as Mexican-American, Cuban, Puerto Rican, etc. Roberto O. González and Michael La Velle discovered this in doing their survey, *The Hispanic Catholic in the United States* (New York: Northeast Catholic Pastoral Center for Hispanics, 1985), p. 7.

7. Two current Hispanic women writers who capture the passion and the spirit of women are Sandra Cisneros, *The House on Mango Street* (Houston: Arte Press, 1988) and Luz del Castillo, *Palabras Chicanas: An Undergraduate Anthology* (Berkeley: University of California Press, 1988).

8. Rudolfo A. Anaya, *Bless Me, Ultima* (Berkeley: Quinto Sol Publications, 1972), p. 4.

9. Sandra Cisneros, *The House on Mango Street.*

10. Orlando Espín and Sixto García, *Proceedings of the Forty-Fourth Annual Convention*, CTSA, vol. 44, pp. 70–90.

11. Interview taken for Gloria Loya's doctoral dissertation with Salvadoran women in San Francisco in 1988.

12. John O. West provides the background to this legend and its variants in *Mexican American Folklore* (Little Rock: August House, 1988), pp. 75–76.

13. Virgilio Elizondo provides a useful overview of the Guadalupe story in *La Morenita: Evangelizer of the Americas* (San Antonio: MACC, 1980).

14. See *The National Pastoral Plan for Hispanic Ministry* (Washington, D.C.: USCC, 1988).

15. See the *Directory* of the Academy of Catholic Hispanic Theologians of the United States for 1990 for numbers of Latinas with doctorates in theology or in doctoral studies.

16. Ivone Gebara, "Women Doing Theology in Latin America," in Elsa Tamez, ed., *Through Her Eyes: Women's Theology from Latin America* (Maryknoll, N.Y.: Orbis, 1989), p. 46.

*Chapter Eight*

# Prayer, Worship, and Liturgy in a United States Hispanic Key

## *ROSA MARÍA ICAZA, C.C.V.I.*

The focus of this study is prayer, worship, and liturgy within the context of the Hispanic communities of the United States. An adequate treatment of this subject requires that careful attention be given to the church's tradition in these matters and to the way in which the Roman rite developed. If we do not know the historical forms and spirit of the liturgical tradition we have received, it is impossible to share it with others or help others understand or appreciate it. In addition to knowing the history of the Roman rite that Hispanics have inherited from their Spanish evangelizers of centuries ago, I also want to stress the importance of the liturgical norms developed by the church since the Second Vatican Council. Bishop Ricardo Ramírez has pointed out that liturgy is the heart of Vatican II's spirituality.[1] That council and the liturgical reform it unleashed continues to be a source for direction and light in the matters to be discussed here. The Vatican II *Constitution on the Sacred Liturgy* is certainly the place to start, but there are many other documents on the adaptation or inculturation of the liturgy that ought to be reviewed before attempting to discuss these issues from a Hispanic perspective.[2]

In the interest of brevity, however, I have decided to go directly to the topic at hand, taking for granted the reader's familiarity with the background I believe to be so essential.

### LINKING LITURGY AND THE EVANGELIZATION OF CULTURE

From the time of the first Spanish missionaries in the Americas, the Hispanic communities have developed many meaningful expressions of faith which harmonize very closely with liturgical feasts and the liturgical year. Who could imagine, for example, the celebration of a *posada* outside the Advent season? Or the simple celebration of the *pésame* or condolences offered to Mary outside Good Friday? The first missionaries found it impossible to communicate verbally with the indigenous people of the American continent, where more than three hundred different languages were spoken. Therefore they had recourse to a well-recognized pedagogical tool: "not only hear, but see and act the truth that must be learned and lived." And following the Western tradition of "mystery plays," they encouraged representations of the mysteries celebrated in the liturgy with active participation of many of the faithful. The end result of this was an effective linking of liturgy with the indigenous cultures.

According to his pastoral letter *Evangelii Nuntiandi*, Paul VI clearly saw these expressions of faith as vehicles for true evangelization;[3] so today in the post–Vatican II era Hispanic pastoral agents are looking into all these practices which have been kept alive by the people. They study them to see how they are rooted in scripture, in tradition, and in the liturgical spirit and use them to make liturgical celebrations alive and relevant to Hispanic communities.

Virgil Elizondo among several other theologians and liturgists maintains that various human families or nations have taken their traditional expressions of faith as part of their cultural identity and have adapted them to their new situations and surroundings.[4] The bishops of the United States express this idea in the *National Pastoral Plan for Hispanic Ministry* when they say: "Culture for Hispanic Catholics has become a way of living out and transmitting our faith. Many local practices of popular religiosity have become widely accepted cultural expressions."[5] Different groups of Hispanics use certain practices more widely than other groups of Hispanics, sometimes influencing one another (like the Mexican custom of celebrating the *quinceañera* now being celebrated by the Puerto Ricans), other times changing them according to their surroundings (for example, the way *luminarias* are fashioned with plastic containers instead of paper bags).

As Edward Kilmartin states: "Christian communities ... draw on elements of the surrounding culture in a selective way, fashioning a new synthesis in which different meaning is given to the symbolic material ... which then becomes a medium of divine epiphany."[6] This accounts for the fact that Hispanic liturgical celebrations in the United States are quite different from those of non-Hispanic communities in this country, and different from those in other Hispanic countries. In Latin American countries they use these ways of celebrating perhaps more freely, because they do not see such practices as part of their identity as a people as consciously as Hispanics living "in exile" from the homeland.

In speaking of liturgy among Hispanics it is important to look deeply into the values of those communities and into their popular expressions of faith.[7] The planning of a liturgical celebration should include Spanish language, art, and environment, music, certain gestures. These would give to it a certain Hispanic flavor, yet the inculturation may still remain on the superficial level. It is important to consider how this particular people relate to God and the sacred, how they pray, and what they consider as an expression of faith. Actions, gestures, and symbols must facilitate this attitude of prayer and participation in the paschal mystery.

## HISPANIC SPIRITUALITY AND VALUES

Hispanic peoples seem to relate to God quite differently from non-Hispanics. Their relationship with the sacred, their *spirituality*, is partly divine and partly human. For them, God is all-powerful, all-seeking, all-just, and very superior to all human beings. God is respected and feared. However, this same God is close to them as part of a family, since God is a loving father and they speak to God in the familiar *tu*. God's beauty is reflected in nature; and God's care and compassion are reflected in the kindness of other human beings. Jesus, the incarnate Word, is truly divine and truly human; for example, he is weak as a baby, feels cold; as an adult, he suffers, welcomes gratitude, enjoys friends, and is in need of company and understanding. The paschal mystery of the passion, death and resurrection of the Lord has been experienced by a true man, a human being like us. Therefore, the spirituality of Hispanics is truly incarnated and their way of praying and relating to God, to Jesus, to Mary, and the saints is a human relationship full of love, compassion, dependence (almost interdependence),[8] and intimacy. This type of relationship calls for a different way of relating to God, praying and celebrating than when God is thought of as "high in heaven," distant, or in more abstract, spiritualized, or unimaginative ways as is sometimes the case among mainstream U.S. Catholics. The God of sophisticated, middle-class people can come across as indifferent toward human needs and joys. The Hispanic perception of God is rich, dramatic, graphic, and populated with images associated with the Trinity, Jesus himself, Mary, and of course the saints.

Together with this spirituality, Hispanics have inherited particular *values* that live in them and guide many of their actions and decisions. These values are naturally going to manifest themselves in prayer and worship: a drive toward the integration of faith and life, the importance of family and community above individuals, the sacredness of ancestral traditions, a depth of symbolic expression, personal relationships before material goods, special devotion to the Virgin Mary, hope and strength in the search for happiness, an appreciation of the beauty of nature, a reverence for the dead, and a desire to belong to and celebrate life.

How do liturgical celebrations foster or hinder these values which are lived or desired by Hispanics? They form an integral part of the fabric of being Hispanic. How are they expressed and how do they characterize liturgical celebrations? As Christians we are called to worship God with all our being. A gesture, a movement, a symbol may be present but devoid of feeling. It is necessary to know the mystery of faith being celebrated and then to express it with gestures, symbols, objects, actions, and movements that convey those truths more clearly and meaningfully to the celebrating community. The following paragraphs specify the nature of the Hispanic values and give some ideas for achieving meaningful and clear liturgical celebrations in the U.S. Hispanic contexts. Examples are given from the Mexican and Mexican-American experience. Similar experiences, however, must be sought from the experiences of other Hispanic communities.

## 1. The Integration of Faith and Life

The liturgical celebration is not truly a celebration of the paschal mystery, if it does not *reflect* and *influence* the life of the community. Participants bring themselves with all their joys, concerns, and sufferings to the celebration of the liturgy, and then leave the liturgical celebration with renewed spirit to continue their lives as followers of Christ. A homily will be meaningful particularly to Hispanics if it relates scriptural readings to the realities and situations of the communities, if it helps the participants to continue in their daily life the truths of faith that they have celebrated in the liturgy. The middle-class, highly professionalized context of mainstream U.S. Catholicism cannot therefore be the norm for discussing the Hispanic world realistically.

## 2. The Importance of Family and Community

In the renewal of the liturgy, the importance of community in all liturgical celebrations is clearly stated. Hispanics, almost naturally, include everyone in all their celebrations. Holding hands at the Lord's prayer, seating the family members together during the celebration, being invited to the celebration of the sacraments, and being called to be *padrinos* are ways of helping Hispanics to worship as a community.

## 3. The Sacredness of Ancestral Traditions

Tradition is part of the Catholic faith, and for many centuries commemorations and rituals have been an integral part of liturgical celebrations. Among Hispanics when an anniversary is celebrated, when small souvenirs are blessed and shared at celebrations of the sacraments, when particular traditional symbols are used in liturgical celebrations, such as the *lazo* and *arras* at weddings and blessed bread and candles on Holy Thursday, respect and honor is given to ancestral traditions. Some small object could be used appropriately at some liturgies to help keep the memory of such celebrations as a reminder at home either of the challenge received through the Word of God or of the commitment made to live as true worshipers of God.

## 4. The Depth of Symbolic Expression

The use of symbols is inherent in all and every liturgical celebration. Hispanics enjoy and understand the use of symbols; therefore, symbols should be used in abundance in the liturgy in a way that they can easily be seen by all present. Blessed *water* is used in the penitential rite at the beginning of the eucharist, baptismal water at baptism not only by immersion but also when water is poured on the head of the baptized, Easter water blessed on Holy Saturday and taken home, holy water when blessing persons and objects. *Light* is used at baptism and at first holy communions, on Holy Saturday, at the funeral vigil and liturgy, before the blessed sacrament on Holy Thursday at the altar of repose. *Oil* is used at baptism and confirmation, and in the anointing of the sick. The *banquet*, mentioned so often in the Bible, is used in the eucharistic liturgy.

## 5. Personal Relationships above Material Goods

The mere gathering of all the faithful to worship God in a liturgical celebration is today one of the greatest symbols of the church; in fact, Vatican II calls this assembly an epiphany of the church, "the preeminent manifestation of the Church."[9] It is difficult to go from the very passive role which the laity had before Vatican II to the active and participatory stance to which all Christians are called today. Hispanics, as many other persons, found this change quite difficult; but once it is experienced, the personal involvement is very meaningful. If given the opportunity, Hispanics like to take an active part as members of the assembly: responding, singing, walking in procession, carrying candles, and so forth. Sharing of roles during a liturgical celebration helps the faithful to take an active part, not only as members of the assembly (which is already a liturgical ministry), but also performing a particular ministry for the community. Naturally there is fear at the beginning of doing something as an individual person, but later there is great pride in being able to participate in this way.

Due to their baroque heritage, Hispanics enjoy seeing rich objects around the church and on the altar, thinking that "God deserves the very best." However, if in a liturgical celebration a personal approach and attitude prevail, Hispanics seem to respond readily and with greater depth—for example, if the communion minister mentions the name of the person who approaches to receive the sacrament. At the prayer of the faithful, Hispanics share more frequently their intentions for friends and relatives. They reveal also their personal relationship and identification with the saints, as they honor particularly those who have been rejected (St. Martin de Porres), who love nature and are poor (St. Francis of Assisi), who are invoked to find lost things (St. Anthony), or are reputed to remedy impossible situations (St. Jude).

## 6. Special Place for Mary in Life and in Prayer

The role that Mary has played in the history of the Mexican and Mexican-American people has been unique. In Our Lady of Guadalupe the indigenous people were able to find a person and a symbol with whom they could identify. She helped the missionaries in their work of evangelization by speaking in Nahuatl, by using indigenous attire and symbols, by calling Juan Diego by name, and sending him with her message of hope and love. Mary has accompanied Hispanics in many of their difficult moments. She is revered as the mother of Jesus and our mother. She always understands, she efficaciously intercedes, she lovingly consoles, and gently leads to Jesus.

In liturgical spaces and celebrations, Mary holds a special place for Hispanics. They have responded to her special care and concern with great joy and gratitude. Her feasts are truly moments of transcendence and deep joy. To even good Catholics, the place that Mary holds in the hearts of Hispanics seems exaggerated; yet *Lumen Gentium*[10] clearly points out the preeminent role Mary has in the economy of salvation and in the church. In the liturgical calendar, Mary has a very important place during the Christmas cycle, particularly in Advent, and in "the remembrance of events of salvation in which the Blessed Virgin is closely associated with her Son."[11] Hispanics celebrate with great enthusiasm, love, and joy the Marian liturgical and nonliturgical feasts.

## 7. Hope and Strength in Search for Happiness

During all life's difficulties and sufferings, Hispanics seem to show special endurance strengthened by hope for a better life. The idea of being a pilgrim people is realistically lived by many immigrant and migrant Hispanics. Their constant moving is inspired by the desire of having a better life, particularly for their children. The Catholic idea that heaven is our eternal and definitive "home" is deeply rooted in Hispanic hearts; they consider this world as a place where we live for a while on the way to heaven. Therefore, participation in processions during liturgical celebrations, particularly on Passion Sunday with the blessed palms, on Holy Thursday with the blessed sacrament, on Good Friday with Jesus on the way to the cross and to his burial, at the Easter vigil with Jesus as the light of the world, is very important for Hispanics.

This same idea inspires them to participate in pilgrimages and in other celebrations related to liturgical seasons and feasts as during the *posadas*, mentioned above, and in certain Marian feasts, particularly in the month of May where there is a procession after each mystery of the rosary to offer flowers, incense, candles. A good entrance procession at a eucharistic celebration is gladly joined in by Hispanics, for they find such symbolic movement very meaningful in their daily life.

## 8. Appreciation for the Beauty of Nature and for the Five Senses

Speaking on liturgical art and environment, the bishops of the United States state: "Flowers, plants and trees—genuine, of course—are particularly apt for the decoration of liturgical space, since they are of nature."[12] For Hispanics, flowers in particular have a very deep meaning as one of the best vehicles to express the truth, and to find the way to God, the giver of life. At liturgical celebrations particular flowers have a special meaning— for example, roses for the feast of Our Lady of Guadalupe, *cempasúchil* (a kind of yellow carnation) for All Souls' Day, *azahares* (orange blossoms) for weddings. Objects that can be appreciated by the senses can be a good way of expressing truths of faith in a liturgical celebration, such as incense, light, sound effects (besides music and song). Even the opportunity to kiss or touch an object (as the statue of the baby Jesus at Christmastime or the cross on Good Friday) are tangible ways to express faith and are meaningful manifestations of reverence and love.

## 9. Reverence for the Dead

From very ancient times in both the Jewish and Christian traditions, as well as in various indigenous cultures that have been christianized, it is important to honor and remember the dead. The church includes this "memory" within the eucharistic prayer itself and celebrates with special care for the faithful departed on November 2. Among Mexicans and Mexican-Americans, the members and friends of the family who have died continue alive in the memories that are kept and shared among the living.

There is a firm belief in the communion of saints and the celebration of All Souls' Day, which in Spanish is called the day of the dead, *el Día de los Muertos*. Particularly for Hispanics, it is an occasion to express publicly the many ways the dead are remembered as human beings (who need food) and as having arrived at the end of their earthly pilgrimage. Not only during the burial vigil (and rosary) but also through the whole wake before the funeral liturgy, it is important to accompany the dead person and the bereaved. It is important to use the name of the deceased person(s) at the "memento" of the dead in the eucharistic liturgy not only on the occasion of the funeral but also in the *novenario* (masses celebrated for nine days after the funeral) and in anniversary masses. Works of mercy are for Hispanics expressions of faith, so at funerals the *puño de tierra* (handful of dirt) is placed on the coffin by the next of kin as a remembrance that it is a work of mercy to "bury the dead."

## 10. Desire to Belong (Affiliate) and to Celebrate Life

A very important aspect of life is a sense of belonging; one must belong to a group in a genuine way and as far as possible from within, by a genuine involvement in its life. In the *National Pastoral Plan for Hispanic Ministry*, the bishops of the United States recognize this desire to belong to the church, a desire to participate, to be called on, to be involved, to be integrated into the different structures.[13] Due to past experiences, many Hispanics are hesitant to come forward offering their personal and community talents; however, when called and supported, they find great affirmation and offer their help with great generosity. One of the most popular practices among Mexican-Americans is the celebration of the *quinceañera* mentioned above. This event almost always includes the eucharistic liturgy in a spirit of thanksgiving for the life of the young girl and for the life she may nurture as a mother. Among U.S. Hispanics, this celebration has acquired greater dimensions and deeper meaning than in Mexico itself. It has become a teachable moment; it is seen as an integral part of the Mexican-American identity. A traditional ritual with great flexibility, the *quinceañera* gives great importance to the mass as the best act of thanksgiving to God.

## MEXICAN-AMERICAN EXPRESSIONS OF FAITH IN LITURGICAL CELEBRATIONS

As is obvious from the above paragraphs, liturgy celebrates the truths of faith within the context of the participating community in order to be meaningful and genuine. What is celebrated in the liturgy remains constant; herein lies the unity and depth of the celebration. How the liturgy is celebrated is open to pluralistic expressions according to the culture and genius of the celebrating assembly, keeping in mind the Catholic (universal) norms for a public, communal, and official Catholic celebration by the total Christ. It is important to remember that after Vatican II, liturgy returned to the people of God and to the theology of the local church. Consequently its function as sacrament of the universal church has become clearer. As D.S. Amalorpavadass states in his book *Towards Indigenisation in the Liturgy*:

Unless each Christian community becomes and is aware of being the local Church and is enabled to accept its full responsibility, the liturgy will neither be relevant to life nor transform it.[14]

In parishes and dioceses where the presence of Hispanics is numerous, some pastoral ministers have encouraged certain Hispanic cultural expressions of faith that enhance the meaning of the liturgical celebrations. This fact helps the community participate with greater joy and understanding. Often, non-Hispanics participating in liturgies "in a U.S. Hispanic key"[15] will comment, "This was a CELEBRATION! There was a palpable joy; the music was beautiful and everyone sang. Here was a real, praying community." What causes the liturgy to be experienced thus? Perhaps it is precisely the fact that the way it is celebrated finds an echo in the life, culture, and identity of the participants, so they can enter into it with mind and heart, soul and body.

Let us see how the different ways of celebrating the Christmas cycle (a liturgical season) foster and affirm Mexican-American values in accord with the directives given in *Lumen Gentium* and *Sacrosanctum Concilium*.[16] These values and customs have been inherited from diverse roots and identify Mexican-Americans as a group, as a people, a people of God.

### Advent

This is a time of preparation for a new coming, a new birth, in our personal and community lives. It is a time of waiting, of expectation, of accompanying the expectant mother and to plan the celebration of a new birth.

> Advent has a twofold character: as a season to prepare for Christmas when Christ's first coming to us is remembered; as a season when that remembrance directs the mind and heart to await Christ's second coming at the end of time. Advent is thus a period for devout and joyful expectation.[17]

Liturgically it begins four Sundays before December 24, which usually falls at the beginning of December.[18] In most parishes and in some homes (including Hispanic homes) in the United States, there is the ritual of the Advent wreath to commemorate the four Sundays of Advent.

On December 3rd, which in some years coincides with the first Sunday of Advent, the novena in preparation for the feast of Our Lady of Guadalupe begins in Mexican-American communities. Since the picture Mary left at Tepeyac represents that of a pregnant mother,[19] the preparation for this Marian feast is particularly fitting for Advent: we accompany the mother as she gets ready to receive her baby. Hispanic spirituality places strong emphasis on the humanity of Jesus, especially when he appears weak and suffering as in the crib.[20]

The liturgical feast of Our Lady of Guadalupe (December 12) is particularly joyful for Mexicans and Mexican-Americans. Her image is the symbol of liberation, understanding, and identity.[21] She is a mestiza (a descendant of the indigenous and the European) as is revealed by the color of her face and hands. She is dressed like an indigenous princess and incarnates the Good News of Christianity in every detail of the painting and of the dialogue with blessed Juan Diego.[22] She announces the birth of Christ in the American continent, since the flower on her womb is the Aztec symbol for a new life, a new era.[23] This picture is likewise described in the Book of Revelation 12:1–2:

And a great sign appeared in heaven: a woman clothed with the sun, and the moon was under her feet, and upon her head a crown of twelve stars. And being with child . . .

The celebration includes: flowers (roses, if possible), the singing of the *mananitas*, processions (sometimes pilgrimages), going all together into the church (temple) and participating in a eucharistic liturgy.

In Mexico it is customary for indigenous people to dance long hours outside the church as an expression of their joy and prayer. In the United States the late Archbishop Francis J. Furey invited the dancers to enter into the church when he heard their dance was their form of praying. Since then, beautiful *danzas* are used within some Sunday and feastday eucharistic liturgies to express the joy of the Gloria, or as a prayer after communion, or as a graceful way of having a procession either bringing the book of the Gospels to the table of the Word or setting the table with cloth, candles, bread, and wine for the eucharistic prayer. In many parishes, the dancers are children. Parents are proud to see their little ones participating and they themselves come to witness their prayer and to join them and other members in the parish for the celebration of the liturgy, singing and praying as a grateful, joyful community. It is truly a festive act of thanksgiving to the father for life ("resurrection") granted to his people through Jesus who came to us through Mary, not only at Bethlehem but also at Tepeyac! This celebration cannot be complete without partaking not only in the eucharistic banquet but also at a simple community table, sharing food carefully prepared and eaten among brothers and sisters honoring their mother.[24]

The Advent liturgy reaches its culmination with the "great O antiphons" for the Magnificat at the liturgy of the hours and for the Alleluia before the Gospel in Advent eucharistic liturgies from December 17 to December 23. Different titles of the incarnate Word are invoked: wisdom of the Most High, shepherd of Israel, flower of Jesse's stem, key of David, radiant dawn, king of all nations, Emmanuel.

In the Mexican-American liturgical calendar, the most intensive days of Advent are from December 16 to December 24—that is, the nine days before Christmas. This novena is celebrated by *Las Posadas* (the inns) accompanying Mary and Joseph in their journey from Nazareth to Bethlehem. According to sacred scripture,[25] there was no room for them in the inn (*la posada*). So, for the Christmas novena the community visits several homes (three to five) where hospitality is denied, thus experiencing rejection and endurance with hope in the journey very similar to their life situation. Finally, there is a home prepared to receive the pilgrims by placing *luminarias* on the road leading to the door, and by rejoicing with the community and with the family privileged to give this hospitality. The entire community participates in the procession with candles, in singing and praying. Everyone is welcome into the final home and together they all enjoy some hot beverage and snacks. There will be the symbolic game of the *piñata*[26] for the children, *colación* (candy, nuts, and fruits) and, perhaps, a dance for adolescents and adults. Prayer and life are symbolically and realistically linked with one another in the liturgical season of preparation for the coming of the Lord.[27]

Continuing the traditions of many centuries in the Catholic Church, Hispanics prepare for the celebration of Christmas in their homes by building a nativity scene, and by decorating the Christmas tree and the house with poinsettias,[28] keeping the domestic church alive and joyful in this liturgical season. But on Christmas eve, Mexican and Mexican-Americans have a ritual for placing the statue of the baby Jesus in the crib. It is called *la acostada del niño*. As mentioned above, faith and life are so closely knit together that one is carried to the other in many ways; therefore many expressions of faith, such as the *acostada del niño*, are taken from real life. A baby is not simply placed in the crib and left there; it is necessary to sing lullabies, to fondle him or her, to rock him or her in loving arms, to tell him or her in many different ways how much he or she is loved so that the baby falls asleep. Only then is he or she placed in the crib. The same things are done with the statue of the baby Jesus, not to the statue, but symbolically to whom it represents. Each member of the family takes turns. It is a concrete and dramatic way of teaching children and of deepening the faith which is celebrated in the liturgy.

In church the entrance procession before midnight Mass is of special meaning for Hispanics, particularly if some of them are called to be the *padrinos*,[29] "godparents" of the baby Jesus for a particular year. These persons may be the ones who prepared the crib or the altar in church, or the ones who contributed in some way to the Christmas celebrations. Again, this is a way of belonging, of giving/receiving personal recognition, of taking active part in the ceremony. Values are affirmed and encouraged to be practiced in daily life within human relationships.

### Christmas

Midnight mass and Christmas day eucharistic liturgies are for Hispanics, as for all Catholics, beautiful celebrations of joy, hope, and love. Family dinner, however, is also quite important. And living in the United States, Hispanics also exchange gifts at this time, perhaps missing the true meaning of this symbolic action. Formerly in Mexico, gifts were given prior to Christmas to those persons who had rendered a service to the family or who had less than the giver, in order that these other families could also have something to share in order to celebrate in their own homes the greatest gift of all, the father's gift of his son Jesus, born for us at Bethlehem.[30]

The octave of Christmas in particular, but it could also extend to the whole Christmas season, is the time to enjoy the *pastorelas*, Christmas plays. In some places within the United States, these plays are very traditional and the actors are adults who have kept this custom in their own families, but perform the plays for the good of the entire community. As scripture tells us, God was first manifested to the marginated, the outcasts of that time — that is, the shepherds.[31] This is symbolically represented by the clothes they wear, which have been discarded by others. The obstacles and temptations we find in life as we try to follow are playfully represented by "devils" telling the shepherds it is late, cold, and difficult. Also this drama helps to illustrate the joy in finding a new family in the neighborhood. Hispanics as well as other groups are to be reminded of the need to welcome others in our church and in our midst.

Other playful, prayerful, and joyful celebrations continue the spirit of the Christmas season among Hispanics, such as Holy Innocents' Day (December 28), playfully making others believe impossible or unreal things (like April Fool's day). The last day of the civic year (December 31) is for prayerfully thanking God as a family for all the graces received in the year that ends and asking God's blessings in the new year. A big family dinner (January 1) is to celebrate joyfully the life given by God to continue in the new year.[32]

## Epiphany

Once more another passage of scripture,[33] another important liturgical feast, is relived and celebrated not only in church, but at home. Children, particularly in urban areas, are taught to be mindful of the animals, for the Magi may find food and lodging on their way to Bethlehem, while their animals may not have anything to eat. Children place straw and water by the window; the Magi find this nourishment for their beasts of burden, take it, and in its place share with the thoughtful children some of the presents they were taking to baby Jesus. Once again, life and faith are united and the truths of faith and the works of mercy (give food to the hungry, even hungry animals) are passed on in a simple but meaningful way from one generation to another.

As in other feasts, some special food could not be lacking with a particular religious, liturgical, overtone: the *rosca de reyes* is a wreath of bread decorated with Christmas colors and hiding either one or three small objects.[34] When this bread is divided, whoever gets one of those objects must help to give a celebration to close the Christmas season. Formerly, this party was held on February 2,[35] but after Vatican II it has been moved to the octave of Epiphany, before the Sunday celebrating the baptism of Jesus.

If official liturgical celebrations keep some of these customs in mind, participation would be more meaningful and relevant for Hispanics.[36] The liturgy would also then give more depth to these religious customs.

### Easter Cycle

During the Easter cycle there are many symbols used in liturgical celebrations that have helped to make these days particularly meaningful to
Hispanics. It would make this chapter too long if these symbols and practices were described here.[37] The principal liturgical symbols and devotional
practices that speak deeply to Hispanics are ashes on Ash Wednesday,
blessed palms on Passion Sunday, blessed bread and candles, washing of
the feet on Holy Thursday; seven visits or holy hour of adoration on Holy
Thursday night; living way of the cross (including the three falls), seven
last words service, adoration of the cross, universal intercessions, burial
procession and *pésame* to accompany Mary in her bereavement[38] on Good
Friday. Fire, light, procession, water, alleluia songs, flowers, white clothing,
family outings in the park, and in some places meetings of Jesus and Mary
on Easter Sunday very early in the morning,[39] all add to the celebration.

### Sunday or Festive Eucharistic Liturgy

Some of the practices that are easily introduced in a eucharistic liturgy
which would help Hispanics to participate more fully are: (1) art and environment that come from the cultural groups, (2) greeting by ushers and
presider that expresses joy in being together and a welcoming attitude, (3)
recognition of guests and visitors by name or place, to which the assembly
responds with an applause, (4) acknowledging by name those persons celebrating birthdays or anniversaries at the end of Mass and perhaps giving
a small "memento," (5) opening the prayer of the faithful to the assembly
for their personal intentions, (6) use of anecdotes and personalized stories
in the homily, (7) use of different musical instruments and of hymns known
by the community so that the entire assembly may participate, (8) inviting
the use of particular gestures like holding hands during the Our Father and
giving an embrace at the greeting of peace, (9) use of incense at the proper
times, (10) use of the aspersion rite, (11) alternating the different eucharistic prayers given in the sacramentary, (12) using the different alternatives
for the penitential rite, including some of the laity for the reading of certain
parts, (13) when the celebration is in Spanish, begining with the long sign
of the cross,[40] (14) at the "memento" of the dead, mentioning the names
of those remembered, (15) encouraging members of the assembly to receive
communion under both species by periodically giving an explanation of this
liturgical action, (16) sometimes using a different word to express the same
idea, such as calling God *Tata Dios* or *Diosito*, (17) occasionally including
a procession and *danzas*, (18) on particular days changing the place of a
particular image of Jesus, Mary, or a saint according to the feast being
celebrated.

All these options and many more are not only permitted but encouraged
in all liturgical documents. As has been stated continually in this chapter,

the purpose of the renewal of the liturgy is to help the faithful, the assembled community, to pray and worship as the Mystical Body of Christ, as the local church, in a way that is meaningful, relevant, and inspiring.

## Celebrations of the Sacraments and Rites of Passage

As mandated particularly by Vatican II and subsequent directives, the celebration of all the sacraments should have a communitarian character.[41] Baptism and matrimony are certainly of special importance particularly for Hispanics. The rite of passage at death is also given great liturgical importance. It is celebrated with a vigil, a funeral liturgy, and the committal. Among Hispanic females, as mentioned above, there is the rite of the *quinceañera*, which celebrates the passage from being a girl to being a young woman.

*Baptism.* Grandparents can play an important role in the baptism of a grandchild, together with the parents and godparents. For example, they can make the sign of the cross on the infant's forehead after the presider has done so. The place where the baptism is celebrated should be big enough so that as many persons as may wish can participate and be able to see what is being done. Not only can the new relationship between godparents and godchild be addressed, but also the one between godparent and parents which is so strong among Hispanics. This elaborate kinship system is called *el compadrazgo*, or "co-parenthood."[42] Brothers and sisters of the baby and other children could be invited to kiss the newly baptized member of the family as a sign of welcome. The presider at baptism may present the newly baptized child to the assembly, which responds with a welcoming applause. At the end of the liturgical celebration the godfather shares his joy by throwing small coins for other children to pick up outside the church. This is called *el bolo*. Naturally the celebration continues at home with sharing of food and good wishes,[43] music, poetry, and dance, and in some instances even including a *piñata!*[44]

*Matrimony.* In this liturgical ceremony many *padrinos*[45] are sometimes needed so that the young couple may have the necessary means for the celebration. Many family members and friends come to the wedding; they have been away from church for a certain period of time. It is a time to make them feel welcomed and to help them become part of the gathered assembly. Simple but meaningful songs are important as well as the use of certain typical symbols in this ceremony. Among these are the *lazo*, a cord often in the form of a rosary, and the *arras*, or coins.[46] When both parents are present it is good to ask both of them to walk with the bride or the bridegroom at the beginning of the ceremony. Members of the marrying couple's families can participate as ushers, lectors, eucharistic ministers, and in any other way conducive to making the ceremony a real family event.

*Funerals.* Once again, the value of family and extended family or community is very important at this moment of grief. It has been customary to pray the rosary at the wake, to sing, and to hear some reflections on the significance of this death. It is also customary to remain with the corpse until the moment of the funeral liturgy and of committal.[47] As with other Catholics, it is important to begin explaining and introducing the liturgical celebration of the vigil or wake, focusing on consoling the family members facing the death of a loved one. The hope of the resurrection should be stressed and appropriate readings from sacred scripture read aloud. Among Hispanics in the United States many of these ceremonies could be bilingual. In this way both young and old may equally participate.

At the funeral liturgy several members of the family can perform some of the liturgical ministries and others can be invited before the final blessing to share some memories of the deceased person. This is the proper place to do so. The sharing would also help the ceremony to be very meaningful and personal for all those present. At the liturgy of committal, which for most Hispanics is still a burial, it is important to allow the coffin to be lowered while the assembly is present, so that the custom of the *puño de tierra* mentioned above can be carried out. Once again, the value of being with, of accompanying, is important at this moment when sympathy is offered with the words: *Te acompaño en tus sentimientos* ("I am with you in the way you feel"). A work of mercy—"console the sorrowful"—is fulfilled not only by offering sympathy at the vigil and funeral liturgy but by taking to the home of the bereaved some food so that they do not have the trouble of cooking on that day. All this involves the community in a very active and meaningful role.

The *novenario*, finally, is a rite performed for the nine days following the funeral. It may consist of a eucharistic liturgy or a rosary.[48] This custom helps the community and friends to have time to express personally their sympathy. It helps the bereaved express their grief and their faith in life after death and in the resurrection. All of these customs provide Hispanics with a profound and extremely helpful way to mourn the passing of a loved one.

The *quinceañera* ceremony helps Hispanic youth be in touch once again with their cultural and spiritual traditions. It has been rightfully called "a teachable moment" and the opportunity to create a lasting memory of the meaning of life and motherhood. It is not strictly liturgical, but more often than not it includes the eucharistic liturgy when many youths and family members participate in its preparation and celebration. Many symbols are used that help evoke an attitude of thanksgiving for the gift of life.[49] Perhaps this ceremony more than any other has been enriched with meaning and symbols as it is celebrated among Mexican-Americans. It seems to have assumed the importance of an identity ritual, which helps young people achieve a real sense of belonging, a crucial developmental task.[50]

## CONCLUSION

All the previous reflections lead to some practical conclusions. First of all, liturgy is the celebration of the paschal mystery as it is lived in a particular Christian community. Therefore it must celebrate the values and beliefs lived by the people themselves. This faith tradition is a gift from God for that particular group. An inculturated liturgy uses some of the external expressions and symbols that characterize the culture of the celebrating community. But, more importantly, it must be an affirmation and celebration of the most meaningful and clear ways of rendering worship to God, of relating to the sacred according to the customs and traditions of the participants.

The norms and directives given by Rome and by ecclesiastical authorities are a great help for truly making the liturgical celebrations occasions of worship of the Father by the total Christ in the power of the Spirit. They serve as the skeleton of the celebration. Within those same documents there are several invitations to adapt, to incarnate, to make more understandable and participatory all the liturgical celebrations. Persons planning, preparing, and presiding at such celebrations must be aware of all those options and opportunities. They must know what is being celebrated and who is celebrating. Liturgy must celebrate the Christian life that is being lived by the community. At the same time it must nourish and inspire the faithful to continue in the following of Christ by serving one another. The liturgy thus assumes a beautiful rhythm, a celebrating of life and a living of the celebration. Prayer and worship within Hispanic contexts often manifest this appealing rhythm that integrates earthly and supernatural life with so much naturalness. Perhaps it is for this reason that the works of mercy play such an important role in the spirituality and prayer life of Hispanics.

Some persons feel that liturgy includes many "legal" requirements and takes away from the spontaneity of expression and depth of religious belief. Instead of looking, for example, at prebaptismal classes, at the RCIA process, or at some particular conditions simply as "legal requirements," consideration must be given to the way one "prepares" for a celebration, such as the birth of a child, a wedding, an anniversary. There is always the element of sacrifice, of doing without, of learning, of practicing. Along with that there comes a sense of expectation for a big day, for a new relationship, a new commitment. Many Hispanics, as well as non-Hispanics, gladly participate in those things which help them to prepare more fittingly for the celebration. So much depends on the attitude we bring to these preparations.

Tangible symbols, joyful music and songs, warm environment, and gestures and meaningful expressions of faith help the liturgy to be more fully lived by the assembly, particularly if it is formed by Hispanics. The participants will truly be nourished in spirit. In their prayer, worship, and liturgy their lives will thus become an "epiphany" of God's love and mercy here and now.

## NOTES

1. Bishop Ricardo Ramirez, C.S.B., conference, "Hispanics in the Church," Seventy-Fifth Anniversary of Assumption Seminary, December 9, 1990, Incarnate Word College, San Antonio, Texas.

2. A useful source for documentation of liturgy is *Documents on the Liturgy, 1963–1979* (Collegeville: Liturgical Press, 1982). It will be cited further below as DOL.

3. Boston: Daughters of St. Paul, 1976, #48.

4. See, for example, Virgil Elizondo, "Popular Religiosity and Identity in the Mexican Community of the United States," in *Concilium*, no. 206, July 1986, pp. 49–56; also Kevin Seasoltz, O.S.B., *New Liturgy, New Laws* (Collegeville: Liturgical Press, 1979), p. 182.

5. National Conference of Catholic Bishops (Washington, D.C.: United States Catholic Conference, 1987), #10.

6. *Christian Liturgy: Theology and Practice* (Kansas City: Sheed & Ward, 1988), p. 39.

7. Among some Hispanic groups, particularly Caribbean, popular expressions of faith mean primarily their practices and beliefs toward saints *(santería)*, particular situations and actions. Among Mexican-Americans, popular religiosity also includes greater emphasis on practices observed during liturgical seasons and celebrations.

8. Perhaps this could be an interpretation of the common "bargaining with God": "If you grant me this, I will give you this particular sanctuary," or "If you cure my child, I will offer you a certain amount of money for the poor," as if God needed our visits and our contributions.

9. *Sacrosanctum Concilium*, #41.

10. *Vatican II* (Baltimore: American Press, 1966), #52–69.

11. Paul VI, *Apostolic Exhortation, Marialis Cultus*, on rightly grounding and increasing Marian devotion, February 2, 1974, *DOL*, #3905. A reading of this entire document is recommended; *DOL*, #3896–945.

12. *Environment and Art in Catholic Worship* (Chicago: Liturgy Training Publications, 1986), #102.

13. *Environment and Art in Catholic Worship*, #3.

14. Bangalore, India: National Biblical, Catechetical and Liturgical Centre, nd.), p. 175.

15. See the title of this chapter. However, Hispanics in general and in particular Hispanic lay persons need more orientation, liturgically speaking, because they have been out of touch with the reforms, in spite of the many efforts made by several pastoral agents and particularly by the Instituto de Liturgia Hispana founded in 1989.

16. See #58 and #37–40, respectively.

17. Sacred Congregation of Rites, *General Norms for the Liturgical Year and the Calendar*, March 21, 1969; *DOL*, #3805.

18. For a historical development of this season, see Aimé Georges Martimort, et al., *The Liturgy and Time* (Collegeville: Liturgical Press, 1986), vol. 4, pp. 90–96.

19. This is symbolically expressed by the ribbon at the waist, tied in the front with its ends hanging in the middle *(está en cinta)*, the way it was worn when expecting a child.

20. National Conference of Catholic Bishops, *Hispanic Presence: Challenge and Commitment* (Washington, D.C.: United States Catholic Conference, 1983), #120.

21. Virgil Elizondo, "The Virgin of Guadalupe as a Cultural Symbol: The Power of the Powerless," *Concilium* (#122, February 1977), pp. 149–60.

22. For a detailed explanation of the symbols in the painting, see Virgil Elizondo, *La Morenita: Evangelizer of the Americas* (San Antonio: Mexican American Cultural

Center, 1980); and for the symbolism in the dialogue, see Rosa María Icaza, C.C.V.I., "Symbolism in the Dialogue between Mary and Juan Diego," paper presented at the Symposium of Guadalupe '90, San Antonio, October 14, 1990. Also see among other studies in Spanish: Mario Rojas Sánchez and Juan Homero Hernández Illescas, *Las estrellas del manto de la Virgen de Guadalupe* (Mexico City: Francisco Méndez Oteo, 1983) and Clodomiro Siller, "Anotaciones y comentarios al Nican Mopohua," *Estudios Indígenas* (Mexico City: CENAMI, 1981), vol. 8, no. 2, pp. 274–314.

23. See in reference to the use of symbols, James Empereur, S.J., *Worship: Exploring the Sacred* (Washington, D.C.: Pastoral Press, 1987), pp. 33–46.

24. A Hispanic celebration, particularly among Mexican-Americans, must include *Misa, Mesa,* and *Musa;* that is, it includes some form of prayer (to celebrate our relationship with the sacred), some things to eat (to celebrate our relationship with other human beings, who by that fact become our companions), and some form of art, like music, song, dance, poetry (to celebrate our relationship with nature and beauty). For most of the liturgical seasons, Hispanics include special dishes or snacks, such as *buñuelos* for Christmas, *capirotada* for Lent, *pan de muertos* for November 2, and so forth.

25. Luke 2:1–5.

26. *Faith Expressions of Hispanics in the Southwest*, revised edition (San Antonio: Mexican American Cultural Center, 1990), p. 13.

27. Among Puerto Ricans, the ritual of the *posada* is celebrated only on Christmas Eve and it is called *asalto* since the final place regularly is the home of an elderly couple or a "shut-in" person. Those who arrive bring along the things needed for the celebration and in this way they share hope and joy with those who otherwise would not be able to join the community's festivities. Another work of mercy: "to visit the sick."

28. This is a Mexican flower brought to the United States around 1850 by Joel R. Poinsett, an American diplomat who "baptized" the flower in English with a variation of his own family name.

29. The strict meaning of this word is restricted to baptismal godparents with all the spiritual, educational, and economic responsibilities toward their godchild. However, it is frequently used to designate any person who helps with the celebration, by donating either money or a particular object.

30. Today consumerism is also evident in the big cities of Mexico and this trend almost forces everyone to buy Christmas presents without remembering the true meaning of such a beautiful action, sharing in God's infinite love and generosity.

31. Luke 2:8–14.

32. Among many families in Mexico there is a beautiful custom of lighting 12 candles at midnight on December 31 while the family members pray three "creeds" in honor of divine providence, a name given to the holy Trinity. At the end of the prayer, all 12 candles are blown out. Then each of these candles is completely used every first of the month to keep alive in the home the idea of God's mercy. It is also customary to offer a monetary gift each first day of the month, giving the same amount to the Father and to the Son and to the Holy Spirit. For this purpose, there is in almost every church in Mexico a place with three open slots in front of an image of the holy Trinity.

33. Matt. 2:1–12.

34. If the community is rather poor, the baker places three small ceramic figures,

or three beans, in the dough. Each of these figures symbolizes one of the Magi who followed the star in search of Jesus. In this way, the three persons who find the figure in their piece of bread share the expense of the following party. If the community is not so poor, the baker places only one object in the dough, symbolizing the baby Jesus whom the Magi found, as the person who receives this object in her or his piece. He or she will give the party.

35. There is also another simple ritual on this celebration: *La levantada del Niño*. The family or the community gathers to take the statue of the baby Jesus from the crib or from Mary's lap, singing joyfully and gratefully. Then, the statue is put away until the following year. However, in some places, the statue, together with some candles, is taken to church particularly on February 2 in remembrance of Mary and Joseph taking Jesus to the temple (Lk. 2:22–24). All these objects are blessed after the celebration of the eucharistic liturgy, then taken home. The statue is kept for the following year and the candles are used as sacramentals.

36. For example, mentioning them in homilies with good scriptural and theological explanations, celebrating some of them in the parish hall or at school, and, if possible, pastors and parish vicars participating in these home celebrations organized and implemented by their parishioners.

37. For those who desire a more detailed explanation, see *Faith Expressions*, pp. 16–19, and in Spanish, *Celebremos Cuaresma* (San Antonio: Mexican American Cultural Center, 1982) and Patricio F. Flores, *Caminando con el Señor* (San Antonio: Archdiocese of San Antonio, 1982).

38. The statue of the sorrowful mother, left alone at the death of her son, is honored with different names which then are given to girls at baptism, such as Dolores, Soledad; sometimes she is represented with a sword piercing her heart, remembering Simeon's prophecy, Lk. 2:35.

39. In the Southwest, the weather is usually beautiful at the beginning of spring. The trees are budding with new life. The children of different families are free to play and run, and perhaps look for the hidden Easter eggs, without anyone conscious of the meaning of this Easter symbol. Birds are chirping and flying. Adults sing and exchange plans. The new life is almost felt in the fresh air and bright sun. A shared picnic puts the final touch to a joyful community/family celebration of new life.

40. See the words and the way it is done together with the great devotion that Mexicans and Mexican-Americans have for the cross in Rosa María Icaza, "The Cross in Mexican Popular Religiosity," *Liturgy* (1981), vol. 1, pp. 27–34.

41. *Sacrosanctum Concilium*, #26–32. It is important to read the general introductions to each of the sacraments and to note the communitarian aspect of its celebration.

42. This relationship has very strong bonds, and godparents truly take seriously their responsibility of being co-father and co-mother to the godchild. Later, as with the word *padrinos*, the words *compadre* and *comadre* are used for persons who are very close to one another in friendship without any relation to baptism. See *Faith Expressions*, pp. 24–25, for a beautiful custom in New Mexico.

43. This "ritual" has taken different forms through the centuries; among the Aztecs, people sat in a circle drinking tea, praying, and wishing or predicting many things about the infant, or in the case of a wedding, about the couple before the marriage ceremony. Among some Mexican-Americans, invited relatives and friends are asked to bring their wish in a small sealed envelope to be placed in a beautiful

box which is locked. It will only be opened on the 15th birthday of the girl or on the 18th birthday of the boy at a family gathering, and the notes are shared with all those present.

44. When considering the baptism celebration of an adult, the process of the Rite for Christian Initiation of Adults offers many opportunities to affirm and foster Hispanic values. See the article, "The RCIA among Hispanics" by Rosa María Icaza, *Liturgia y Canción* (Tiempo Ordinario I, 10 de junio–8 de septiembre de 1990), pp. 7–8.

45. See note #42 above for the "extended" use of this word.

46. See *Faith Expressions*, pp. 25–27, for the meaning and history of these symbols and for other rituals that accompany the celebration of this sacrament in Hispanic communities.

47. National Conference of Catholic Bishops, *Order of Christian Funerals* (Collegeville: Liturgical Press, 1989).

48. Arturo Pérez, *Novenario* (Chicago: Liturgy Training Publications, 1987).

49. For this celebration, see particularly *Religious Celebration for the Quinceañera* by Angela Erevia, M.C.D.P. (San Antonio: Mexican American Cultural Center, 1980) and the Diocesan Pastoral Guidelines for Preparation and Celebration of the *Quinceañera*. Several dioceses have published bilingual editions of their own guidelines.

50. Other faith expressions among Hispanics could also be examined as far as they relate to liturgy, such as novenas in preparation of liturgical, patronal feasts; medals or symbols worn on certain feasts; banners or paintings carried in special processions. Some good resources for these practices are: Arturo Pérez, *Popular Catholicism: A Hispanic Perspective* (Washington, D.C.: Pastoral Press, 1988); Rosa María Icaza, "Spirituality of the Mexican American People," *Worship*, 63 (1989), pp. 232–46; Ricardo Ramírez, C.S.B., *Fiesta, Worship and Family* (San Antonio: Mexican American Cultural Center, 1981), idem, "Liturgy from the Mexican American Perspective," *Worship*, 51 (1977), pp. 293–98, and "Reflections on the Hispanicization of the Liturgy," *Worship*, 59 (1985), pp. 26–35; some taped materials from the National Conferences on Hispanic Liturgy sponsored by the Instituto de Liturgia Hispana, particularly in October 1990; and the recent magazine, *Liturgia y Canción*, published by Liturgy Training Publications.

*Chapter Nine*

# Culture, Spirituality, and United States Hispanics

## JUAN-LORENZO HINOJOSA

If one walks into the San Fernando cathedral in San Antonio, Texas, one walks into an integral part of Texas history. Begun at the founding of the city in the 1700s and further expanded in a Romanesque style in the nineteenth century, it reflects its origins as the oldest church in Texas. One is met with the coolness and quiet of a place in which generations of Hispanics, starting in 1731, have worshiped. To the left are the remains of some of the defenders of the Alamo. One of them, James "Santiago" Bowie, was married here to Señorita Ursula de Vermendi in 1831. If one walks forward, one sees on the left a baptismal font which has been used to baptize thousands upon thousands. A gift in the Spanish colonial period by the king of Spain, probably Phillip V, its beauty and dignity befit this parish which has continuously been a source of pastoral care since its founding.

This is not one of the modern, simple, austere churches, which are now in favor. Statues are very prominent and lifelike as candles flicker at their feet. As one adjusts one's eyes and looks more closely, one notices that the statues here have papers stuck in the cracks — notes written in supplication and thanksgiving. Hanging from the hands or tucked into the nooks and crannies are small amulets depicting arms, legs, eyes, or people at prayer. These *milagros* denote expressions of petition or thanksgiving for oneself or loved ones. Although this would appear to be a traditional church such as one might see in many places, these are signs that many of the worshipers have been Hispanic.

But this is only part of the story. One must understand that although popular religion and classic Catholic piety are integral to Hispanic-American spirituality, there is another dimension of that spirituality. As people who have entered into the ethos of the dominant U.S. culture, Hispanics

154

are also truly children of that culture. This dimension is expressed in the life and struggles of a young Mexican-American woman, Mary Fernandez.

Mary Fernandez is a well-educated women in her mid-20s. She has surpassed her family in education, having earned a college degree. Though her English verbal skills are excellent, her Spanish is halting and she finds reading and writing it difficult. She has moved away from the barrio, the neighborhood in which she grew up, and has a nice house in the suburbs. She is as much at home with a "folk Mass" as she is uncomfortable with certain expressions of Hispanic folk religion, such as *curanderos*, the faith healers so common in her parents' religious culture.

## ISSUES FACING HISPANICS WITHIN U.S. CULTURE

The faith expressions found in the San Fernando cathedral and in hundreds of other places where Hispanic Americans worship testify to the abiding influence of Spanish and, in this case, Mexican, spiritual influences. Although Mary Fernandez is as Hispanic as those who place their notes and *milagros* on the statues, her spirituality exemplifies the influences of the dominant culture upon Hispanic spiritual practice and experience. She is not alone. There is a growing assimilation of great numbers of Hispanic Americans whose spirituality more closely resembles that of the mainstream culture than that of their culture of origin. A core spiritual issue facing each and every Hispanic, whether he or she be of Mexican, Cuban, Puerto Rican, or of other Latin American extraction, is how to relate to the dominant culture and to one's culture of origin. Many issues in the spirituality of Hispanic Americans, as such, relate to this core issue.

These reflections are more than simply impressionistic. They are supported by the most extensive study of its kind to date, "The Hispanic Catholic in the United States," which is based on interviews with 1,010 Hispanic Catholics from around the country.[1] According to this study, first-generation immigrants are more likely to consider religion very important to their lives, while those who have been in the country for more than one generation find religion less central. Compared to foreign-born Hispanic Catholics, "a sharp decline in intensity of religious belief and practice takes place among U.S. born Hispanic American Catholics."[2] Those born in this country have a clear preference for worship in English. These survey results point to the acculturation issues related to spirituality which inevitably confront those who have immigrated to this country.

Hispanics, and other ethnic minorities for that matter, face a potent force in mainstream culture. The channels through which it inexorably exerts itself are the media, especially television, the work context, and the schools. Even with Hispanic Americans who live in a milieu in which all speak Spanish, sooner or later the children will grow up having English as their dominant language. This shift brings with it more opportunities in terms of education and therefore advancement in their work life. This inevitably also leads to a degree of alienation from their culture of origin, often including a tension both with their family, especially parents, and with their spiritual roots. The level of acculturation and assimilation will determine to a great extent the nature of the spiritual issues with which the person will deal.

For discussion's sake, I propose four levels of acculturation and assimilation. The first is that of the immigrant. The second is that of the partially acculturated/assimilated, usually someone in the second generation. The third is that of the strongly acculturated/assimilated, and the final level is that of the fully bicultural individual.

Immigrant individuals or families usually carry with them the religious customs, perspectives, and spirituality which were theirs from their culture of origin. In the case of most Hispanic Americans, this will include a spirituality with a strong piety, which is usually not institutionally based but family and home centered, and which includes a strong sense of the sacred. This sense of the sacred finds expression through having an *altarcito*, a home altar or shrine, which includes pictures, statues, candles, and perhaps momentos. A keen awareness of the supernatural results in an emphasis on blessing and curse, a sensitivity to spiritual forces of good and of evil, and a need to align oneself and family with the spiritual forces of good and seek protection from those of evil. Communal piety revolves around rites of passage such as baptisms, first communions, and *quinceañeras*, the celebration of a girl's fifteenth birthday. Devotion to Mary and other special saints will often call forth a desire for pilgrimage to sacred places where the power of God can be felt and experienced. Those with this least assimilated spirituality will tend to experience a great shock when confronted by the mainstream culture. Not only does this culture not validate their spirituality, it depreciates it as superstitious and backward. Recent immigrants will have little societal support for their spirituality unless they live in enclaves with fellow Hispanic Americans, where they can find some validation and support. Their very plausibility will come into question. Parishes that emphasize cultural sensitivity will include a place for the popular religious practices which Hispanic Americans have brought to this country. The dilemma is that if one wants to enter into the mainstream of U.S. society and advance oneself economically and socially, then these very practices will become problematic. The fact that many Hispanic Americans defect to Protestant groups reflects the need they see to leave behind what they have known as Catholicism in order to advance. Andrew Greeley reports that there are significant differences in income ($19,000 vs. $25,000) between those Hispanics who remain Catholic and those who become Protestant.[3] This would lead one to wonder if, for some Hispanic Americans, leaving their traditional piety is part of the process of "making it" in the mainstream culture.

A major issue faced by each of these groups, but particularly the first group, from the standpoint of spirituality, is how to relate to the mainstream culture, a culture which tends toward either a secularist or an anti-Catholic bias, either of which denies the validity of their religious experience and expression. Some choose to isolate themselves and live in Hispanic enclaves. Others choose to enter the mainstream and face the challenges of the second group, the partially acculturated/assimilated.

Among this second group, there will be an ability to function to some extent in the dominant cultural milieu, and to continue to draw from some of the elements of their culture of origin. A pervasive spiritual issue faced by this group is a sense of dislocation. Truly poised between two worlds, they are not totally at home in either culture. Since the dominant culture's normative projection of what is "good," "beautiful," and even "true" does not match either the thinking, background, or looks of most of the Hispanic Americans in this country, there will tend to be very painful feelings of alienation, which often include feelings of inferiority. In many cases, dealing with these feelings will involve jettisoning elements of the culture of origin, including many aspects of the religious practice. This may leave them adrift, or it may lead to the substitution of Protestant religious expressions, which will better fit the mainstream milieu. Some will respond by clinging to the spiritual expressions of their origins. Many upwardly mobile Hispanic Americans will take the option of beginning to move away from religion altogether, into a secularist framework.

Those in the third group, the more fully acculturated/assimilated group, like Mary Fernandez, will be able to deal with the mainstream culture in a comfortable manner, being rather at home in it. In some cases, a vestige of Spanish-language ability remains; in others it may have been virtually lost, while in yet others, some degree of proficiency will remain. A primary issue for this group will be the recovery of what was of importance and value from their culture of origin, and beginning the process of sorting through what of the dominant culture they will retain and what they will abandon. This clarifying, sorting through, and choosing, although apparently a nonreligious event, can be understood as an instance of spiritual discernment. For there are elements in each culture that conform themselves more fully to gospel values and those that do not. The process of beginning to recover Spanish as a language which one values usually begins at this stage. Other elements of the culture of origin which might have been neglected or lost will be examined and possibly recovered. An example of sorting out what one wants to take from the dominant culture can be well illustrated by a young woman who, being pregnant for the first time, must deal with attitudes from both the dominant culture and the culture of origin. Cultural values around childbirth and breast-feeding are quite different in the Mexican and Mexican-American community than in the dominant culture. It is usual to hear loud shrieks and anguished yells in maternity floors where they give birth. A prevalent attitude among Mexican Americans is that giving birth is something akin to a curse which one must endure and which will be excruciatingly painful. Loud shrieks and anguished yells during labor and childbirth are quite common. Mary Fernandez, however, has acquired from the mainstream culture a very different attitude and perspective. For her, birth, although painful, is a joyous experience. This attitude clashes with the values of her family and friends. A similar issue emerges with regard to breast-feeding. Generally speaking, Mexican Americans do not value breast-feeding and are not comfortable with it. Men will leave the room when a woman begins to breast-feed. A more acculturated woman, if she chooses to buck the cultural assumptions of family and friends, will have to deal with the feelings associated with being different.

The final group consists of those who have come to terms with being both Hispanic and a part of the dominant culture. This group, while continuing to discern what to keep and what to leave in both cultures, has reached a level of consolidation in their identity as hyphenated Americans (as in Cuban-American, or Mexican-American). They will neither be alienated from nor romanticize either the dominant culture or their culture of origin. In a very real sense, there will be the claiming of a new identity. This identity will be neither Cuban nor Mexican nor Puerto Rican, nor that of one who identifies totally with the dominant culture. What is coming to birth, in Virgilio Elizondo's term, is a *mestizaje* — a new reality made up of parts of the old.[4] A continuing spiritual issue will be coming to terms with and finding meaning in being a person who is discriminated against. Regardless of one's educational, economic, or social attainment, there remains in this country a pervasive prejudice against Hispanics. A deep level of maturity will have been reached when the person who has entered this stage becomes an advocate and prophetic figure for the powerless in the Hispanic community.

## PAUL RICOEUR AND SYMBOLS

The previous material has attempted to sketch some of the issues facing those who are Hispanic as they traverse various stages of contact with the dominant U.S. culture. As should be evident from what has come before, there is a tremendous diversity of response to the dominant culture. The thought of Paul Ricoeur can help make sense of much of what has been discussed with regard to the shifts that occur in a person as he or she confronts the modernity of the mainstream culture, with its accompanying attitudes and perspectives. Ricoeur has developed a theoretical framework which elucidates some of the processes and passages which a person traverses in her or his contact with modernity. The main focus of his work, a theory of language, and in particular the symbolic nature of certain types of language, serves as an avenue for understanding the shifts that happen in those who encounter the key cultural trends in the mainstream culture.

The study of symbol, a central focus of Ricoeur's, cuts across many contemporary disciplines which attempt to understand religion. One can find a keen interest in symbol in anthropology, the history of religions, the sociology and psychology of religion, and other fields. Understanding the role of symbol is an important key for understanding the faith development of Hispanic Americans. In one sense, the entire spiritual enterprise is predicated upon our ability to enter into symbolic experience. The sacred comes to manifestation in and through symbol. Symbol is the very locus of our encounter with God, the privileged avenue for religious experience. Whether in parable, in ritual action, or in Christ himself, we are dealing with a symbolic economy—a web of symbols that makes up the narrative which creates meaning vis-à-vis the foundational questions facing the individual and society.

Symbol is both the *cause* and the *effect* of revelation. As cause, it leads to disclosure of a reality which we designate as "the holy." As effect, it is the sedimentation of that experience, and reaches us in our inherited tradition as scripture, ritual, theology, icons, and so forth. Unfortunately, we are in a time in which these symbols have either stopped speaking for some, or have begun to speak in ways that are less than adequate to reality. They have stopped speaking in the secularized culture which cannot accept the transcendent, and have begun to speak in inadequate ways in the fundamentalist solution to the distress of modernity. Paul Ricoeur addresses us in the context of this contemporary situation.

Ricoeur's own interest in symbol arises in part from his sense of our existential situation as children of modernity. He aims at a recovery of a sense of the sacred which has been lost in the sophisticated milieu in which many of us operate. He maintains that the tragedy of much of contemporary Western culture, especially that which has been touched by the influence of the "masters of suspicion," Marx, Nietzsche, and Freud, is the loss of what he calls a first naïvety. In terms of influence on our contemporary worldview, these three giants of modern thought helped call into question many of the previously held certainties with regard to religion. Each one, in his own way, raised the question of the very genesis of religion and its practice, and answered the query with an interpretation which ultimately destroys the possibility of faith by positing a critical and reductive hermeneutic of the faith experience. These reductionisms would explain religion as simply reflections of intrapsychic or societal processes, with no referent to a transcendent reality.

In addition to the effects of this reductive hermeneutics of the "masters of suspicion," our age has also seen the beginning of a purely literal understanding of language and a positivistic science which denies the real beyond the observable and quantifiable. The result is a forgetfulness—of hierophanies, of signs of the sacred, and finally of the sacred itself. We face a loss of a sense of the sacred, precisely because our symbols and myths have lost their power to evoke the sacred. When one reduces religion to what is known, the possibility of a transcendent reality is denied, and the symbols which mediated that reality are silenced. This forgetfulness of the sacred is a part of humankind's process of coming to itself, Ricoeur believes, and should not be viewed absolutely negatively. Ricoeur does not aim at a return to a more innocent age, but rather for a recharging or re-creation of language which is itself a gift of "modernity." A movement through the "desert of criticism"—that is, the purifying use of contemporary critical consciousness—will lead to a new ability to experience the sacred in what he calls a second naivety.

### First and Second Naivety

As he reflects on the situation in which we find ourselves as children of modernity, Ricoeur introduces these two rather odd terms which hold potential as helpful tools of understanding: the first and second naivety. I believe they have important heuristic value in the attempt to understand the transitions undergone by Hispanic Americans affected by the dominant culture. Ricoeur begins to develop his thought on the first and second naivety in *The Symbolism of Evil*, and in his next major work, *Freud and Philosophy*.

A primary or first naivety is an immediacy of belief or access to symbol which has been unchallenged by modernity's criticism. In one sense, the millions of people who have lived and who currently live without questioning their religious symbolic economy were or are in a first naivety. These are people who have not suffered the distantiation that comes from the powerful and increasingly dominant strands of contemporary Western consciousness, which call uncritical religiosity into question. For someone in the first naivety, the symbolic encounter is immediate and uncritical. Although there is an enviable simplicity and directness to their sense of the sacred, this manner of apprehension of the sacred is not without its ambiguity, for there is also the danger of mystification. When the symbolic life becomes explanatory of reality in such a way that reality is actually obscured, mystification has occurred. A religious culture which canonizes injustices in the name of God, or in which people are passive in the face of suffering and injustice, because of a spirituality which encourages this, is afflicted by mystification. The pathologies of religion are multiple, but mystification is one of the most serious because it hinders human and social development, as both Marx and Freud demonstrated.

Those in the first naivety have yet to be challenged by the influences which Ricoeur aptly calls the "acids of modernity." These acids are the influences which break the first naivety. Though there are certain groups, such as the least acculturated/assimilated Hispanics, who are less influenced, it is extremely difficult to be a part of mainstream culture without being influenced by these acids, either explicitly or implicitly. How can one respond to the challenge which stems from the "acids of modernity?" Three possible responses are common; only one of them adequate.

One possible response to the breaking of the immediacy of the first naivety is the reductionistic fallacy—that is, the loss of the condition of openness to the spiritual. In reductionism, whether sociological, such as Marx's, or psychological, such as Freud's, there is the mistaken notion that the symbol can be explained simply as an expression of a societal process or an intrapsychic event. Marx reduces the human religious experience to an expression of false consciousness which arises out of the thwarting of legitimate aspirations as historical agents. Freud reduces religious experience to the working out of the Oedipal complex. In all reductionism, symbol is reduced to a sign which tells us what we already know or can discover. Symbols are only reminders of what we can come to know rationally, either through the social/political revolutionary process or through psychoanalysis. For the reductionist there is no such thing as mystery or a transcendent reality which can be pointed to and made present through symbol.

A second possible response to the threat of the loss of the first naivety is the concretist fallacy. The concretist fallacy is a response to modernity, which is a reentrenchment out of fear. As modern influences push their way into the consciousness of an individual or a society, there often will arise a deep fear of loss; a fear of losing faith. The concretist fallacy emerges as a possible solution to dilemmas and tensions in what is an anxious and tense time. It can arise out of what Eric Fromm has called a "lust for certitude." As our worldview is challenged by modernity, our well-structured universe can begin to collapse, eliciting a response of fear and a "lust for certitude" which can lead to fundamentalism. A prominent example of this process or dynamic occurrence is the events in Iran which led to the fall of the shah. As the shah attempted to introduce westernization in Iran, he provoked a reaction which eventuated in a fundamentalist theocracy.

How does this fallacy operate? A symbol, when understood and experienced properly, opens up meaning beyond itself and can become a means for transcendent experience. In the concretist fallacy, the interpretive process leads to seeing the symbol in such a manner that it becomes opaque and no longer points beyond itself. Instead of a means, the symbol has become an end. Spiritually speaking, a form of idolatry has occurred. All fundamentalism and inappropriate literalisms are a product of this fallacy: there is an engagement with the symbolic which tames the symbol rather than allowing it to point to the transcendent. This image of taming is apt, for when the symbol has not been domesticated, it has a life of its own similar to that of a wild creature and can serve to undermine our human certainties and securities. The fundamentalist option is extremely common. It can be a stage in the process leading to a more "dark" faith, much akin to what St. John of the Cross refers to in his mystical writing. When fundamentalism is a transitional phase in one's faith development, one will move beyond the "lust for certitude" into a quality of faith which involves a radical entrustment of one's self beyond one's own vision. This quality of faith comes only through moving out of a first naivety into the uncertainty and loss which precedes the birth of the second naivety.

The second naivety emerges as the only legitimate long-term answer to the challenges of modernity. In the second naivety, one experiences the transcendent through the symbolic again, but in a different way. A new self-possession has taken shape. The mystification which might have been part of the first naivety will have been purified through contact with the "acids of modernity." These acids have created a critical perspective, but if the second naivety has developed, there will be a deep respect for symbol and an access to the sacred through the symbolic. As the term second naivety implies, this access to the sacred will be characterized by a certain simplicity and immediacy. One can never return to the same manner of access to the sacred as one had in the first naivety, but a new access will be gained in and through traversing the purifying critiques of religion found in modern thought without becoming mired in them. Ricoeur aims at recapturing the symbolisms of the sacred in a second naivety which occurs in partnership with criticism. The second naivety is a postcritical mind-set which reopens the possibility of hierophany in and through the symbolic. It is the result of the spiritual movement through our modern dilemma with the help of modern critical hermeneutics. Ricoeur tells us that "it is through interpreting that we can hear again."[5] The process into the second naivety demands a critical hermeneutics as "the 'modern' mode of belief in symbols, an expression of the distress of modernity and a remedy for that distress."[6] Although most of us will not be involved in serious hermeneutical study, each of us *is* dealing with the corrosive effects of modernity. The passage into the second naivety comes through trial and anguish, but finally emerges as a solution to the pressing problem of recognizing the truth found in the modern criticisms of religion, yet at the same time being open to God's revelation through the symbolic medium.

The division between fundamentalists and "modernists" in almost all Christian communions is a sign of the distress we live in today. Some Hispanic Americans will be in a first naivety and some will be in a second, and some between them. Ricoeur's distinctions are useful, illuminative, and suggestive because different issues will emerge, depending on whether one is in a primary or secondary naivety or between them, in fundamentalism or a postcritical limbo. Many highly acculturated Hispanic Americans have moved beyond the first naivety and find themselves in a circumstance in which the symbolic no longer "speaks." They will tend to disparage and look down on those in a first naivety for whom the symbolic is alive. At the very least, there will be a lack of understanding and appreciation of what appears to them as superstition. Likewise, they will not understand those who are in the second naivety. They will tend to see them as conservative and unenlightened.

Generally speaking, Hispanic Americans still are taken up with a sense of the sacred and of a supernatural reality. Their religious life finds expression in many ways, one of the most prominent being popular piety. Hispanic Americans often come out of a traditional religiosity which has not been deeply challenged by the "acids of modernity," the influences which tend to break the first naivety. As many of the Hispanic American youth are touched by mainstream culture, those "acids" will inevitably begin to have their effect, making the issues they face similar to that of mainstream individuals.

This breaking of the first naivety can be extremely alienating and frightening. The experience will tend to include feelings of loss, creating a good deal of anxiety and confusion. It has many of the characteristics associated with what St. John of the Cross has described as the passive dark night of the spirit: a sense that the very basis of faith is being eroded and undermined. If it can be traversed, a deeper level of faith will be reached and the alienation which accompanies the rupture of the first naivety will give way to a new response to symbol facilitated by contact with those who have an ongoing encounter with the symbolic in a second naivety.

Another key avenue of breakthrough into the second naivety is through the reevangelization that can happen precisely through popular religiosity, for authentic symbols are embedded in its forms. Popular religiosity arises out of a first naivety and carries the primordial symbols in all their simple power. One of the great insights which has come to the church through liberation theology would appear to be related to this: the poor and marginalized evangelize those open to them. It is the poor who carry the primordial symbols and through whom contact can be made with these primordial elements of the gospel.

*Summary*

To summarize, Ricoeur's articulation of what he calls the first and second naivety serves as a useful heuristic model for understanding both the dilemma facing much of contemporary Western culture in its relationship to the sacred, and the challenges which modernity poses to Hispanic Americans. As mentioned earlier, a core spiritual issue for Hispanic Americans is their relationship to the dominant culture and their relationship to their culture of origin. For some, there will be a capitulation to the dominant culture, which may include a fundamentalist or a secularist option. For others, the "ghetto" option will be a solution: clinging to a first naivety. Those, however, who want to engage the dominant culture and at the same time be faithful to their roots will need to make the journey which honors the truth in both realities. It is these who will make the most significant contribution to the church and to society.

**NOTES**

1. Andrew Greeley, "Defection Among Hispanics," *America*, July 30, 1988, pp. 61–62.
2. Roberto O. González and Michael La Velle, *The Hispanic Catholic in the*

*United States: A Socio-Cultural and Religious Profile* (New York: Northeast Catholic Pastoral Center for Hispanics, 1985), p. 176.

3. Greeley, "Defection."

4. Virgilio Elizondo's groundbreaking theological reflection can be found in *Galilean Journey: The Mexican-American Promise* and *The Future Is Mestizo: Life Where Cultures Meet.*

5. Paul Ricoeur, *The Symbolism of Evil* (Boston: Beacon Press, 1967), p. 351.

6. Ibid., 352.

# Select Bibliography

The following entries were selected from a larger bibliography researched by Arturo Bañuelas and Eduardo Fernández. A few additions were also made by the editor of this collection. Only Roman Catholic Hispanic writers have been included. It must be acknowledged, however, that the writings of U.S. Hispanic Protestant theologians like Justo L. González and the late Orlando Costas deserve as much attention as the Roman Catholics receive here.

Ongoing developments in this field can be followed in *Apuntes*, published at the Perkins School of Religion at Southern Methodist University. Both Protestant and Roman Catholic Hispanic theologians are contributors to this review. The annual newsletter of the Academy of Catholic Hispanic Theologians of the United States (ACHTUS) provides news on current publications and projects in the field of U.S. Hispanic theology. Father Kenneth Davis, O.F.M.Conv., writing in the *Review for Religious* published in St. Louis, has inaugurated an annual resumé of trends and recent works on U.S. Hispanic Catholics in the March-April 1991 issue. In selecting the following works special attention was given to the contributors to this volume and to those works which reflect a more explicit theological focus.

Aquino, María Pilar, ed. *Aportes para una teología desde la mujer*. Madrid: Ediciones Biblia y Fe, 1988.
———. *Nuestro clamor por la vida*. San José, Costa Rica: DEI, 1992.
———. " 'Sin contar a las mujeres' toca su fin: la contribución de la mujer a la teología," in *La situación de la mujer en América Latina*. San José, Costa Rica: DEI, 1989.
———. "Mujer y praxis ministerial hoy: la respuesta del tercer mundo," in *Biblia y Fe* 46 (1990).
Aymes, Ma. de la Cruz. *Fe y cultura* Mahwah, NJ: Paulist Press, 1987.
———. *Los Sacramentos*. Allen, TX: Tabor Publishing, 1990.
Deck, Allan Figueroa. "A Christian Perspective on the Reality of Illegal Immigration," in *Social Thought*, Fall 1976.
———. "Proselytism and the Hispanic Catholic: How Long Can We Cry Wolf," in *America*, December 10, 1988.
———. *The Second Wave: Hispanic Ministry and the Evangelization of Cultures*. Mahwah, N.J.: Paulist Press, 1989.
———. "Hispanic Theologians and the United States Catholic Church," in *New Theological Review*, 3, no. 4, November 1990.
———. "The Spirituality of United States Hispanics: An Introductory Essay," in *U.S. Catholic Historian*, 9, nos. 1 and 2, Winter 1990.
Elizondo, Virgilio P. "A Challenge to Theology: the Situation of Hispanic Americans," in *Proceedings of the Catholic Theological Society of America*, vol. 30, 1975.

————. "La Virgen de Guadalupe como símbolo: el 'poder de los inpotentes'," in *Concilium*, 122, Madrid: Ediciones Cristiandad, 1977.

————. *The Galilean Journey*. Maryknoll, N.Y.: Orbis Books, 1983.

————. C. Geffrée and G. Gutiérrez, eds. "Different Theologies, Common Responsibilities: Babel or Pentecost," in *Concilium*, Edinburgh: T. & T. Clark, 1984.

————. *The Future Is Mestizo: Life Where Cultures Meet*. New York: Meyer-Stone, 1988.

————. "Elements for a Mexican American Mestizo Christology," in *Voices from the Third World: Christologies in Encounter*. Sri Lanka, 1989.

————, with Leonardo Boff, eds. "The Voice of the Victims: Who Will Listen to Them?" in *Concilium*, Philadelphia: Trinity Press, 1990.

Espín, Orlando. "Religiosidad Popular: Un Aporte para su Definición y Hermenéutica," in *Estudios Sociales*, 17, no. 58, October-December 1984.

———— and Sixto J. García. "Hispanic American Theology," in *Proceedings of the Catholic Theological Society of America*, vol. 43, 1988.

———— and Sixto J. García. " 'Lilies of the Field,': An Hispanic Theology of Providence and Human Responsibility," in *Proceedings of the Catholic Theological Society of America*, vol. 44, 1989.

García, Sixto J., and Orlando Espín. "Hispanic American Theology," in *Proceedings of the Catholic Theological Society of America*, vol. 43, 1988.

———— and Orlando Espín. " 'Lilies of the Field,' An Hispanic Theology of Providence and Human Responsibility," in *Proceedings of the Catholic Theological Society of America*, vol. 44, 1989.

Goizueta, Roberto S. *Liberation, Method and Dialogue*. Atlanta: Georgia Scholars Press, 1988.

————. "Liberation Theology: Retrospect and Prospect," in *Philosophy Today*, vol. 3, no. 1, Fall 1988.

————. "Liberating Creation Spirituality," in *Listening: Journal of Religion and Culture*, vol. 24, no. 2, Spring 1989.

————. "The Church and Hispanics in the United States: From Empowerment to Solidarity," in Michael Downey, ed., *That They May Live*. New York: Crossroad, 1991.

Guerrero, Andrés G. *A Chicano Theology*. Maryknoll, N.Y.: Orbis Books, 1987.

Herrera, Marina. "Popular Religiosity and Liturgical Education," *Liturgy*, vol. 5, no. 1, 1985.

————. "Providence and Histories: One Hispanic's View," *Proceedings of the Catholic Theological Society of America*, vol. 44, 1989.

———— and Jaime Vidal. "Evangelization: Then and Now," *New Theology Review*, vol. 3, no.4, November 1990.

Icaza, Rosa María. "Spirituality of the Mexican American People," in *Worship*, vol. 63, 1989.

Isasi-Díaz, Ada María. "La Mujer Hispana: Voz Profética en la Iglesia de los Estados Unidos." *Pro Mundi Vita*, Brussels, 1982.

————. "Toward an Understanding of *Feminismo Hispano* in the U.S.A.," in Barbara Hilkert Andolsen, Christina Gudorf, and M.D. Pellauer, eds. *Women's Consciousness, Women's Conscience*. Minneapolis: Winston Press, 1985.

————." 'Apuntes' for a Hispanic Women's Theology of Liberation," in *Apuntes*, Fall 1986.

————— and Yolanda Tarango. *Hispanic Women: Prophetic Voice in the Church*. San Francisco: Harper and Row, 1988.

—————. "The Bible and Mujerista Theology," in Susan Brooks Thistlewaite and Mary Brooks Engel, *Lift Every Voice: Constructing Christian Theologies*. San Francisco: Harper and Row, 1990.

Romero, C. Gilbert. "Teología de las Raíces de un Pueblo: Los Penitentes de Nuevo México," *Servir*, vol. 15, 1979.

—————. "On Choosing a Symbol System for a Hispanic Theology," in *Apuntes*, vol. 1, no. 4, 1981.

—————. *Hispanic Devotional Piety: Tracing Biblical Roots*. Maryknoll, N.Y.: Orbis Books, 1991.

Segovia, Fernando. "A New Manifest Destiny: The Emerging Theological Voice of Hispanic Americans," in *Religious Studies Review*, vol. 17, no. 2, April 1991.

Tarango, Yolanda and Ada María Isasi-Díaz. *Hispanic Women: Prophetic Voice in the Church*. San Francisco: Harper and Row, 1988.

Vidal, Jaime R. "Popular Religion in the Lands of Origin of New York's Hispanic Population," in *Hispanics in New York*, vol. 3. New York: Office of Pastoral Research, 1982.

—————. "Popular Religion among the Hispanics in the General Area of the Archdiocese of Newark," in *Presencia Nueva*. Newark, N.J.: Office of Pastoral Research, 1988.

# Contributors

**María Pilar Aquino,** director of the Hispanic Pastoral Ministry Program at Mount St. Mary's College in Los Angeles, California. She is the first native Mexican Roman Catholic woman to earn the doctorate in theology at the University of Salamanca. She wrote a dissertation on women's perspectives on Latin American theology of liberation. Among her many publications is *Apuntes para una teología desde la mujer.* She currently serves on the board of directors of ACHTUS.

**Allan Figueroa Deck, S.J.,** currently the coordinator of Hispanic pastoral programs and lecturer at Loyola Marymount University in Los Angeles, California. He earned the Ph.D. in Latin American studies at St. Louis University and the S.T.D. in missiology at the Gregorian University. He co-founded the Academy of Catholic Hispanic Theologians of the United States (ACHTUS) and was its first president. Author of *The Second Wave: Hispanic Ministry and the Evangelization of Cultures,* he has written in several journals. Currently he serves as president of the National Catholic Council for Hispanic Ministry (NCCHM).

**Virgil P. Elizondo,** rector of San Fernando cathedral in San Antonio, Texas. Founder of the Mexican-American Cultural Center, he is the author of more than seventy articles and books. He earned the doctorate at the Catholic Institute of Paris and received the doctorate *honoris causa* from the Jesuit School of Theology at Berkeley. The annual Virgil Elizondo Award of the Academy of Catholic Hispanic Theologians of the United States was established in his honor and he was the first recipient.

**Orlando O. Espín,** a priest of the diocese of Venice, Florida. He is associate professor of theology at the University of San Diego and author of several studies on popular religiosity. He earned the doctorate in theology at the Pontifical University of Rio de Janeiro. He is currently on the board of directors of the Catholic Theological Society of America (CTSA) where he has been active in developing a Hispanic presence. He is the president-elect of ACHTUS.

**Sixto J. García,** associate professor of systematics at St. Vincent de Paul Regional Seminary in Boynton Beach, Florida. He earned the doctorate at the University of Notre Dame. He is an active member of the Catholic Theological Society of America and of ACHTUS. With Orlando O. Espín, he has lectured on Hispanic popular religiosity from the perspective of a Hispanic systematic theologian.

**Roberto S. Goizueta,** vice-president of the Aquinas Center of Theology and associate professor at Emory University in Atlanta, Georgia. He earned the doctorate

169

in theology at Marquette University. A past president of ACHTUS, he is author of *Liberation, Method and Dialogue*.

**Juan-Lorenzo Hinojosa,** director of the Central Texas Pastoral Center in Austin, Texas. A native of Bolivia with many years residence in the United States, he earned the doctorate at the Graduate Theological Union. He has written several articles on spirituality and ministry.

**Rosa María Icaza, C.C.V.I.,** member of the faculty of the Mexican-American Cultural Center in San Antonio, Texas. She earned the doctorate in Spanish literature at the Catholic University of America. A leading liturgist, she is currently president of the Institute of Hispanic Liturgy.

**Gloria Inés Loya, P.B.V.M.,** completing the doctorate in pastoral theology at the University of Salamanca. She is currently a member of the faculty at the Jesuit School of Theology at Berkeley where she supervises students in field education and teaches pastoral counseling and Hispanic studies.

**C. Gilbert Romero,** a priest of the archdiocese of Los Angeles. He earned the doctorate in the Hebrew scriptures at Princeton Theological Seminary. He is currently professor of biblical studies at the major seminary of Trujillo, Peru. His book *Hispanic Devotional Piety: Tracing Biblical Roots* and his several articles are important contributions to a specifically biblical approach to Hispanic theological concerns.

# Index